IMAGES
of America

SAND LAKE

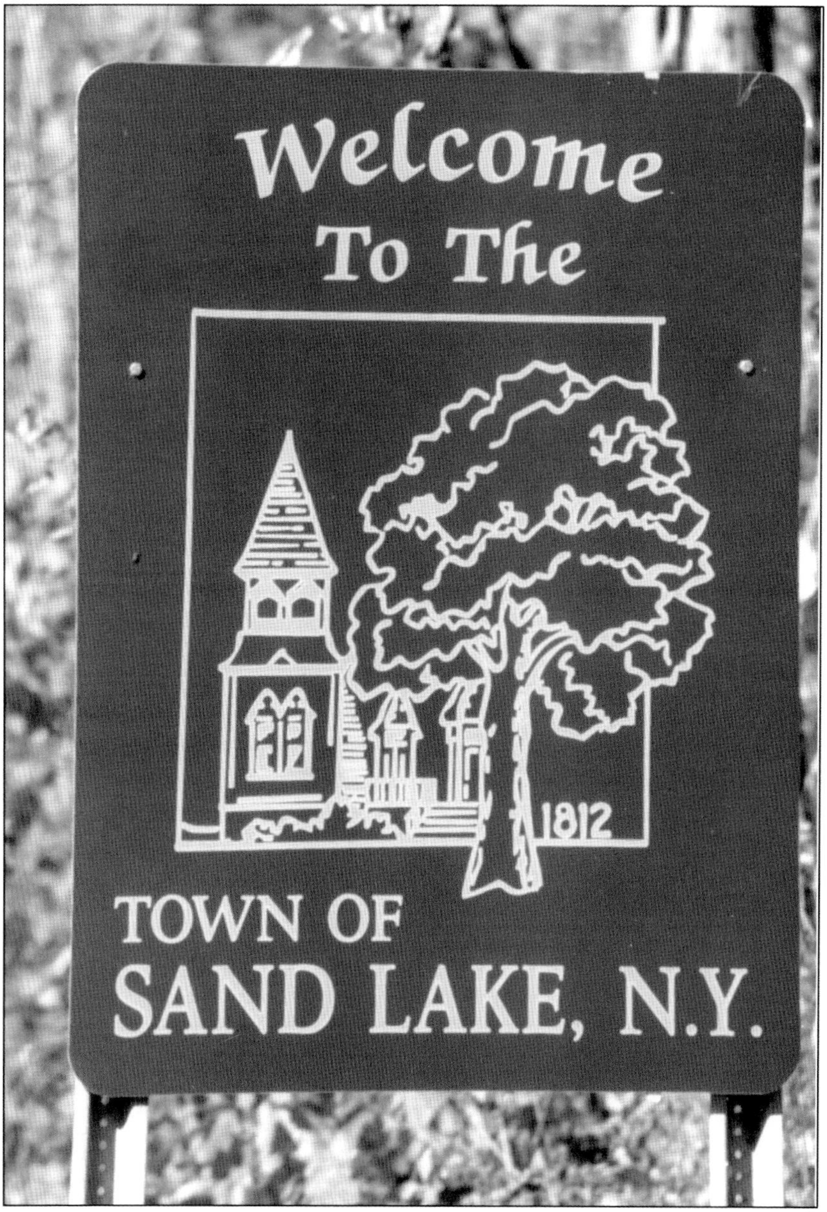

TOWN LOGO. Signs showing the town hall and the large oak tree in front welcome persons to Sand Lake at each major entry point. The large oak tree was designated the Liberty Tree with residents' names nailed to it during the bicentennial celebration. In 1985, a contest to choose a town logo was held. This design by Patricia Brock was chosen. (Courtesy Sand Lake Historical Society Collection.)

IMAGES
of America

SAND LAKE

Mary D. French & Robert J. Lilly
for the Sand Lake Historical Society

ARCADIA
PUBLISHING

ISBN 978-0-7385-0540-4

Published by Arcadia Publishing
Charleston, South Carolina

Printed in the United States of America

Library of Congress Catalog Card Number: 2001088817

For all general information contact Arcadia Publishing at:
Telephone 843-853-2070
Fax 843-853-0044
E-mail sales@arcadiapublishing.com
For customer service and orders:
Toll-Free 1-888-313-2665

Visit us on the Internet at www.arcadiapublishing.com

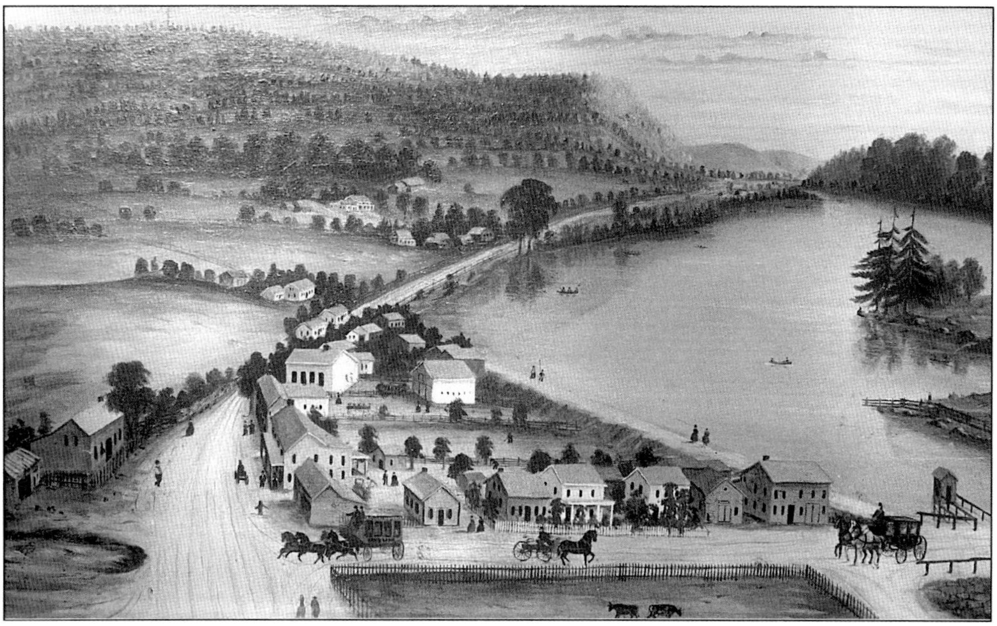

HIDLEY'S PAINTING OF GLASS LAKE. Joseph Hidley, a local folk artist, painted two scenes of Glass Lake. This picture can be dated after 1865 because the gatehouse to control the water flow is shown in the lower right corner. Along that same road, to the left, is District No. 8 School and on the far right is a warehouse from the glass factory. The road in the foreground that runs along the lake is the current Routes 43 and 66. The largest of the buildings on the right side of the road is Mechanics Hall, which later became Glass Lake Hotel. The original painting of this scene is at the Rensselaer County Historical Society. Hidley lived in Poestenkill and painted four scenes of that hamlet. (Courtesy Rensselaer County Historical Society.)

Contents

Introduction 7

1. West Sand Lake 9

2. Averill Park and the Burden Lakes 41

3. Sand Lake, Glass Lake, and Crooked Lake 79

4. Taborton 99

5. Townwide Events and Organizations 109

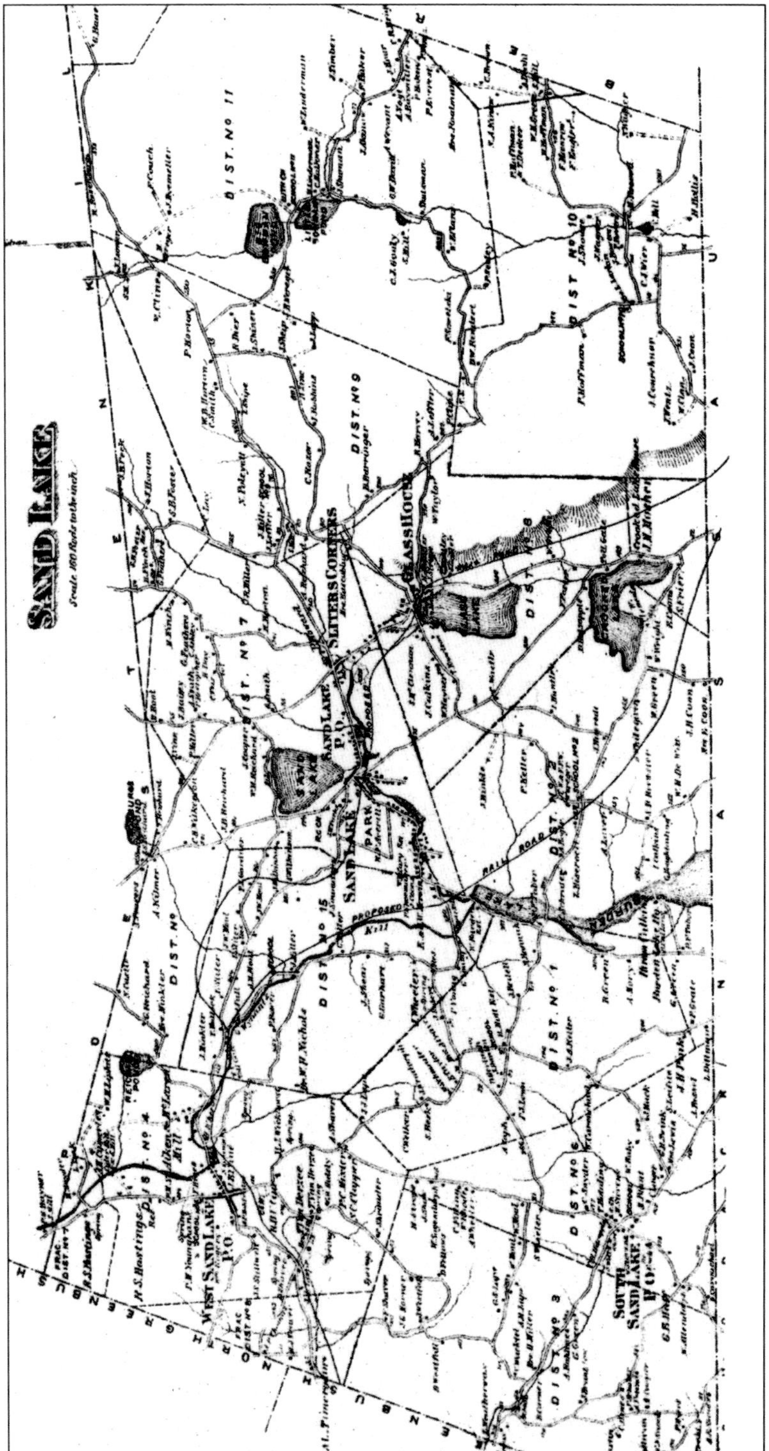

TOWN OF SAND LAKE MAP. This map shows the town lines and school districts as they were in 1876. It is from the *Rensselaer County Atlas*, by F.W. Beers, copyright 1876.

Introduction

Where was Sand Lake? Where is Sand Lake? Crystal Lake was previously named Sand Lake. Today, we refer to Sand Lake as the township within Rensselaer County, New York. It is about equidistant from Troy and Albany. Within the township there is also the hamlet of Sand Lake.

Prior to 1791, it was part of Albany County, within the Manor of Rensselaerwyck, which extended east and west from the Hudson River. In 1791, it was declared part of Rensselaer County. By 1812, Sand Lake had been formed from the towns of Greenbush and Berlin. Present boundaries were finally established when sections were removed to Greenbush in 1843 and to the town of Poestenkill in 1848.

For a detailed and in-depth account, *Sylvester's History of Rensselaer County* relates Sand Lake's earliest beginnings. Perhaps you missed the historical society's house tour booklets, which are now out of print: *Sand Lake History,* begun by Madolyn Carpenter and Charles Viens in 1979, and *Pictorial History of Ulinesville 1776 to West Sand Lake 1976*, by Sanford Young and Charles Viens. Some of the pictures in those booklets are included in the chapters of this book. The very popular method of preserving photographs on postcards provided a multitude of images. The collections of Lawrence Herzog, Joseph Connors Jr., Alice Tifft, Ada and Wesley Miller, the town of Sand Lake, and the Sand Lake Historical Society, as well as individual offerings from a multitude of persons, were used extensively. Courtesy acknowledgment was given to the original source of the photograph whenever possible.

From this generous outpouring of photographs, we have selected those images from the 19th and 20th centuries that capture the distinctiveness of the town's hamlet areas. The first chapter begins at West Sand Lake—rich in farmland, gravel, and water-powered mills. Cedarhurst, Brookside Park, and the Brewster House were popular spots. In the next chapter, we travel eastward along the town's main creek, the Wynantskill, to the Burden Lakes, formed by dams, with the water used for local woolen, grist, paper, and hosiery mills. Ultimately, that same water was used to power the largest waterwheel in North America at the Burden Iron Company in Troy. Nearby is Averill Park, a hub of activity, with the Troy & New England Railway terminal, a carousel ride at Crystal Lake Park, Scram's Collegiate Institute, Traveler's Rest, and the Lake View Hotel. Thence, we go to Sand, Glass, and Crooked Lakes, replete with vacation spots and hotels. For starters, we pick the Crooked Lake Hotel and pay a visit to Crist Crape's Central Hotel. On a tour of the area, we visit the site of the Rensselaer Glass Factory, from which Glass Lake got its name. Then we head up to Taborton, with its mountains yielding much wood for sawmills and charcoal. The earliest wood lease on record was 1798. We climb to the Kipple, the town's highest point. It is a clear day, and we can see a panoramic westward view of the Hudson Valley and Helderberg Mountains. Townwide organizations, government, and events are found in the last chapter.

As their stories are recounted, the people and activities remembered bring each hamlet to life. Ulinesville, as West Sand Lake was formerly known, is still remembered by that name, especially when family members meet at their reunions. Faith Mills, the largest employer in town, contributed not only to the town's growth and social life but also to its prestige when the mill and each of the employees received the E Award in 1943 for providing long woolen underwear for the war effort. Looking back, some persons can say, "I was served ice cream by a soda jerk named Jerry Lewis."

With the passage of time, the area changed. The many water-powered mills, so prevalent along the Wynantskill, became obsolete or ravaged by fire. The advent of the automobile brought freedom to travel to new places and to commute to work. Several of the hotels, no longer a mecca for tourists, either were razed or they burned. Summer camps were winterized for year-round use. Gradually, Sand Lake became a residential community, with most merchants in businesses for the maintenance of the local population.

Throughout its history, Sand Lake has been an involved community.

In 1844, at the height of the Anti-Rent War, Dr. Smith Boughton, known as "Big Thunder," led a major resistance to the Van Rensselaer landlords on both sides of the Hudson River. In 1984, Big Thunder Day began at Smith Boughton's grave in Sand Lake Union Cemetery. Local residents dressed in calico and Indian face masks, and by blowing tin horns they remembered the victorious resistance.

During the Civil War period, there was much clandestine activity on the Underground Railroad. Church pulpits gave coded messages for the movement of slaves. The Lutheran Church in West Sand Lake split over the issue of slavery.

In 1976, Sand Lake was recognized as an official Bicentennial Community. A highlight of the celebration was the reenactment of the Declaration of Independence, depicted by the men of the town in Colonial costumes.

Much of this book comes from the legacy of the 20 years of work (1975–1995) by town historian Madolyn Carpenter. The present town historian, Judy Rowe, has been an invaluable source of encouragement, naming persons to contact and relating her seemingly limitless information on the town's history. The cooperation and enthusiasm of the people within the town to share their treasures to make *Sand Lake* a reality was heartening and made the task enjoyable. Another diligent worker was Ross French, who did the rephotographing of the pictures loaned to us. We especially thank the Rensselaer County Historical Society, the New York State Museum, Capital Newspapers, and the Record for permission to include their pictures.

As you read *Sand Lake*, coeditors Mary D. French and Robert J. Lilly invite you to enjoy the collective efforts of all who contributed toward its coming to fruition and, in the process, carried out the motto of the Sand Lake Historical Society: Preserving the past—enriching the future.

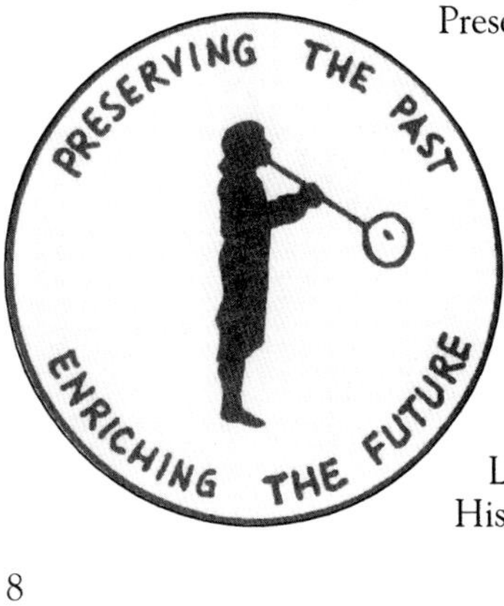

SAND LAKE HISTORICAL SOCIETY LOGO. Our motto and the glassblower have been combined to represent the Sand Lake Historical Society as its logo. (Courtesy Sand Lake Historical Society Collection.)

One

West Sand Lake

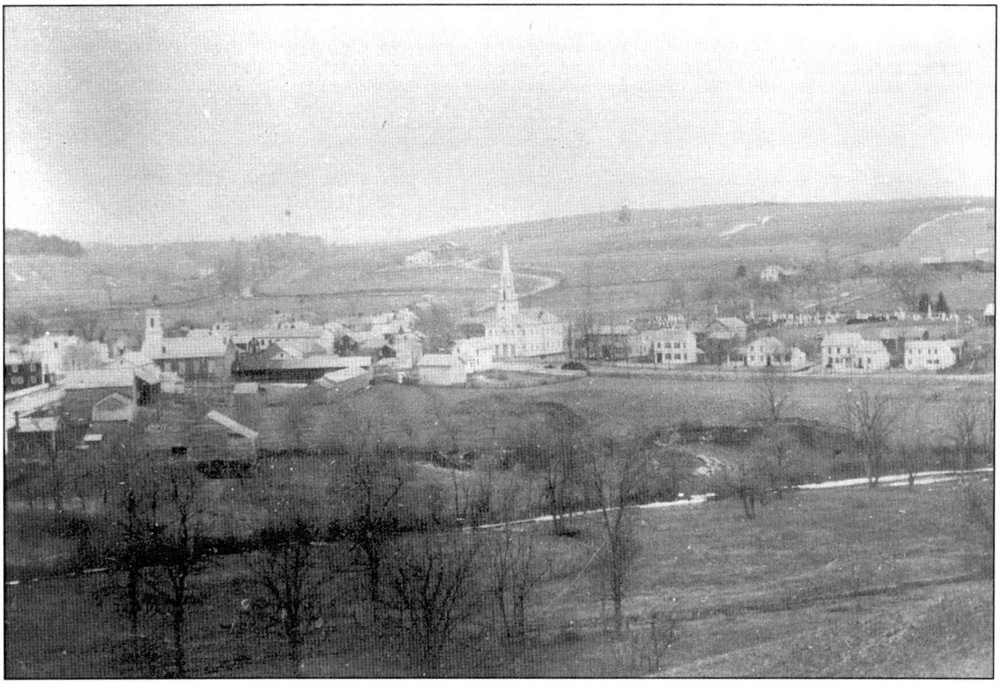

A View of West Sand Lake, 1900s. West Sand Lake was named in 1834 because it was the next hamlet west of the former hamlet of Sand Lake, now Averill Park. Here in the foreground you can see the Wynantskill Creek. The church spire on the left is the Second Evangelical Lutheran Church on Route 43, and the one in the middle is Trinity Lutheran Church on Route 150, with the cemetery in the back. Most of the action begins at what is commonly known as the Four Corners, where Routes 43 and 150 intersect. Albany Street, now Route 43, makes an ess westward up the hill out of the village. The 1778 John Van Alen Survey Map shows 14 farms surrounding the Four Corners, with the smallest being 140 acres and the largest being the Uline farm of 325 acres. One has to ask when looking at this scene, "Where has all the farmland gone?" (Courtesy Charles Viens.)

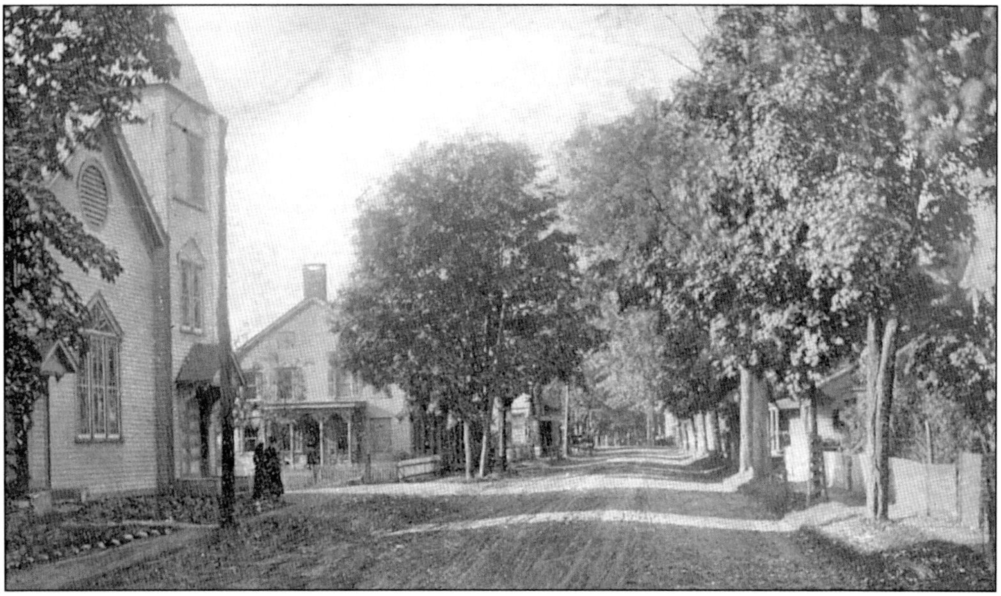

A VIEW NORTH ON SOUTH STREET. Looking north on Route 150, or South Street, the West Sand Lake Methodist Church and parsonage is on the left. Many trees line the dirt road. (Courtesy Sand Lake Historical Society Collection.)

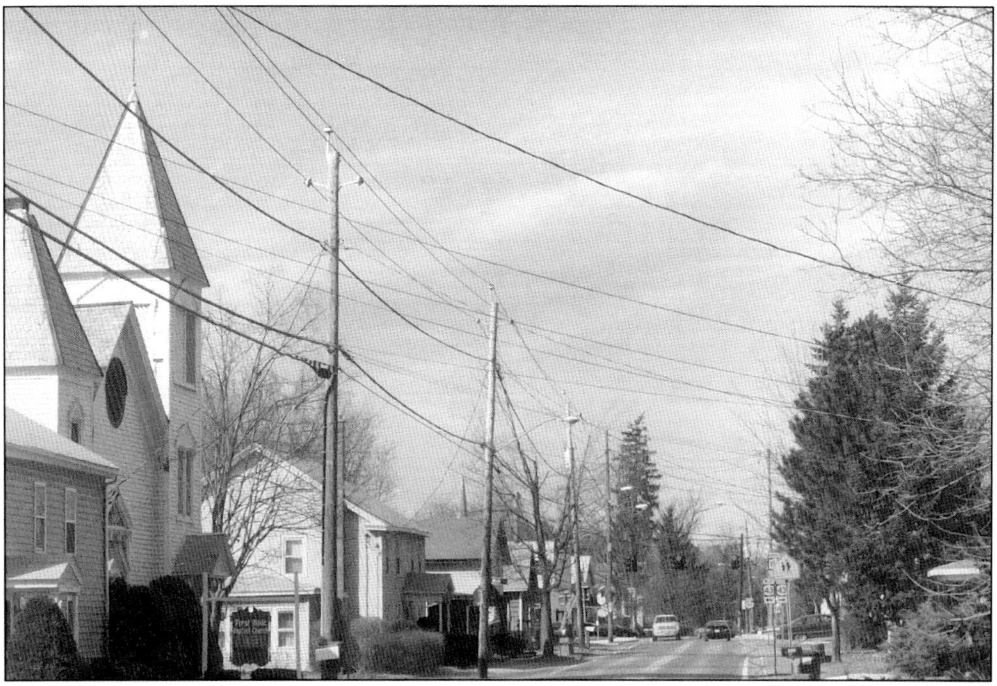

LOOKING NORTH ON ROUTE 150, 1990S. As we view this same scene in the 1990s, the West Sand Lake Methodist Church is now the First Bible Baptist Church. The road is well paved, and trees have given way to telephone and electric poles and wires. (Courtesy Sand Lake Historical Society Collection.)

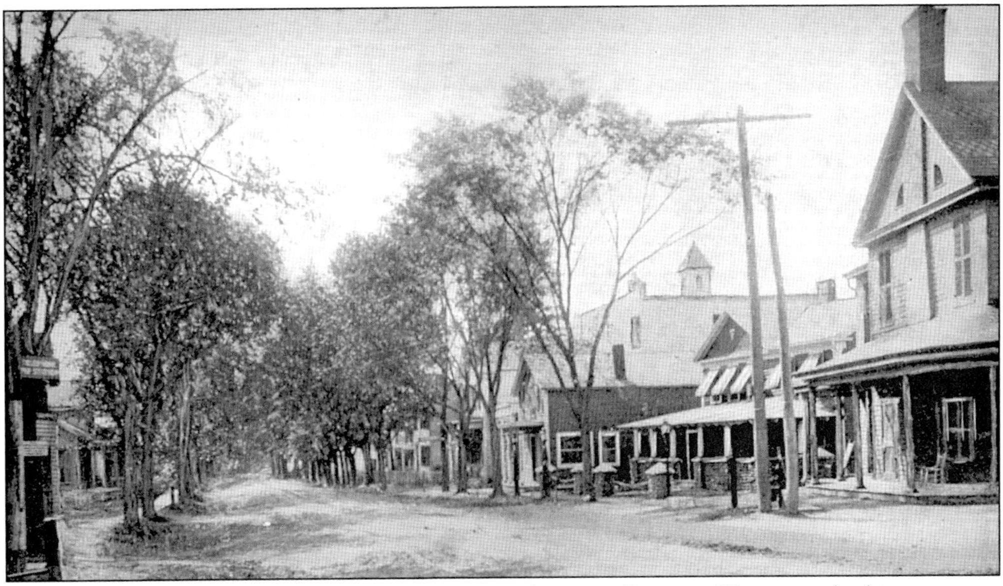

A View from the Four Corners, West on Albany Street. This view looking west on Albany Street (now Route 43) shows the Brewster House, the former Archie Wolfe home behind the stone wall, a house that was later moved farther down across Albany Street and became Dr. Walter Meeler's home, and C.H. Lewis's Store. (Courtesy Lawrence Herzog.)

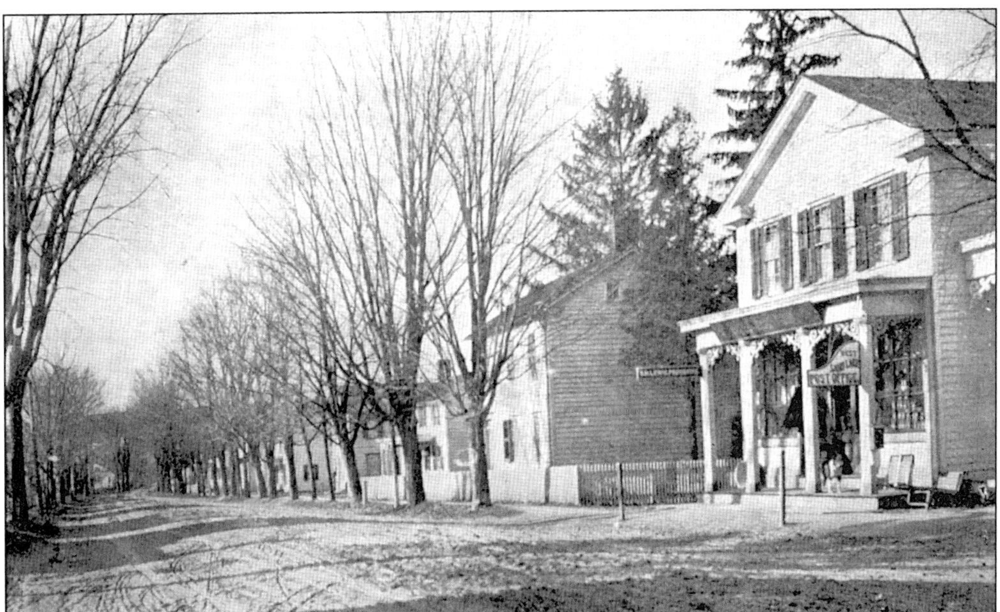

A View Farther West on Albany Street. Now in full view is C.H. Lewis's Store and the West Sand Lake Post Office. It had many proprietors over the years. George Lewis was postmaster from 1905 to 1921. Charles Ryemiller served as postmaster in the building in which he ran his store. The post office relocated to the 43 Mall in 1978. (Courtesy Sand Lake Historical Society Collection.)

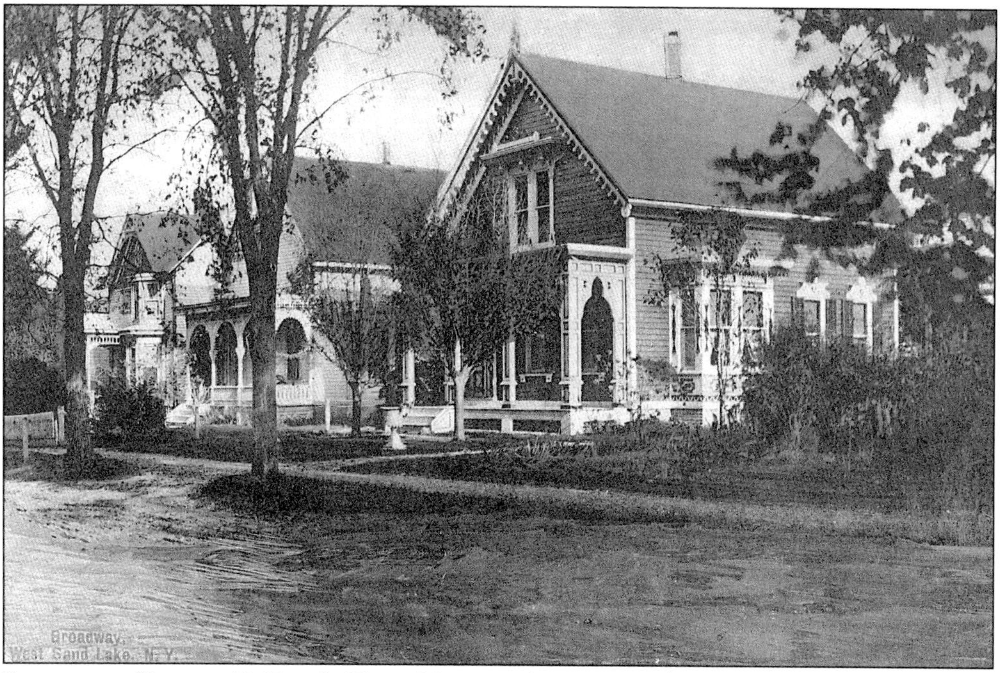

BROADWAY (ROUTE 43 EAST). These Victorian houses were located on the site of the new West Sand Lake Firehouse. (Courtesy Ada and Wesley Miller.)

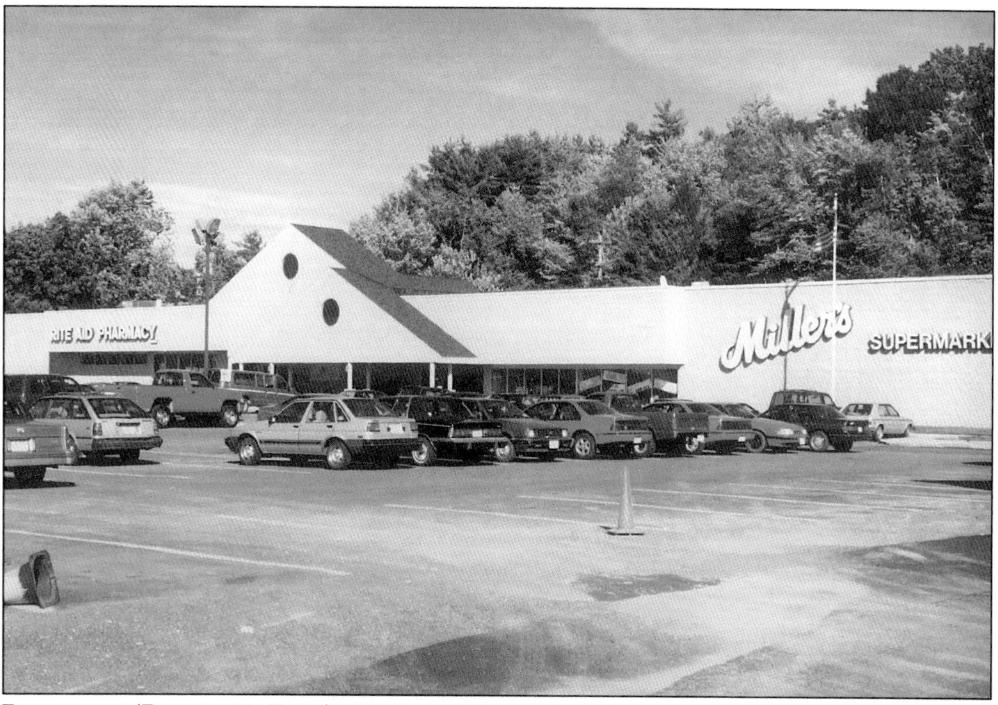

BROADWAY (ROUTE 43 EAST), 1990S. With ample parking space, a modern and spacious Miller's Market, Rite Aid Pharmacy, and Key Bank now occupy the northeast corner of the Four Corners. (Courtesy Sand Lake Historical Society Collection.)

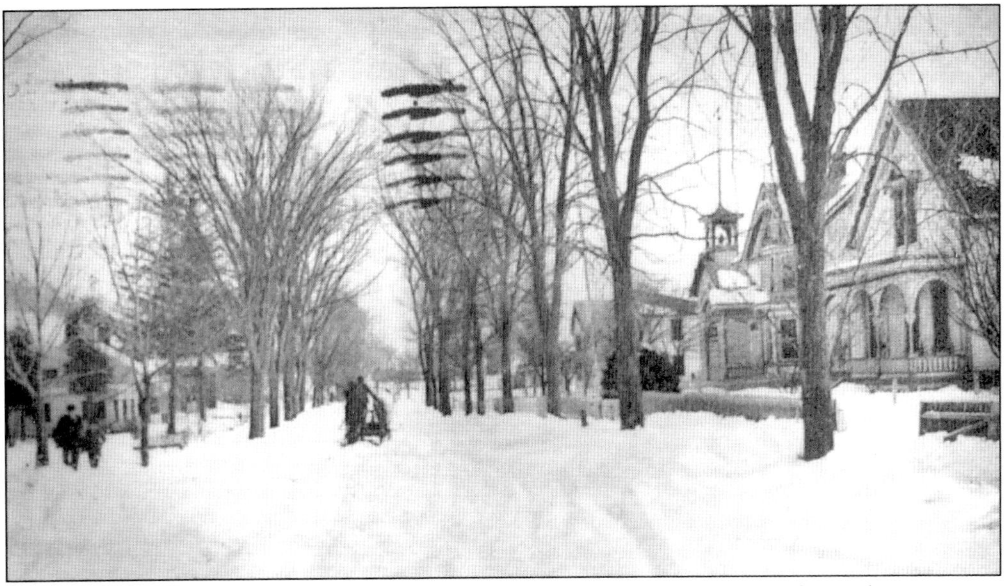

BROADWAY (ROUTE 43 EAST) IN WINTER. Looking farther down Broadway, the Victorian houses shown on page 12 can be seen to the right of the old West Sand Lake Firehouse bell tower. (Courtesy Lawrence Herzog.)

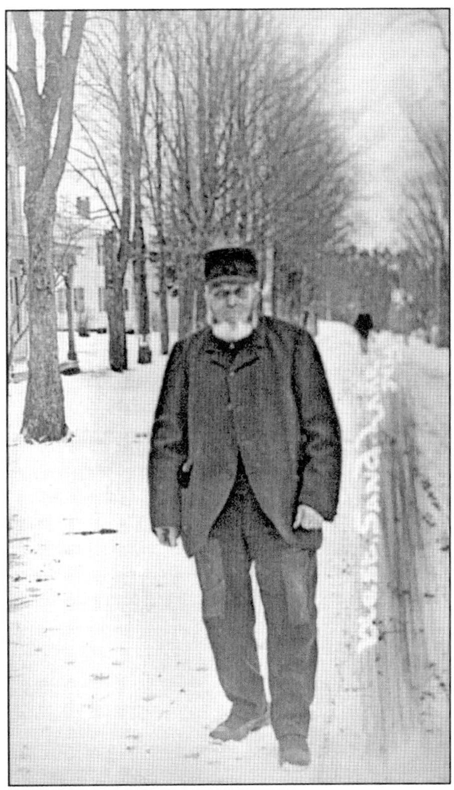

WILHELM ZWEIG. A commercial photographer took this picture of Wilhelm Zweig, who was taking a walk in the village. At the time, Zweig was living with his daughter, Hattie Bower, across from the Salem Evangelical United Brethren Church. Later, he was upset to find himself on a postcard. (Courtesy John Zweig, great-grandson of Wilhelm Zweig.)

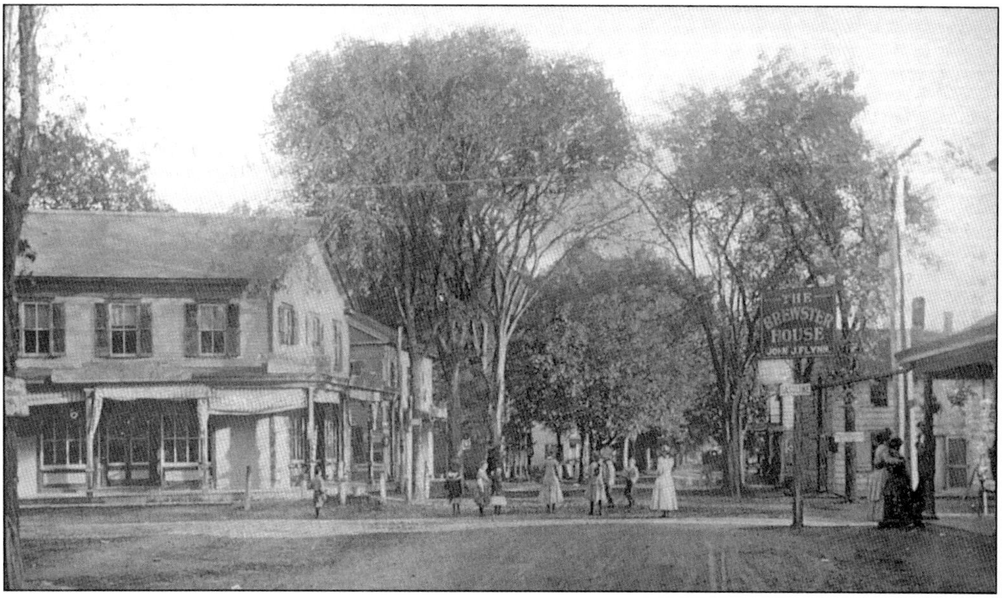

LOOKING SOUTH ON SOUTH STREET (ROUTE 150). On the left at the Four Corners, looking south on the present Route 150, is the original Miller's Market. Diagonally across from Miller's Market is the Brewster House sign. (Courtesy Sand Lake Historical Society Collection.)

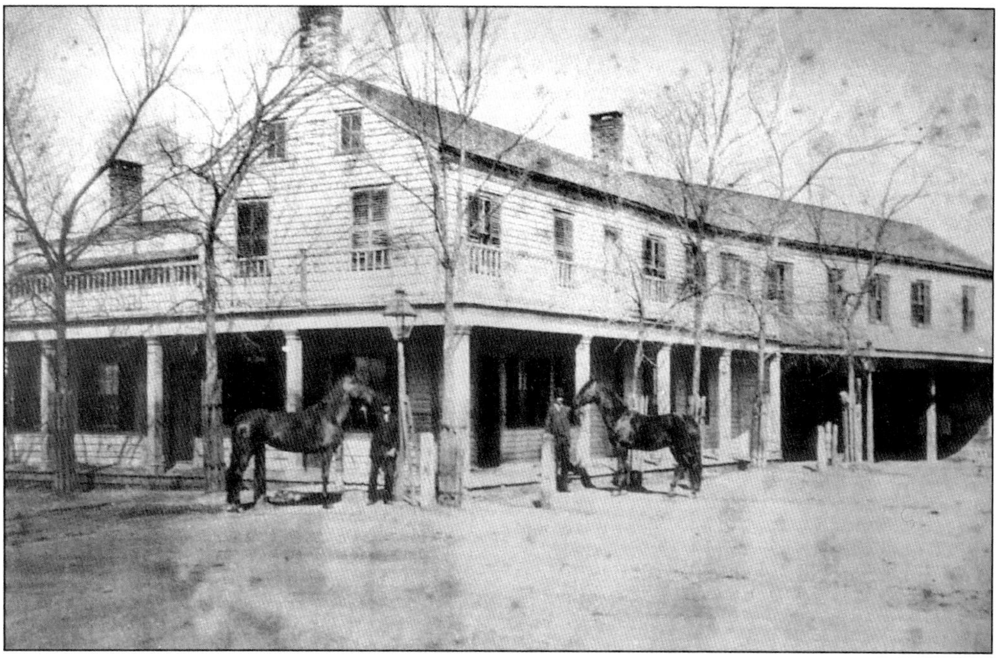

THE BREWSTER HOUSE. Begun as a tavern and then enlarged as a hotel, this building had several owners before it was acquired by Fred Brewster and became the Brewster House. In 1897, it burned and was rebuilt. Subsequently, it housed various businesses, including a bus garage for the KLWM Bus Company (see page 61). The building was demolished in the early 1930s. Several gas stations and A.K. Wolfe's Appliance Store have since occupied this corner. (Courtesy Charles Viens.)

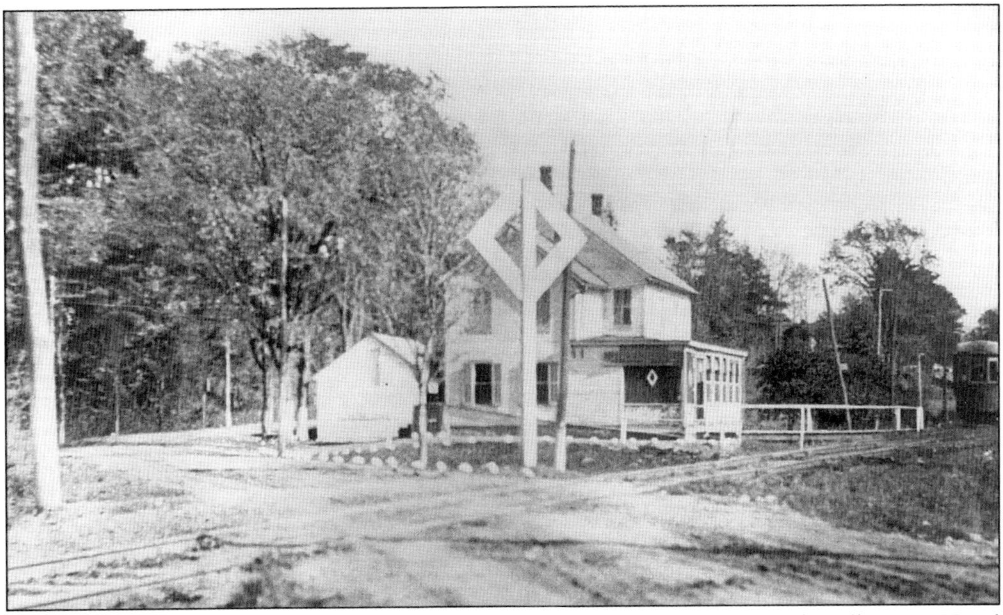

THE JOURNEY'S END HOTEL. The hotel built *c.* 1890 was also known as the Elk Horn Hotel and the Arlington Hotel. It was a trolley stop for the Troy & New England Railway Company. The tracks ran close to what was then the rear door of the hotel. The front door of the hotel was on old Route 43, now Werger Road. Route 43 now runs where the old trolley tracks did; thus, the former rear door of the old Arlington Hotel became the front door of the Journey's End Hotel. (Courtesy Dorothy Leitgeb.)

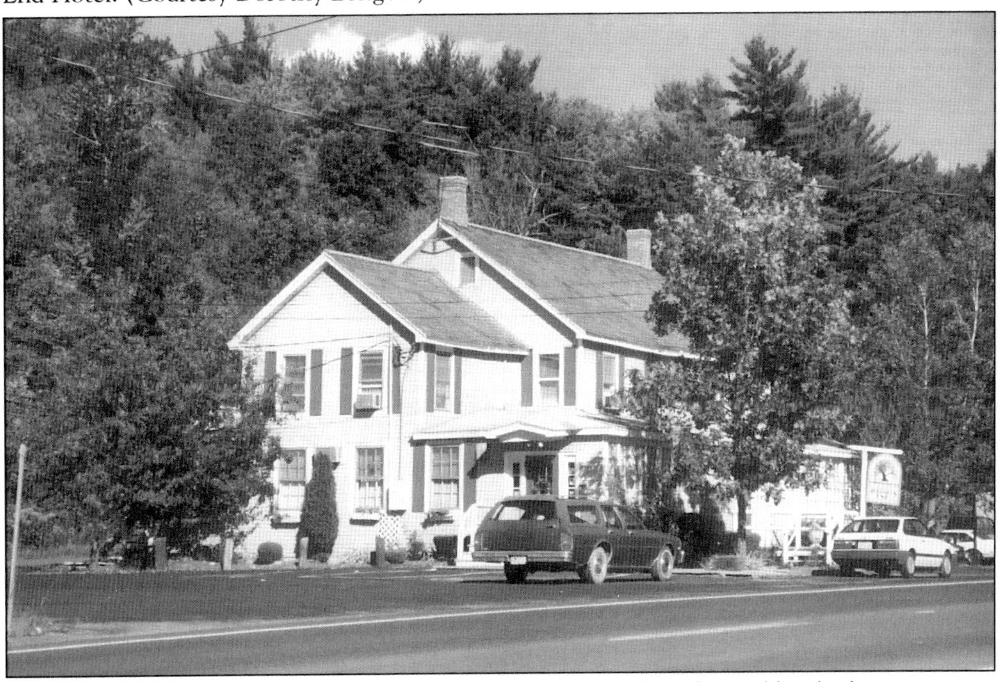

THE NEW OLD JOURNEY'S END. Over the years, the Journey's End Hotel has had many owners and a variety of cuisines. It has been known as the "Old Journey's End" and the "New Old Journey's End." (Courtesy Sand Lake Historical Society Collection.)

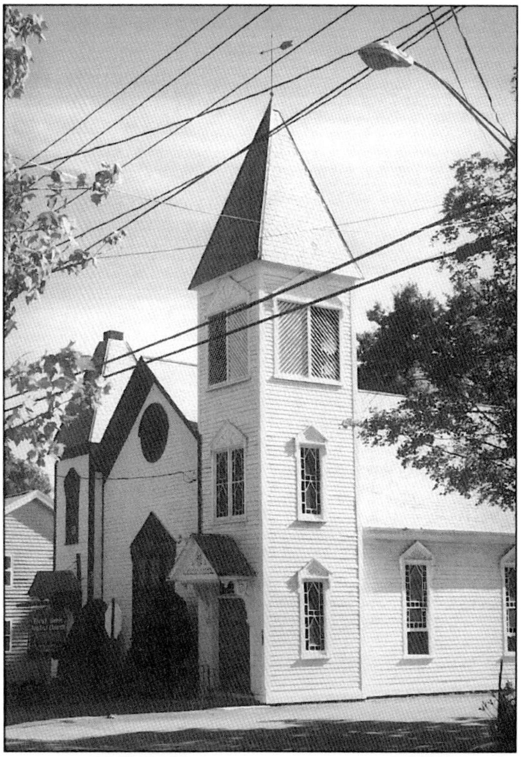

THE WEST SAND LAKE METHODIST CHURCH. The West Sand Lake Methodist Church opened on January 27, 1836 (see page 10). It was remodeled in 1894. In 1968, the congregation merged with the Salem Evangelical United Brethren Church. This church is now the home of the First Bible Baptist Church. (Courtesy Sand Lake Historical Society Collection.)

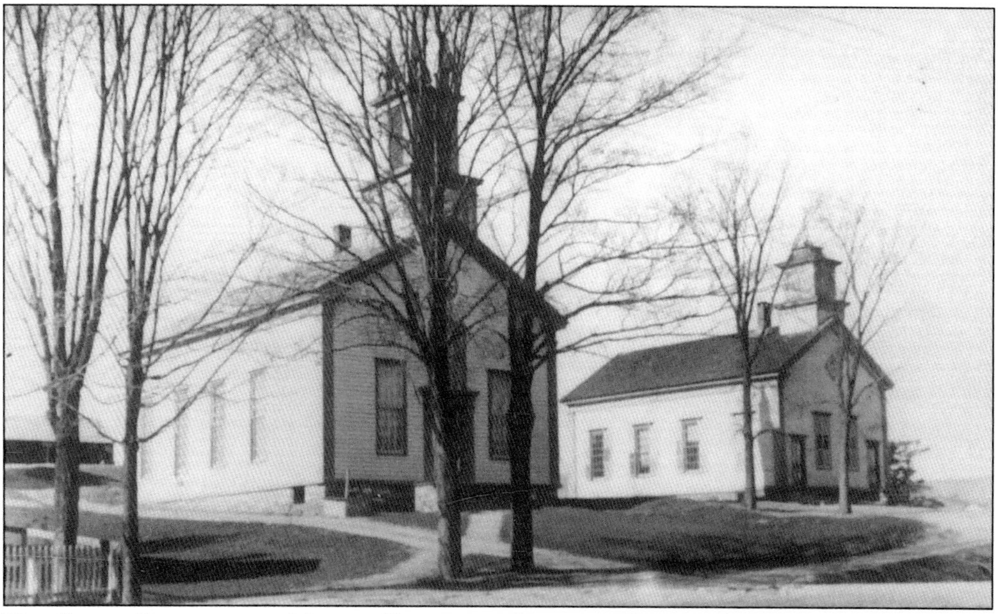

THE SALEM EVANGELICAL UNITED BRETHREN CHURCH. Organized in 1845, the church met in the parsonage until the church building was erected in 1865. Class pictures for the District No. 4 School next-door were often taken on the church steps (see page 19). The congregation merged in 1968 with the West Sand Lake Methodist Church and became the Salem United Methodist Church. An example of building reuse, it is now the home of the Chester Gavryck family. (Courtesy Town of Sand Lake Collection.)

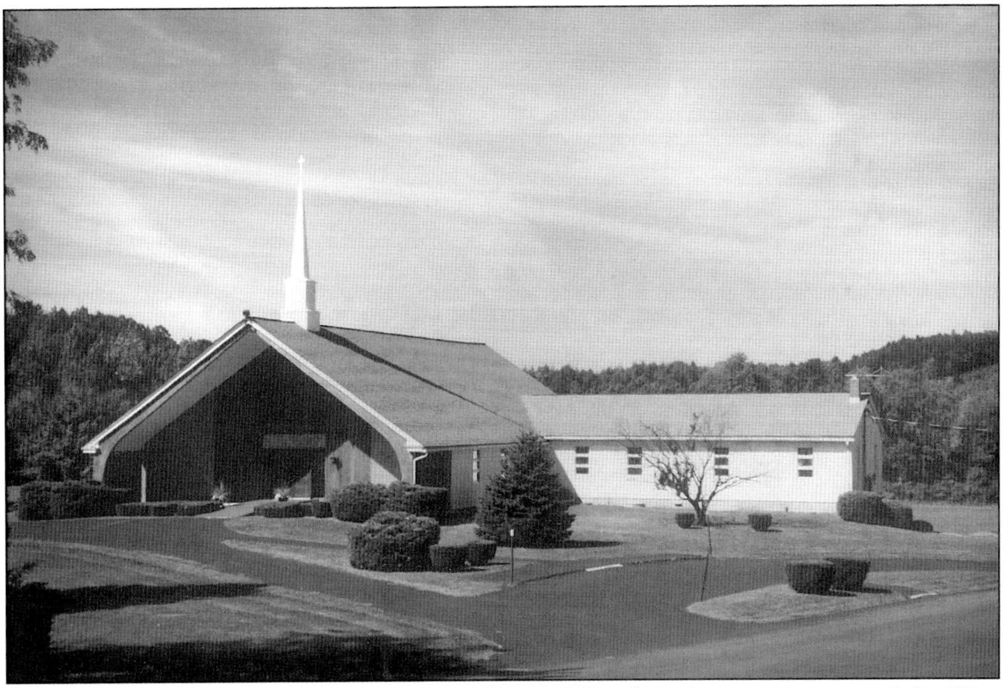

THE SALEM UNITED METHODIST CHURCH. From 1968, when the congregations of the West Sand Lake Methodist and the Salem Evangelical United Brethren Churches merged, until the new church was dedicated in 1971, worship was held in the West Sand Lake Methodist Church. The new building on Shaver Road combines traditional church and modern architectural lines. (Courtesy Sand Lake Historical Society Collection.)

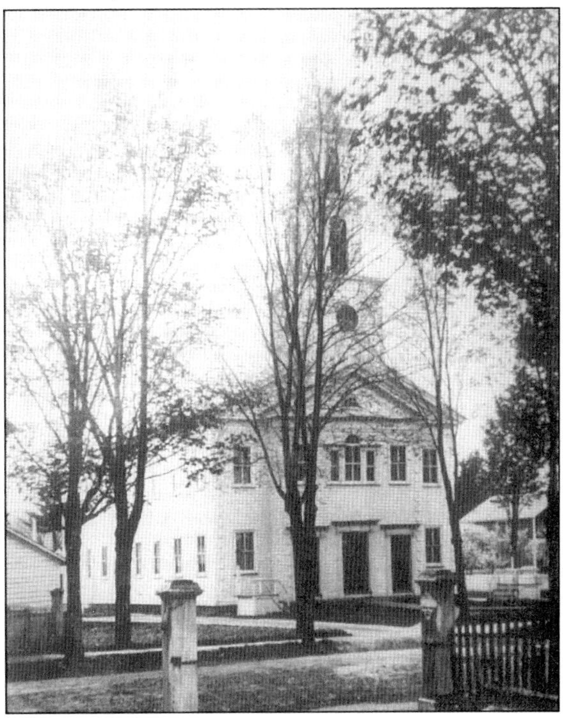

ZION EVANGELICAL LUTHERAN CHURCH. Lutheran families from Sand Lake and Poestenkill who had attended Gilead Lutheran Church in Brunswick left because of its Tory leanings when the Revolutionary War began. They erected a log church in 1776 on the present Thomas I. Cipperley property. Later, the building was taken down and Zion Evangelical Lutheran Church opened in 1816. In 1838, when there was a church split, the structure then became the First Evangelical Lutheran Church. (Courtesy Town of Sand Lake Collection.)

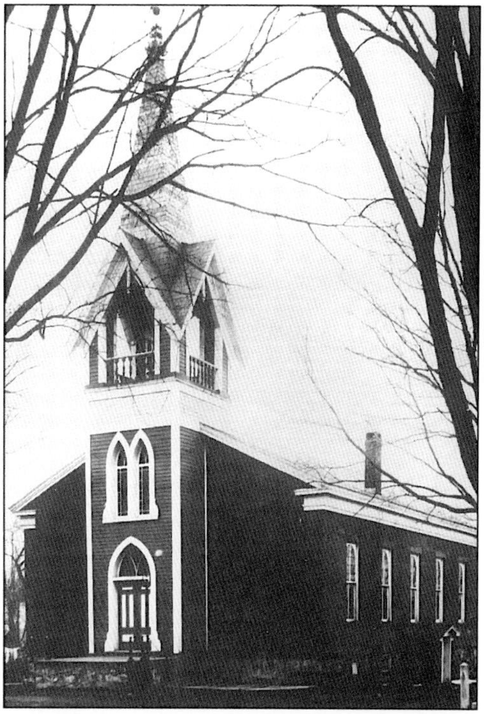

THE SECOND EVANGELICAL LUTHERAN CHURCH. In 1838, parishioners left the Zion Evangelical Lutheran Church over the issues of antislavery and temperance and formed the Second Evangelical Lutheran Church. This church was a station on the Underground Railroad for fugitive slaves. Rev. Nickolas Van Alstyne, with the secret name "Paul," gave messages in code during Sunday sermons for abolitionists' meetings and the movement of slaves to freedom. (Courtesy Charles Viens.)

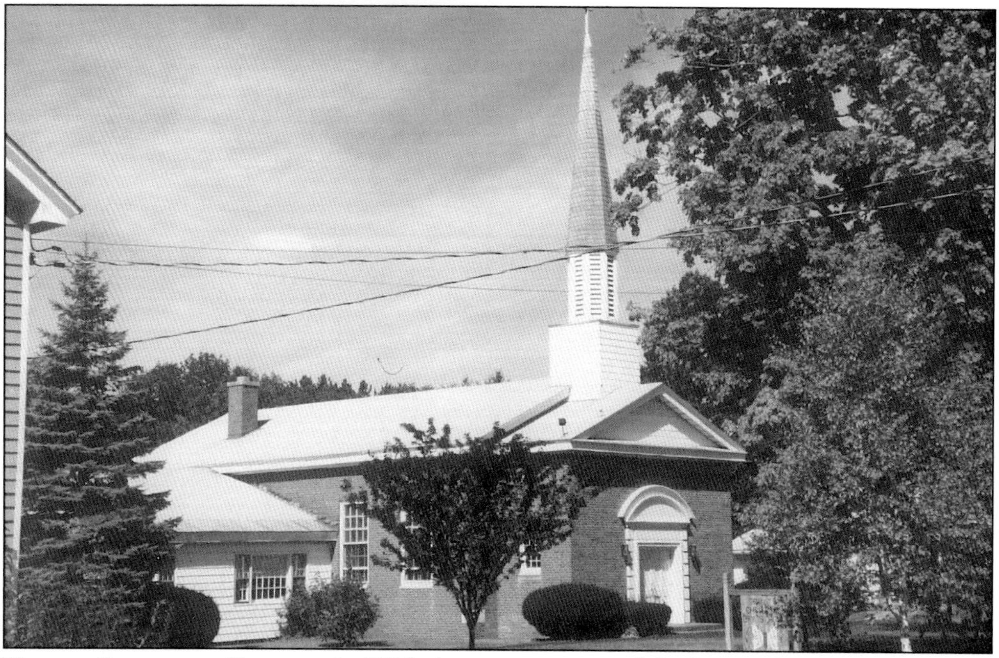

TRINITY LUTHERAN CHURCH. In 1926, the congregations of the First and Second Evangelical Lutheran Churches reunited and became Trinity Lutheran Church. Services were held in the original Zion Evangelical, or First Evangelical, Lutheran Church (see page 17). The building was struck by lightning and burned on August 14, 1944. Between 1944 and 1954, services were held in the Second Evangelical Lutheran Church building while the present brick building was being completed. (Courtesy Sand Lake Historical Society Collection.)

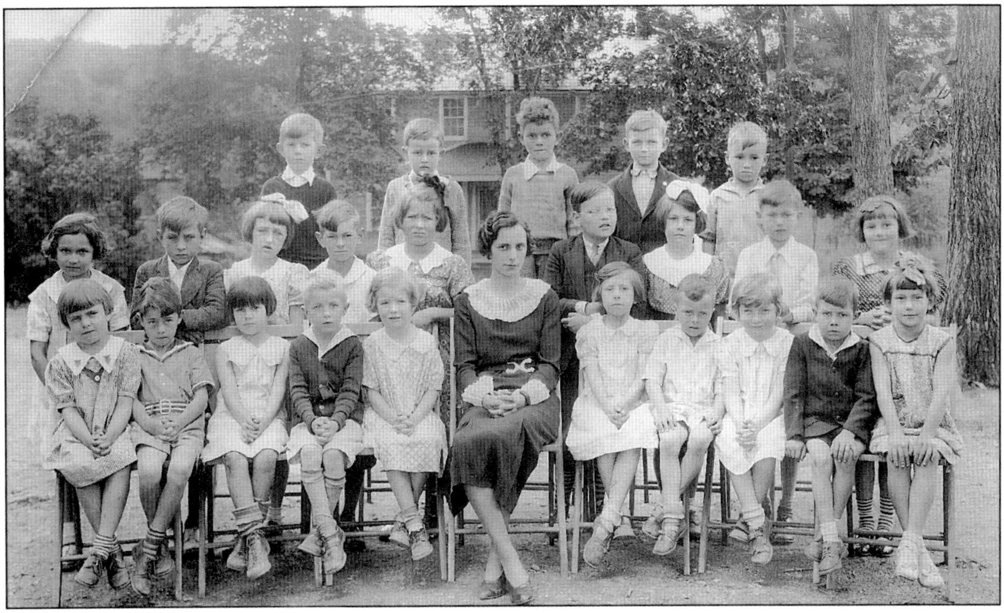

DISTRICT NO. 4 SCHOOL CLASS PICTURE, C. 1935. From left to right, are the following: (front row) Doris Hogle, Raymond "Jug" Lape, Grace Oechsner, Walter Wehnau, Marilyn Mittler, Mrs. Crane, Emma Williams (Wicks), Ralph "Doc" Wehnau, Betty Harrington (Ramella), Irving Sewell, and Dorothy Samjohn; (middle row) Frances Konopka, John Therrien, Jane Reid, Raymond Barnes, Shirley Sisson, Harry "Senator" Werger, Eleanor Reid, Charles Knapp, and Joan Rescott; (back row) Kenneth Wehnau, Charles Werger, William Collins, Robert Middleton, and James Platt. (Courtesy Irving Sewell.)

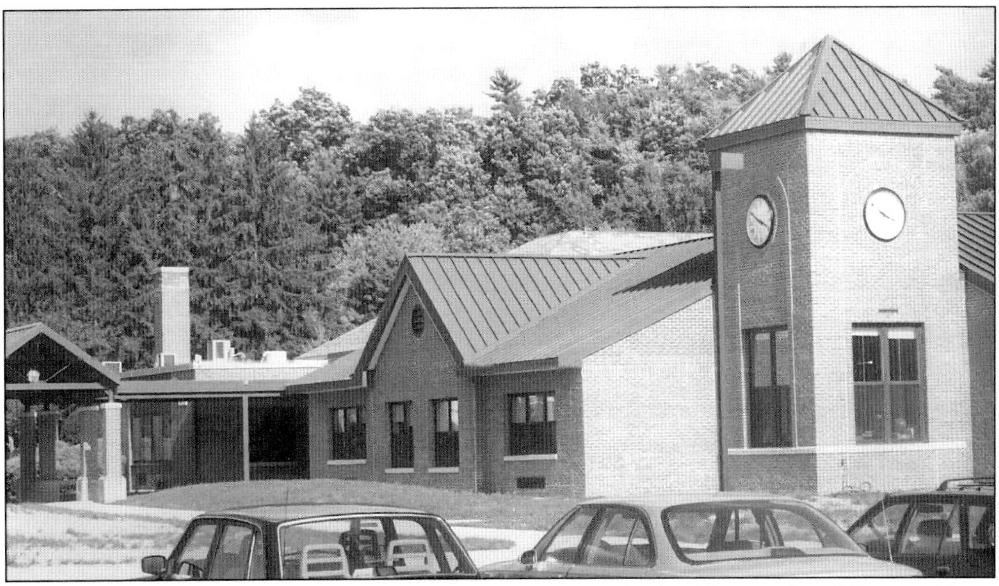

WEST SAND LAKE ELEMENTARY SCHOOL. Built in 1935, this building replaced District No. 4 School (see page 16). As enrollment expanded, additions were made in 1939, 1951, and 1967. The latest renovation occurred in the late 1990s, during the extensive work done to all the schools when the district merged with the George Washington Elementary School of the Town of Brunswick (see pages 56 and57). (Courtesy Sand Lake Historical Society Collection.)

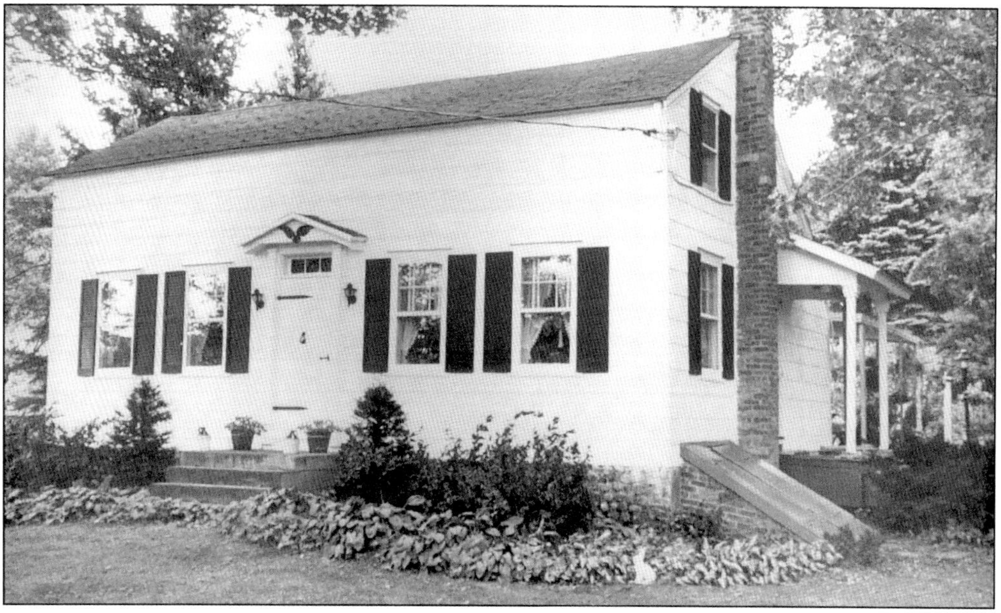

The Philip Krist House. This saltbox house was built on property leased to Philip Krist and Karol Mickel in 1789 by Stephen Van Rensselaer. As stated in the deed, annual rent was "two bushels of wheat, twenty pounds of good clean merchantable winter wheat, one day's service with carriage, and four fat fowls." Located on Shaver Road, the house has been the Frank Morlock home since 1954. (Courtesy Frank and Ruth Morlock; photograph by the *Times Record*.)

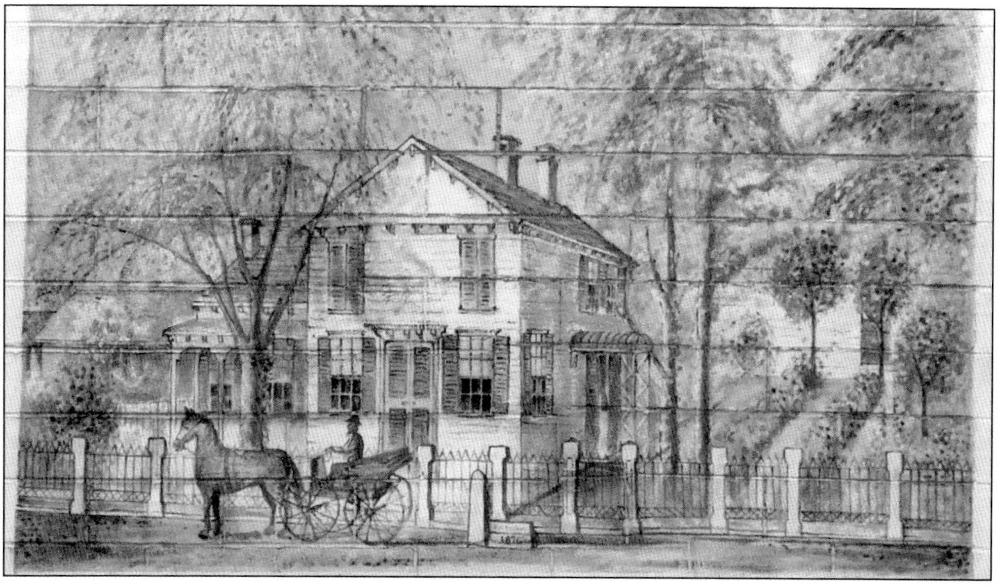

Burton A. Thomas Home. This mural of the Burton A. Thomas home was painted in 1976 for the bicentennial celebration on the exterior wall of Lake Pharmacy, the site of his home. Thomas, a surveyor and civil engineer, engineered the building of the Burden Lakes and the enlarging of Glass Lake for hydraulic water control along the Wynantskill. He was also secretary of the Anti-Rent Association in Rensselaer County. (Courtesy Sand Lake Historical Society Collection.)

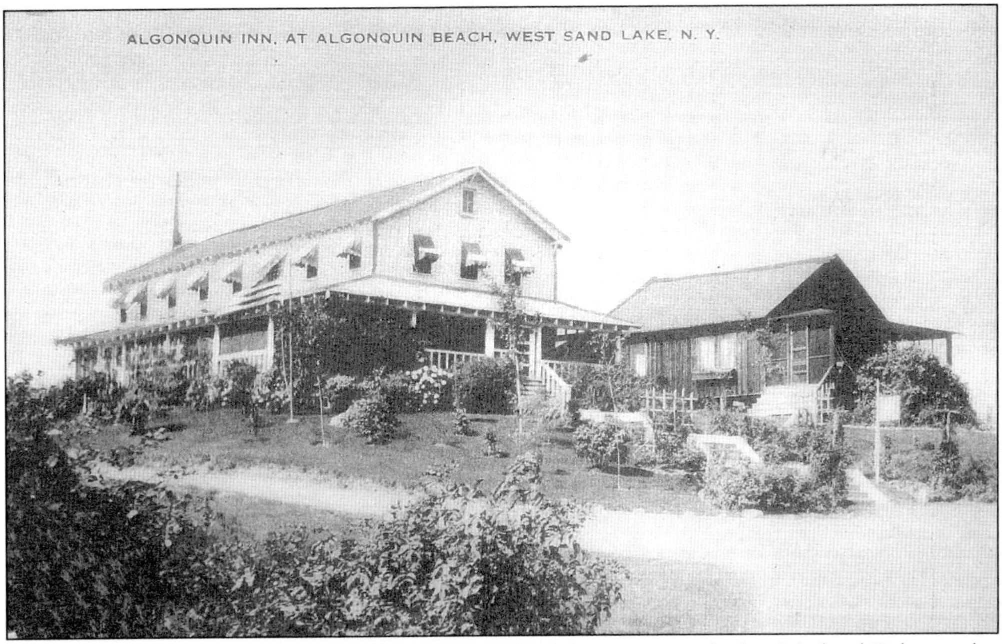

THE ALGONQUIN INN AT REICHARD'S LAKE. The lake was named after Michael Rykert, who leased a 159-acre farm in 1790 on a pond called Drie Kante Lackie, which in Dutch means "three-cornered lake." A popular resort was the Algonquin Inn, which had a large hotel with a dance hall and 28 cottages on the lakeshore. Canoeing, swimming, bird hunting, and fishing were choices during summer vacations. (Courtesy Muriel DeRosa.)

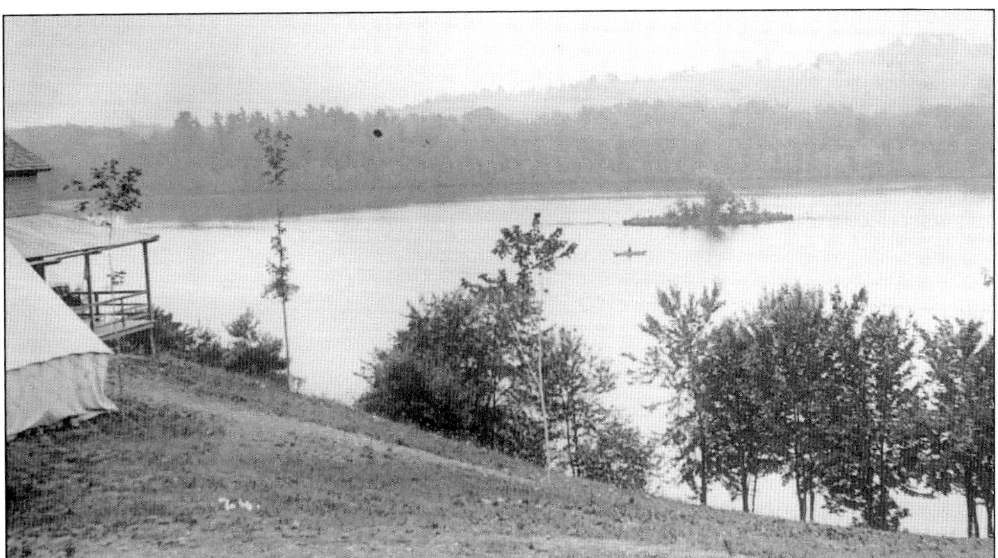

REICHARD'S LAKE. Since 1955, the town has maintained for its residents a town beach at Reichard's Lake, a popular spot. Today, most of the camps and homes along the lake have been converted to year-round residences. (Courtesy Alice Tifft.)

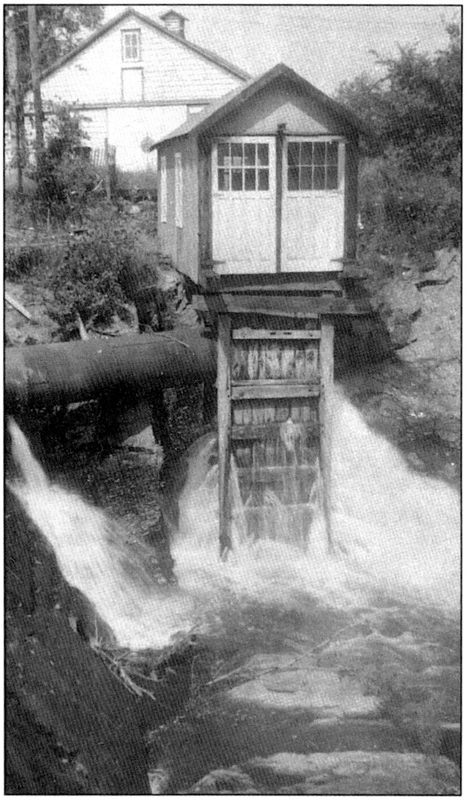

THE WYNANTSKILL HYDRO-ELECTRIC COMPANY. The town's first hydroelectric generating plant was built by Clifford Hastings in 1910. He converted his father's gristmill and cider mill by installing a water turbine and shafting to drive a 50-kilowatt generator. This picture shows the gatehouse that controlled the water flow. The company was sold to New York State Electric and Gas in 1926. (Courtesy Richard Hastings.)

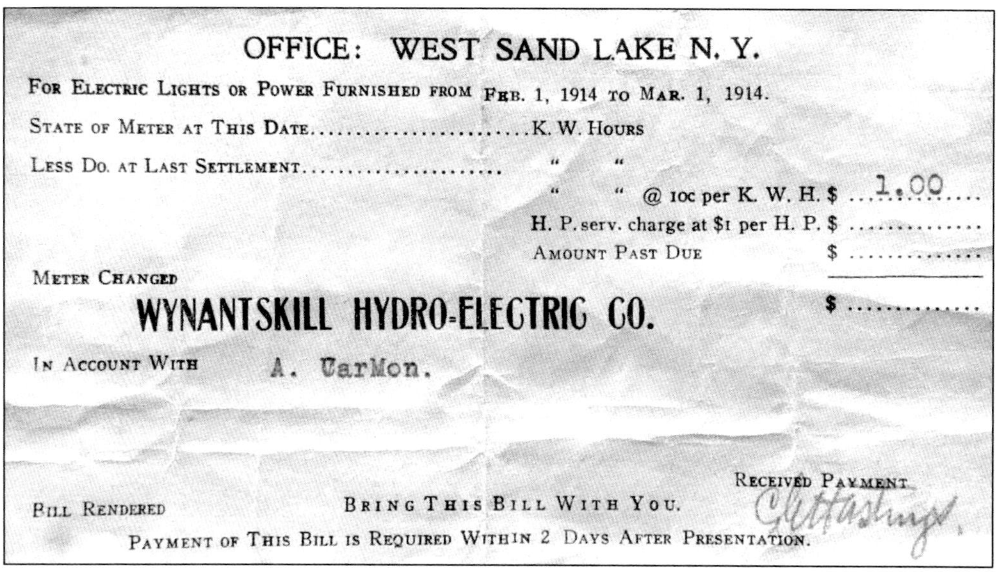

OFFICE: WEST SAND LAKE N. Y.

FOR ELECTRIC LIGHTS OR POWER FURNISHED FROM FEB. 1, 1914 TO MAR. 1, 1914.

STATE OF METER AT THIS DATE........................K. W. HOURS

LESS DO. AT LAST SETTLEMENT...................... " "

" " @ 10c per K. W. H. $ ...1.00...

H. P. serv. charge at $1 per H. P. $ ....

AMOUNT PAST DUE $ ....

METER CHANGED

WYNANTSKILL HYDRO-ELECTRIC CO. $ ....

IN ACCOUNT WITH A. CarMon.

RECEIVED PAYMENT C. H. Hastings.

BILL RENDERED BRING THIS BILL WITH YOU.

PAYMENT OF THIS BILL IS REQUIRED WITHIN 2 DAYS AFTER PRESENTATION.

A WYNANTSKILL HYDRO-ELECTRIC COMPANY BILL. A. Carmon bought 10 kilowatt hours of power for $1 during the month of February 1914. Upon receiving his bill, he had two days to pay. (Courtesy Town of Sand Lake Collection.)

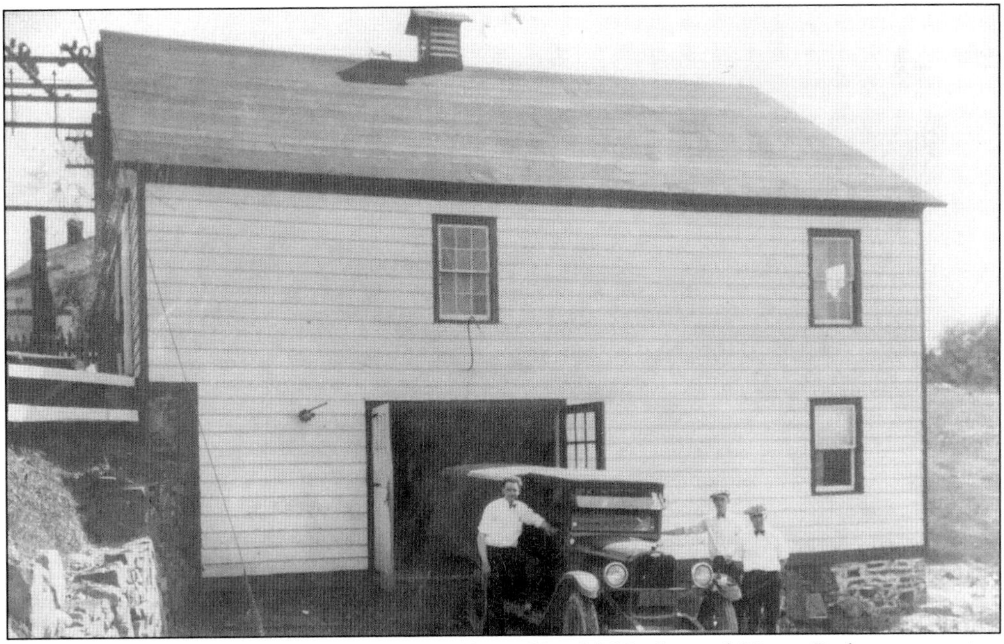

SAND LAKE SPRINGS. Employees Lemon Ewig, Harold Hogle, and Harry Bailey are getting the truck out at Sand Lake Springs to load for a delivery. Springwater, noted for its purity, and many flavors of soda were delivered to local and city customers until 1960. (Courtesy Richard Hastings.)

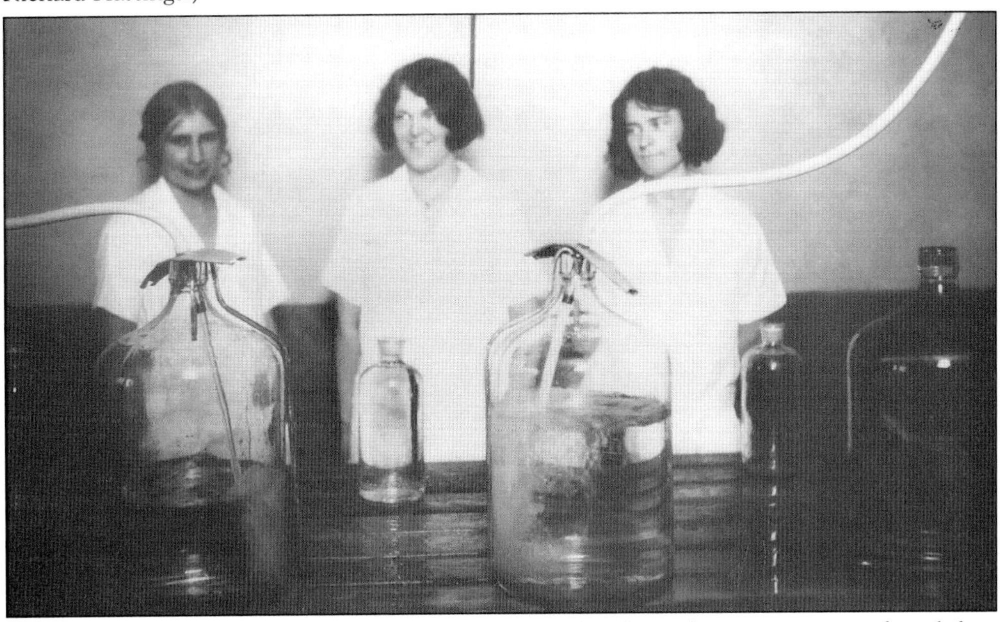

BOTTLING SAND LAKE SPRINGS WATER. Filling large bottles with springwater are, from left to right, Myra Hogle, Eleanor Ewig, and Rossetti Hastings. An October 7, 1931 advertisement in the *Troy Record* has a testimonial from Margaret King, who was "astonished at the pains taken to safeguard good health," and was "Enthusiastic in Her Praise of This Fine Soft, Pure, Spring Water and Heartily Recommends To The Housewives of Troy and Vicinity Its Use in the Home Daily." (Courtesy Charles Viens.)

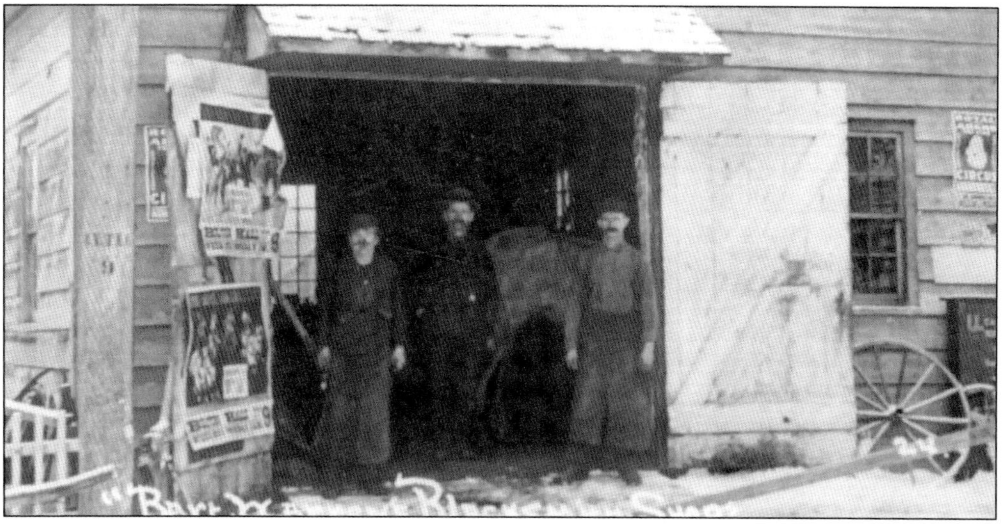

Bart Warren's Blacksmith Shop. This blacksmith shop was on Route 150 south, near the Four Corners. From left to right are Dennis Warren, William Mielenz, and Bart Warren (see page 83). Bart Warren was the father of Joseph Warren Sr., former town clerk and supervisor. (Courtesy Town of Sand Lake Collection.)

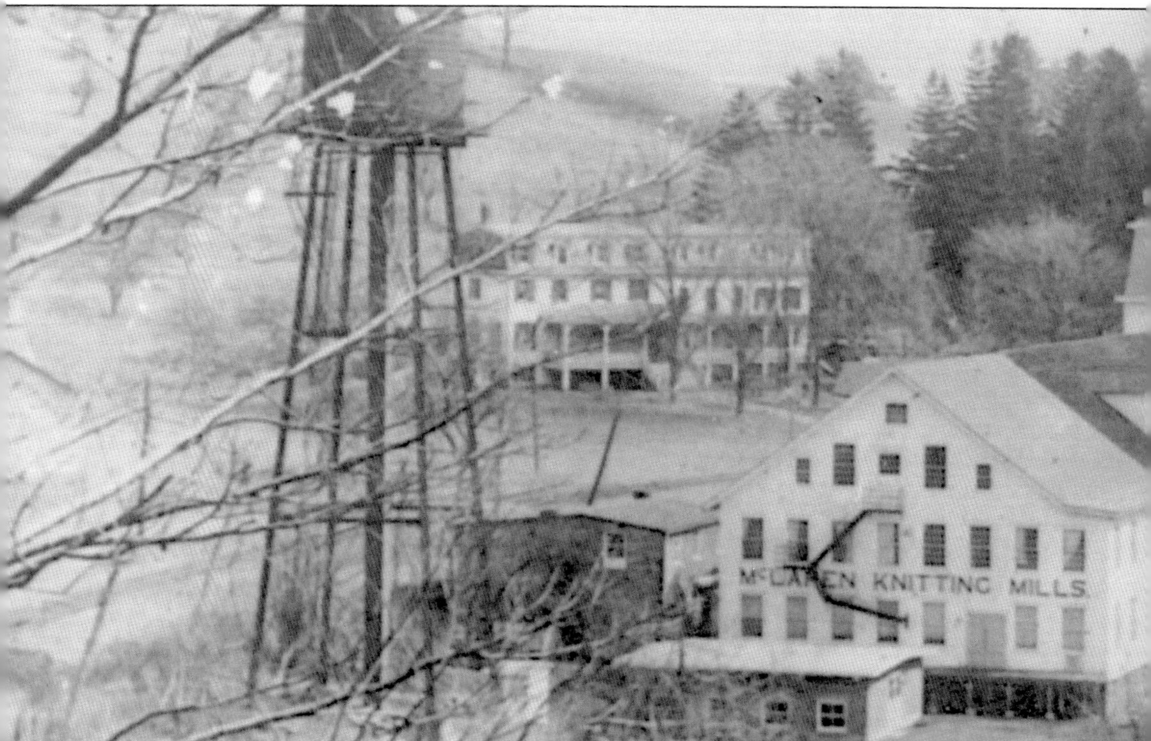

The McLaren Knitting Mill and the Thermo Knitting Mill. Shown, from left to right, are Cedarhurst, McLaren Knitting Mill, Thermo Knitting Mill, and Route 43. The trolley tracks ran between Cedarhurst (see page 30) and the McLaren Knitting Mill. Both mills occupied the site of the Cipperley Mill, a cloth-dressing factory that dated back to 1788.

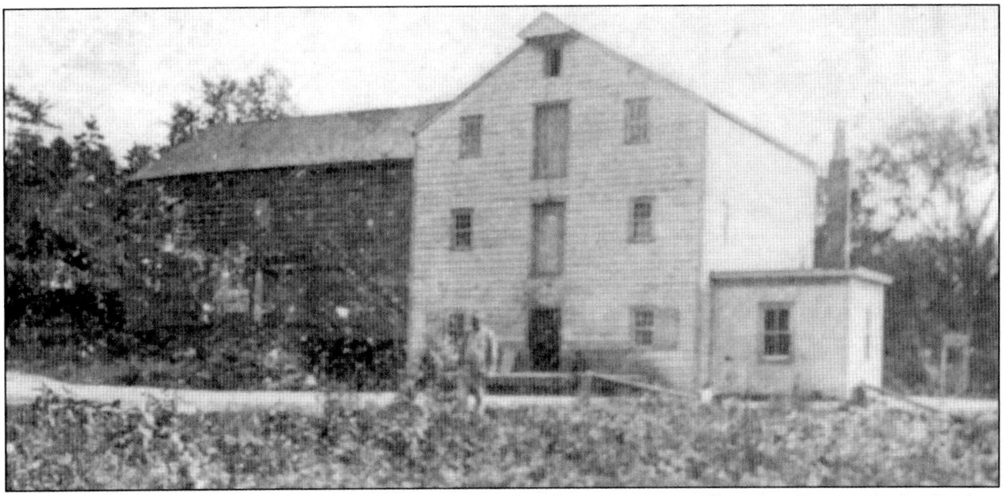

The Old Uline Mill. Barant Uline settled on his farm in 1798. Shortly afterwards, he built a gristmill and fulling mill, to shrink and thicken woolen cloth into felt by moistening, heating, and pressing. The mill operated until the 1950s. The flour mill shown here was built in the 1880s and was located across from the Thermo Mill (Bonded Concrete). (Courtesy Town of Sand Lake Collection.)

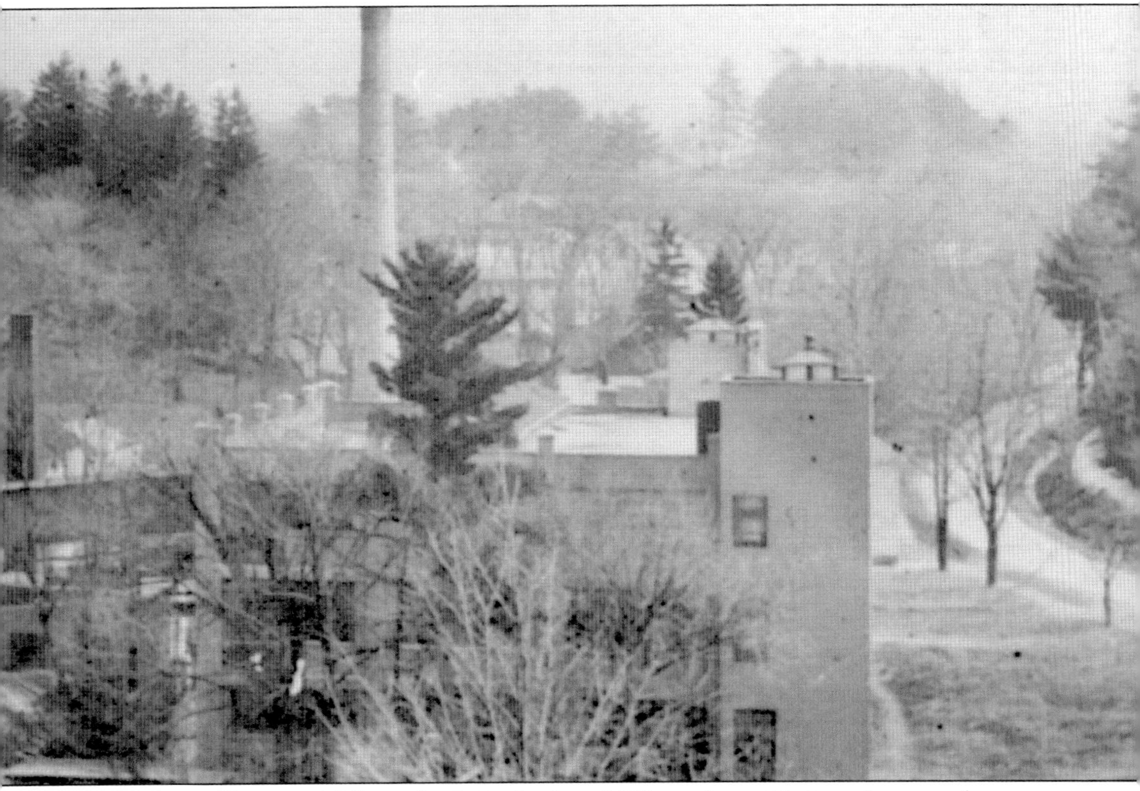

The McLaren Knitting Mill was built in the late 1800s and provided employment for many of the town's people. It became the Union Piece and Dye in the 1920s. The mill burned in a spectacular fire in 1956. The Thermo Knitting Mill was a concrete structure built *c.* 1910. Today, it is Bonded Concrete. (Courtesy Richard T. McLaren.)

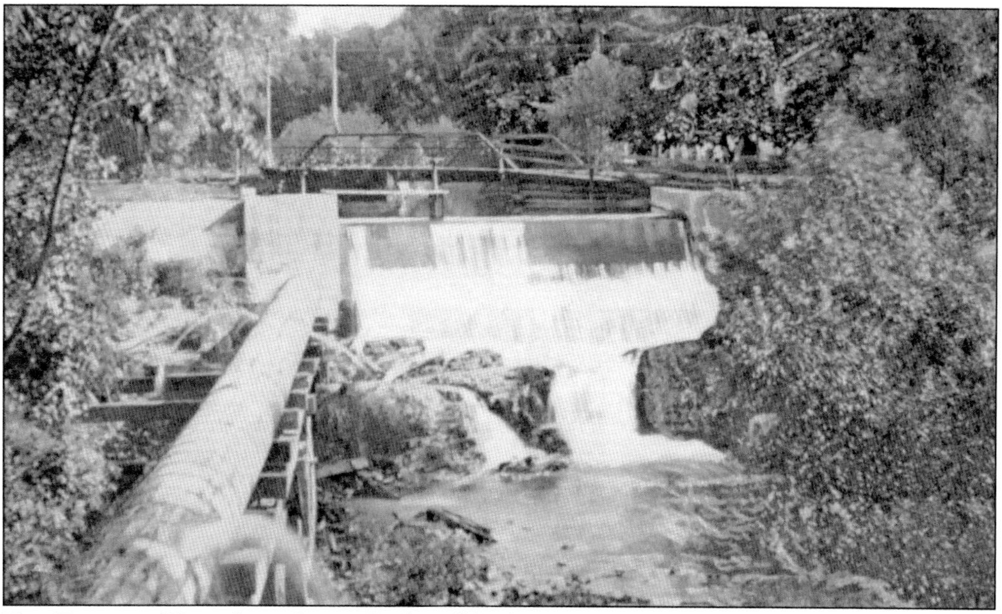

THE FALLS AT WEST SAND LAKE. Each mill had its own millpond. The McLaren Dam created the falls, and the wooden raceway carried water to the waterwheel. Today, the bridge in the background is on Route 43. (Courtesy Alice Tifft.)

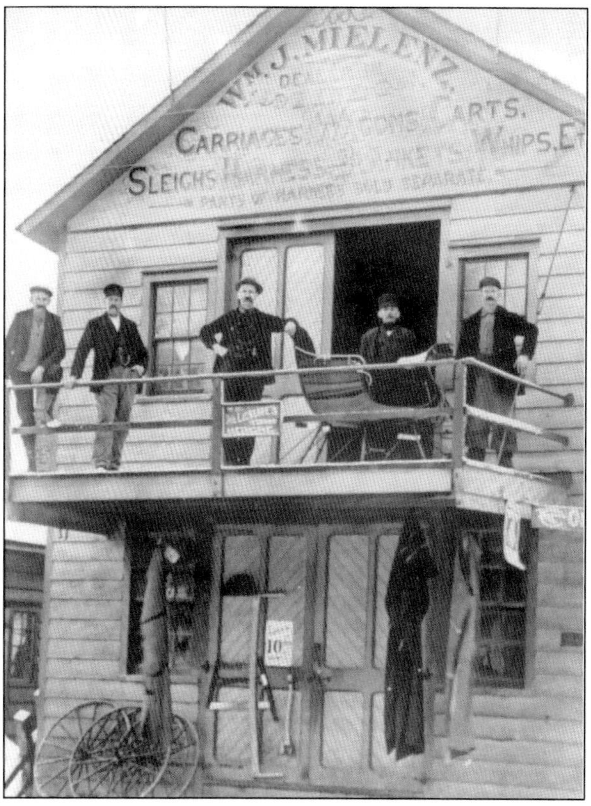

WILLIAM MIELENZ'S WAGONMAKER'S SHOP. Mielenz's carriage shop operated from 1874 to 1917 and was located on the southwest corner of the Four Corners. It provided carriages, wagons, sleighs, harnesses, blankets, and whips. Proudly displaying one of their sleighs are, from left to right, Albert Cipperly, Albert Goewey, William Mielenz, George Eweg, and Bart Warren (see page 83) . (Courtesy Town of Sand Lake Collection.)

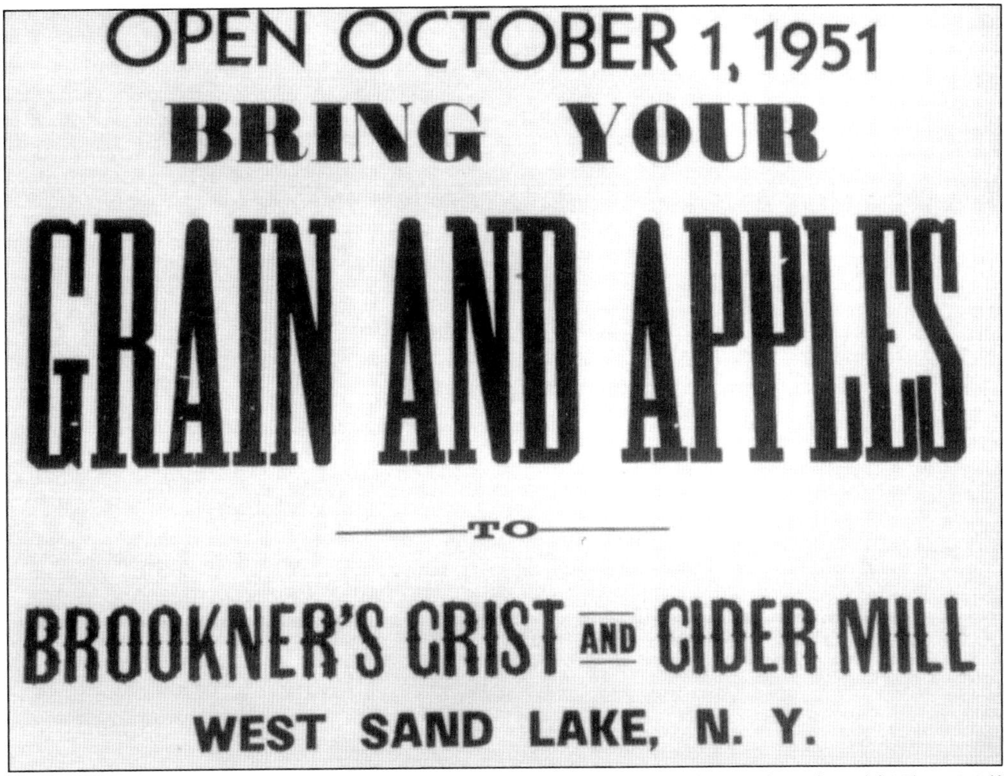

OPEN OCTOBER 1, 1951
BRING YOUR
GRAIN AND APPLES
TO
BROOKNER'S GRIST AND CIDER MILL
WEST SAND LAKE, N. Y.

BROOKNER'S GRISTMILL AND CIDER MILL. Brookner's Mill was located in the old Uline Mill (see page 25). This broadside encourages local farmers to bring their grain and apples to be processed into flour and cider. (Courtesy Town of Sand Lake Collection.)

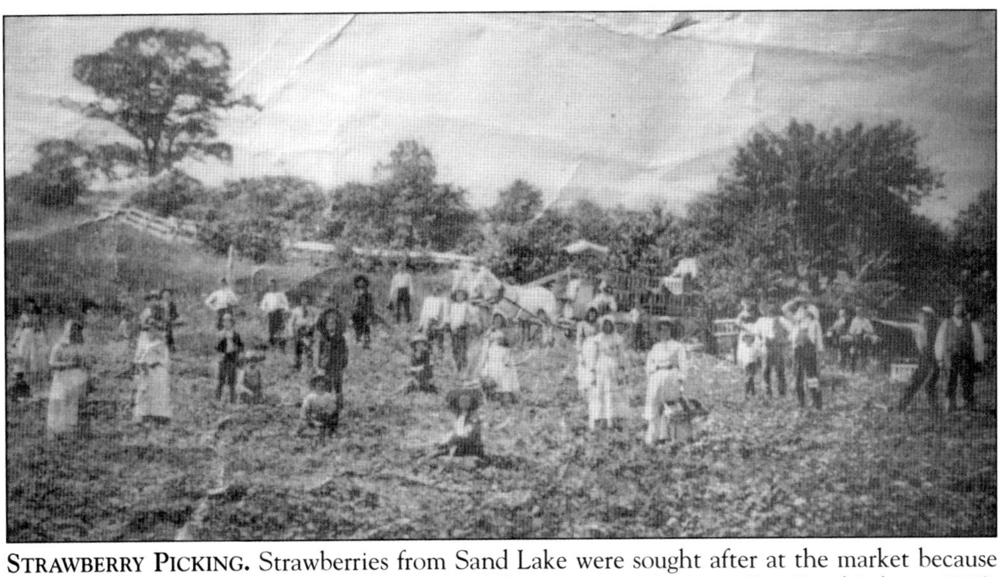

STRAWBERRY PICKING. Strawberries from Sand Lake were sought after at the market because of their fine flavor. Pickers are shown at the Albert Hastings farm in West Sand Lake in 1910. One history of the town states that "in one day, 2600 quarts were gathered at the Uline farm and 5000 quarts from the Hastings farm." (Courtesy Town of Sand Lake Collection.)

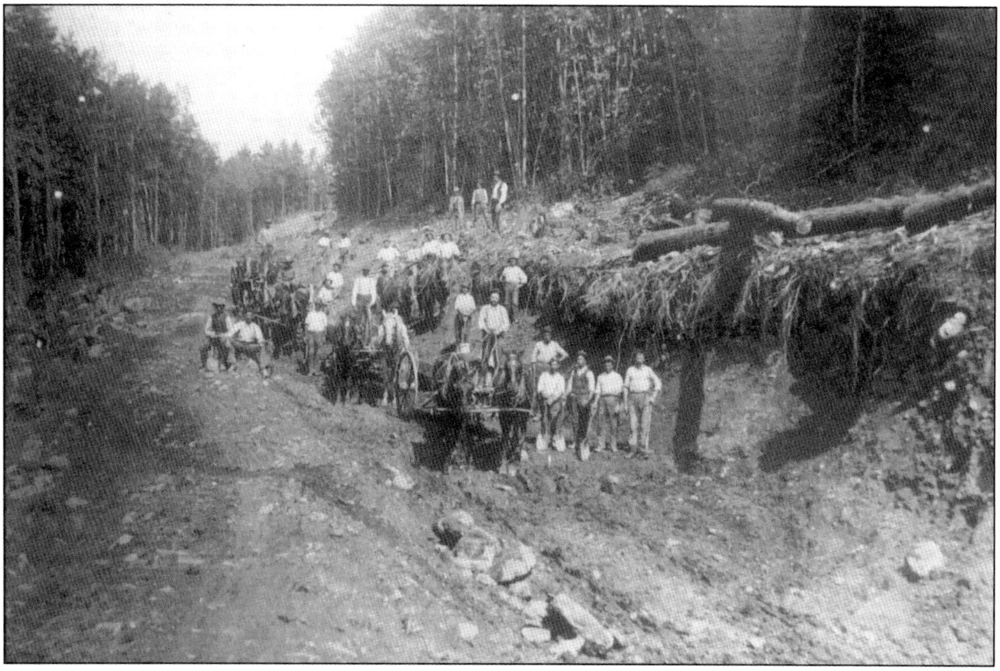

A Troy & New England Railway Work Crew. The work crew is shown preparing the roadbed for the trolley tracks for the Troy & New England Railway. Men, horses, picks, and shovels excavated at a pace as fast as a man could dig and horses could haul. (Courtesy Town of Sand Lake Collection.)

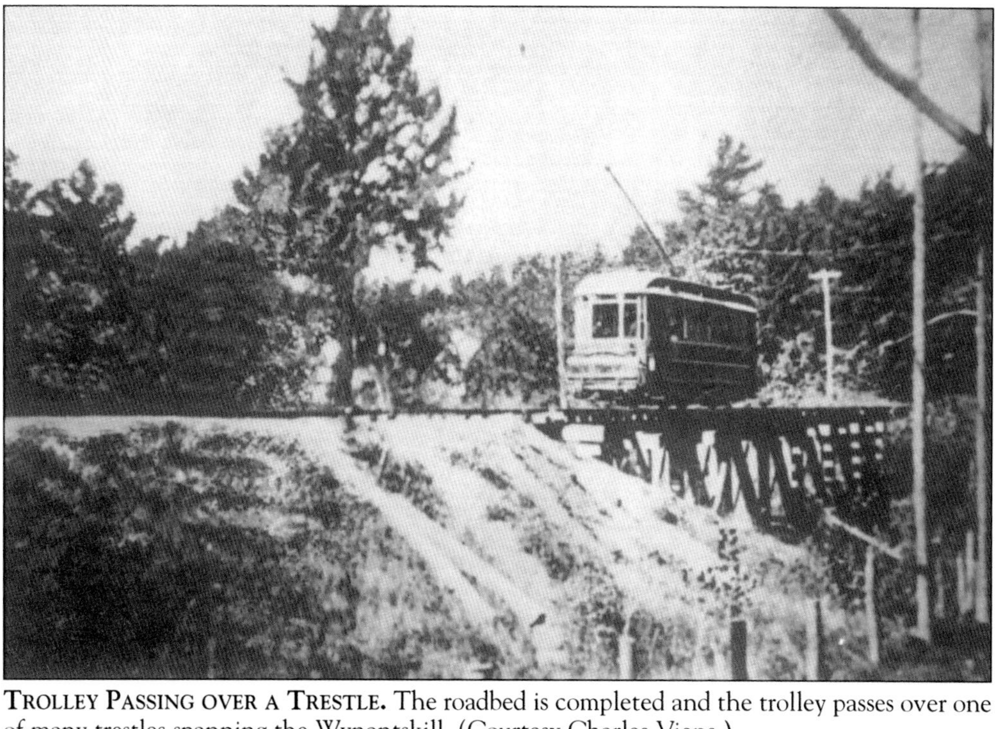

Trolley Passing over a Trestle. The roadbed is completed and the trolley passes over one of many trestles spanning the Wynantskill. (Courtesy Charles Viens.)

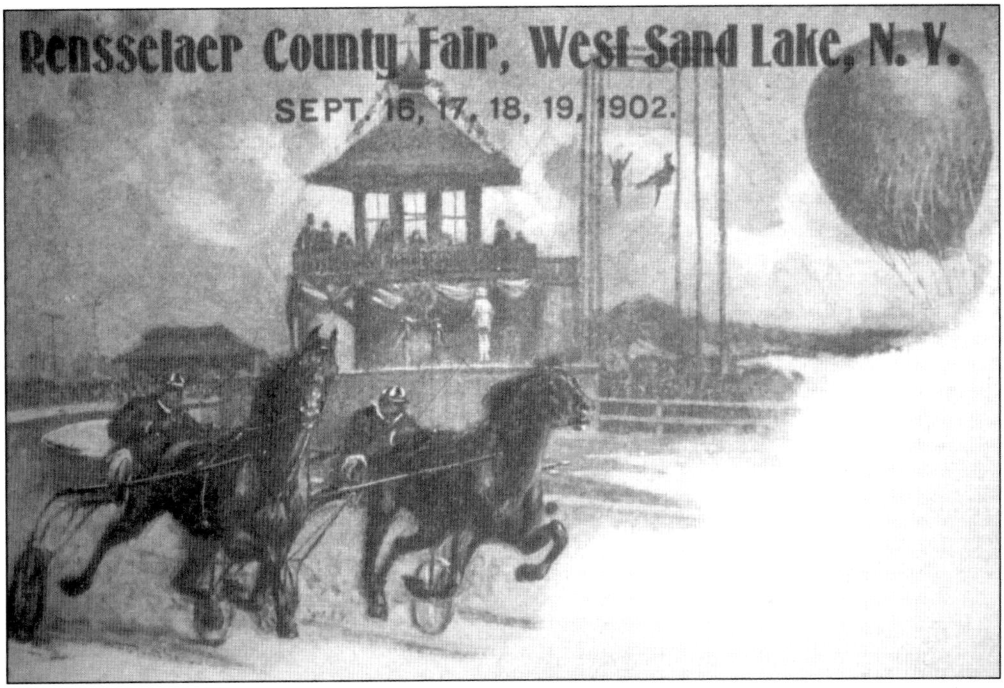

THE RENSSELAER COUNTY FAIR. This broadside advertises the Rensselaer County Fair, which was held in 1902 at Younghan's Race Track in West Sand Lake. (Courtesy Town of Sand Lake Collection.)

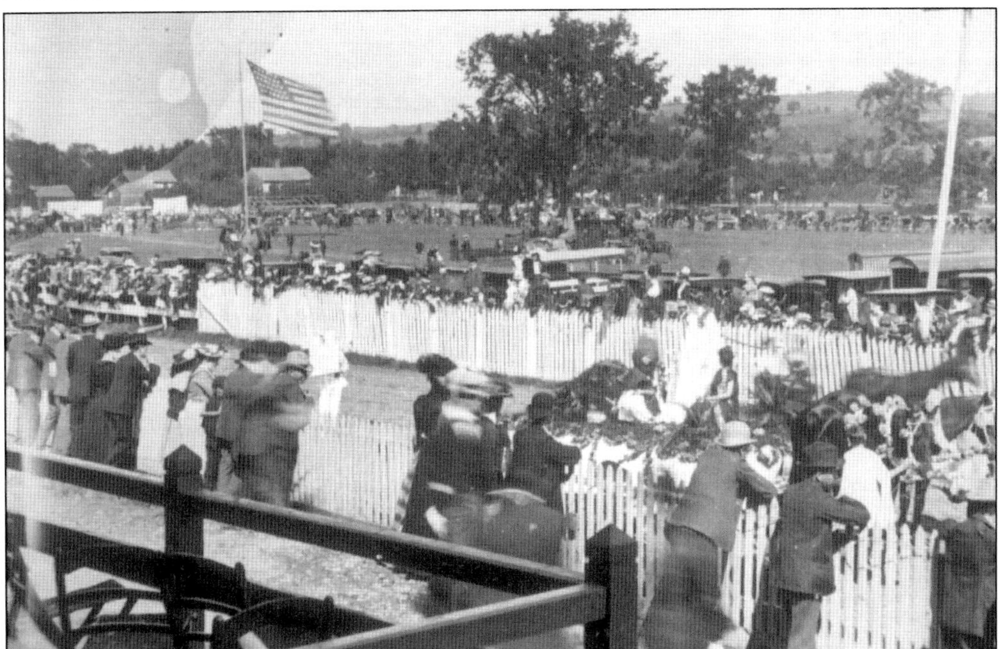

YOUNGHAN'S RACE TRACK, 1909. This fairgrounds and racetrack was located at the present site of the West Sand Lake Elementary School (see page 19). It looks like there was standing room only. (Courtesy Charles Viens.)

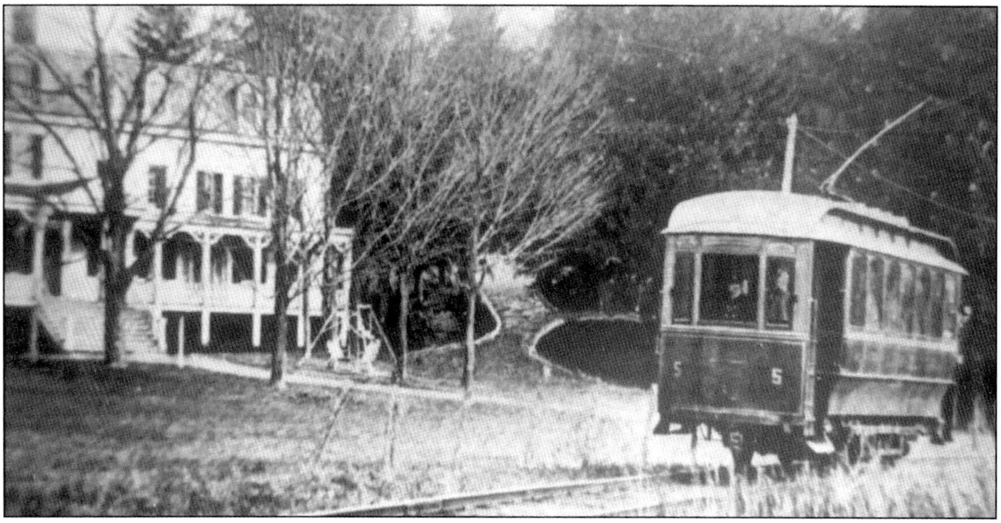

CEDARHURST. Cedarhurst stands on land leased by Hendrick Cipperly in 1795 from Stephen Van Rensselaer. In 1833, a log cabin was replaced with a brick house, and a clapboard addition was built in 1895. Used as a trolley stop until 1925, Cedarhurst was a well-known rooming house for mill workers and summer boarders. Owned by West Sand Lake Grange No. 949 from 1932 to 1968, it was called Grange Hall. It now houses the administrative offices for Bonded Concrete and Troy Sand & Gravel Companies. (Courtesy Charles Viens.)

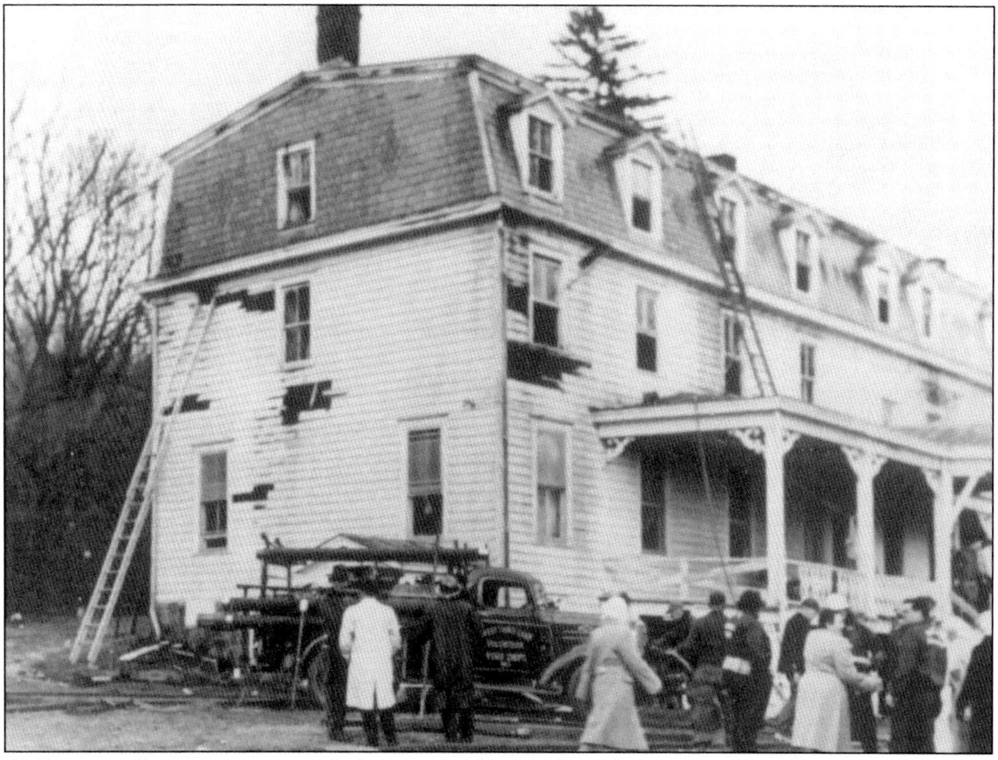

A FIRE AT CEDARHURST. Cedarhurst was damaged by fire on April 4, 1963. Another fire occurred in 1985. After the more recent fire, the building was renovated and used by NAPA Auto Parts. (Courtesy Town of Sand Lake Collection.)

THE KNIGHTS OF PYTHIAS. The cornerstone for this building, known as the Pythian Castle, was laid in 1927. The upper hall with the stained-glass windows and murals painted by C.G. Davidson was the organization's meeting room. The lower floor has been an elementary school, dance studio, furniture store, and Four Doors—a mission of clothing and food for needy persons. The building is owned by James Bonesteel and located on Route 150, south of the Four Corners. (Courtesy Sand Lake Historical Society Collection.)

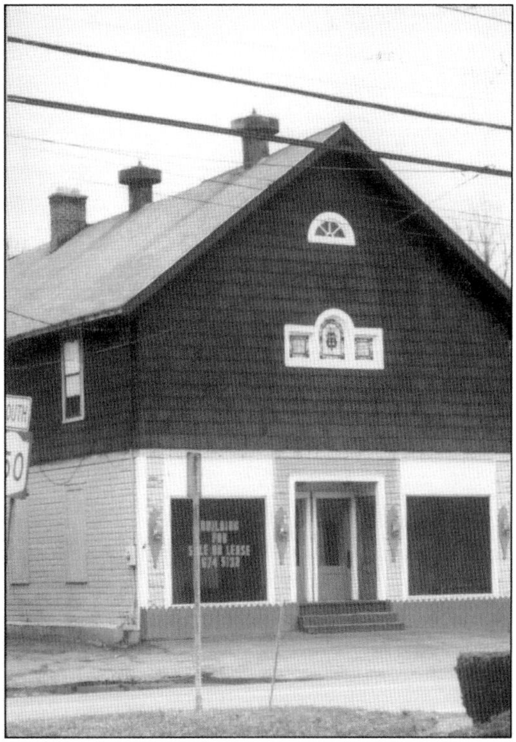

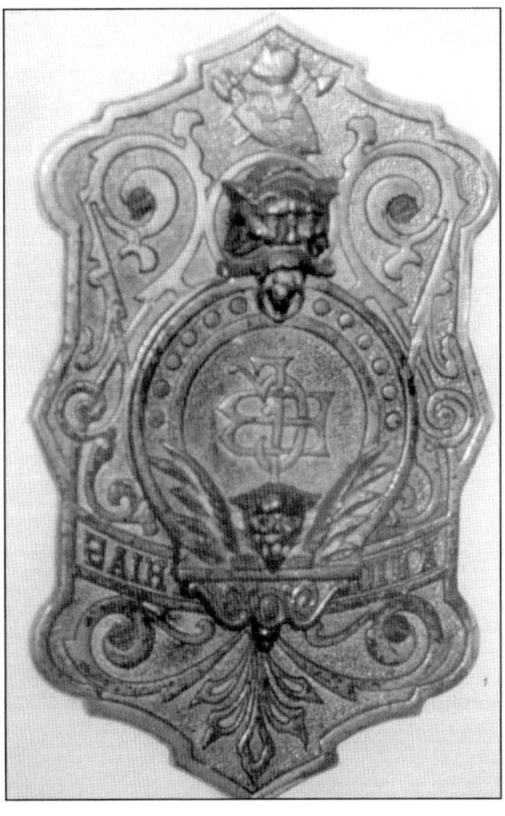

THE DOOR TO PYTHIAN CASTLE. Before a Pythian knight was allowed to enter the meeting room of the Pythian Castle he was identified by the outer guard to the inner guard through the slide opening in this door shield. (Courtesy Sand Lake Historical Society Collection.)

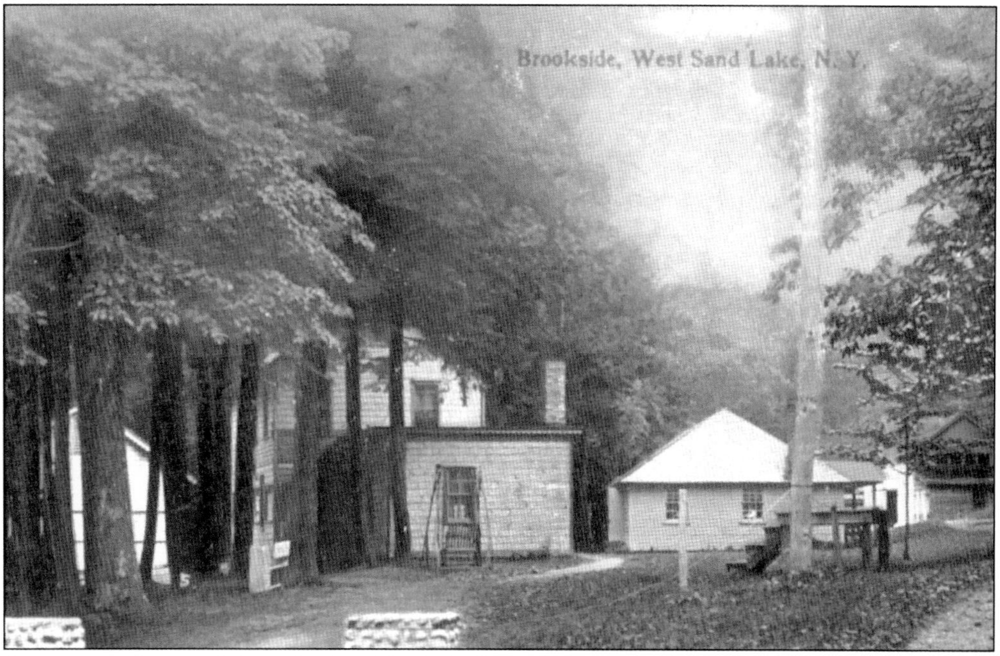

BROOKSIDE PARK, 1914. A New Year's Ball was advertised for December 31, 1897, when George Fredenburgh ran a dance hall at Brookside Park. Clam steams were a specialty and continued with Harry G. Werger, as owner. Brookside Park was a favorite place for businesses, groups, and churches to have their picnics. This is a 1914 view of the entrance. (Courtesy Ada and Wesley Miller.)

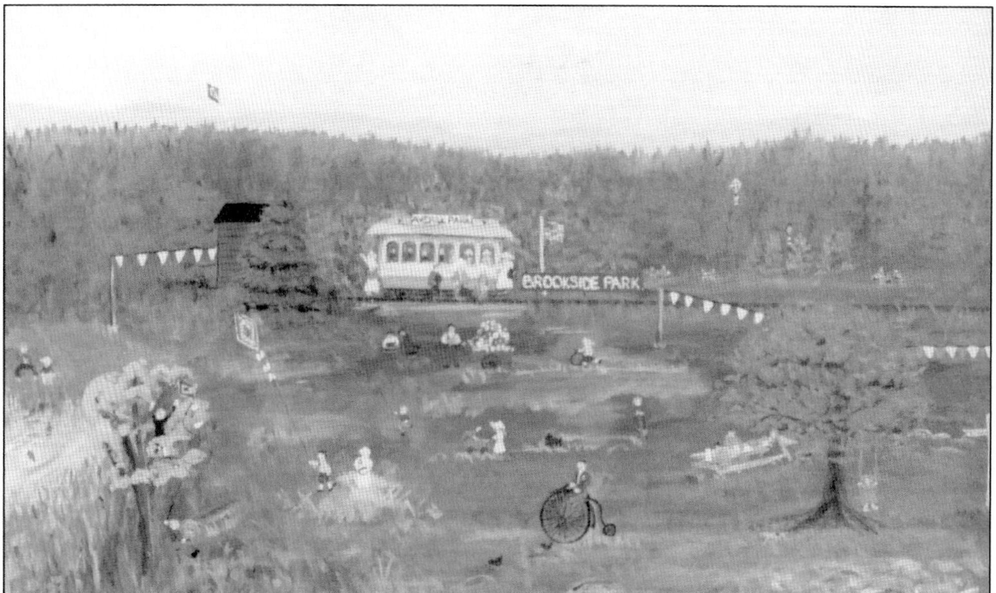

A PAINTING OF BROOKSIDE PARK. Beryl Vannier captures a variety of activities in this painting of Brookside Park. Persons getting off the trolley will be joining the fun. The trolley stopped here beginning in 1895. (Courtesy Beryl Vannier; painting displayed at Key Bank, West Sand Lake.)

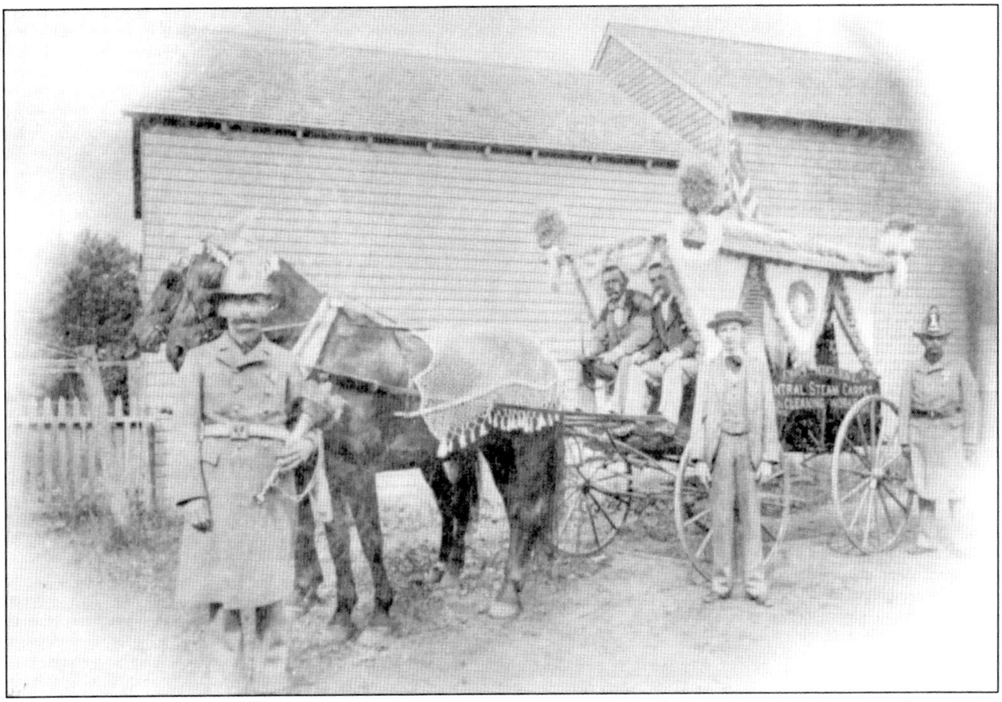

C.E. MIELENZ STEAM CARPET CLEANING. Steam carpet cleaning is not a new business. C.E. Mielenz and his crew are decked out for a parade and stand ready to serve "after the parade is over." (Courtesy Dorothy Leitgeb.)

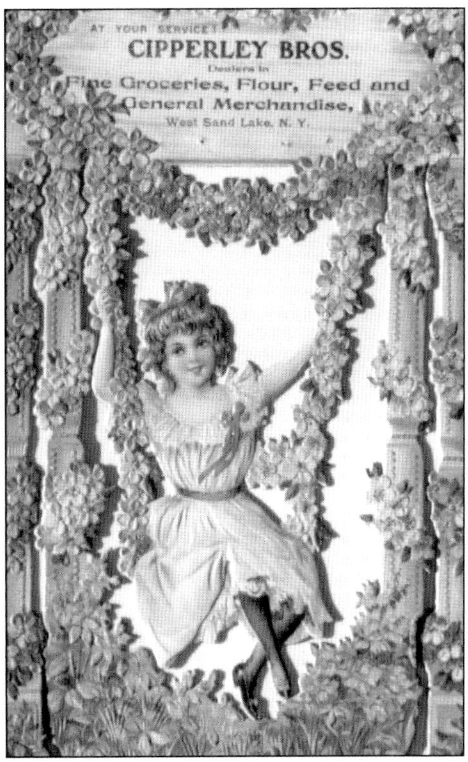

A CIPPERLEY BROTHERS ADVERTISEMENT. A valentine-like advertisement displays the Cipperley Brothers as dealers in fine groceries, flour, feed, and general merchandise. The business was located in the lower floor of the former Pythian Castle, or Bonesteel's Furniture. (Courtesy Mary Margaret A. "Meg" Cipperley.)

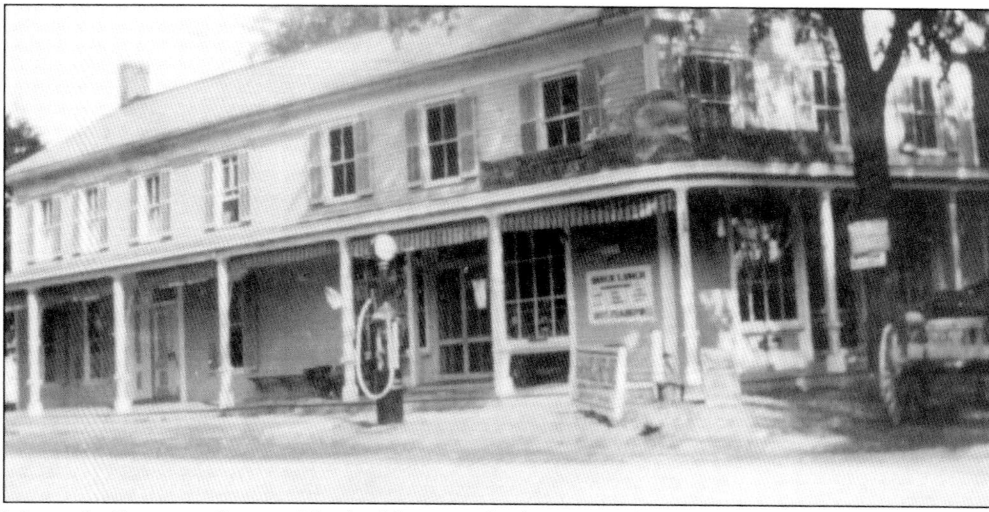

Miller's General Store. The building was built in 1878 by Washington Snyder and ran for many years as a store and Seymour's Hotel. It had many owners before it became Mike Miller & Sons Meats, Groceries. At one time, the entire second floor extended the length of the building and was a ballroom. Many village affairs, including trials, were held there. It was demolished in 1956 for the parking lot of the new Miller's Market. (Courtesy George Breigle.)

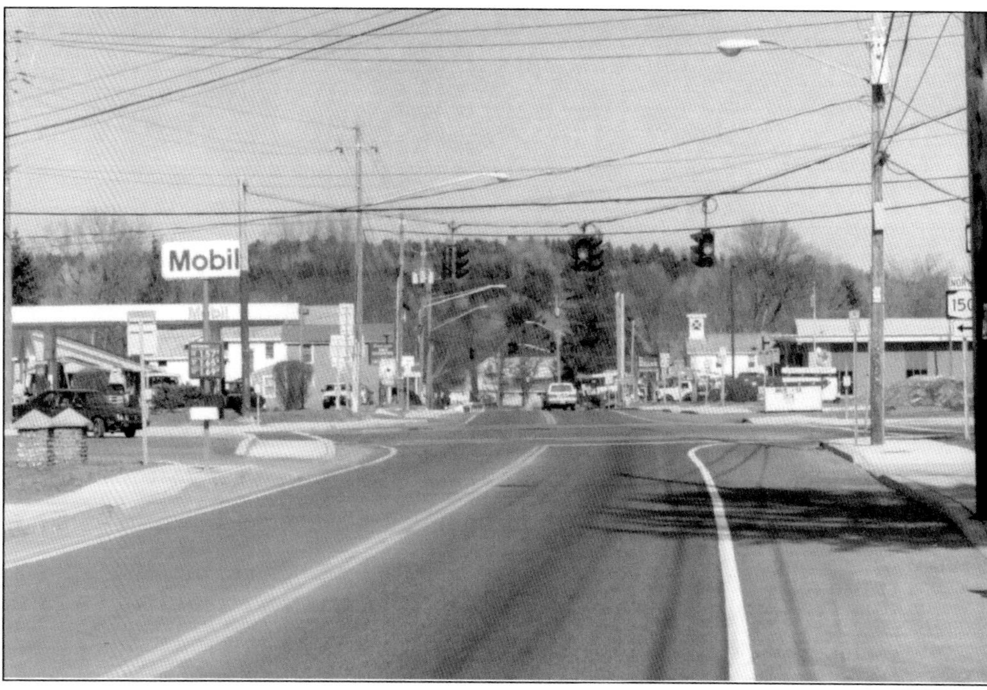

Looking East on Roue 43 at the Four Corners, 1999. Traffic is so heavy during commuting hours that a stoplight is now needed. The southeast corner is now the parking lot for Miller's Market. Visible farther down on the right is the new firehouse and still farther, the side and bell tower of the old firehouse. (Courtesy Sand Lake Historical Society Collection.)

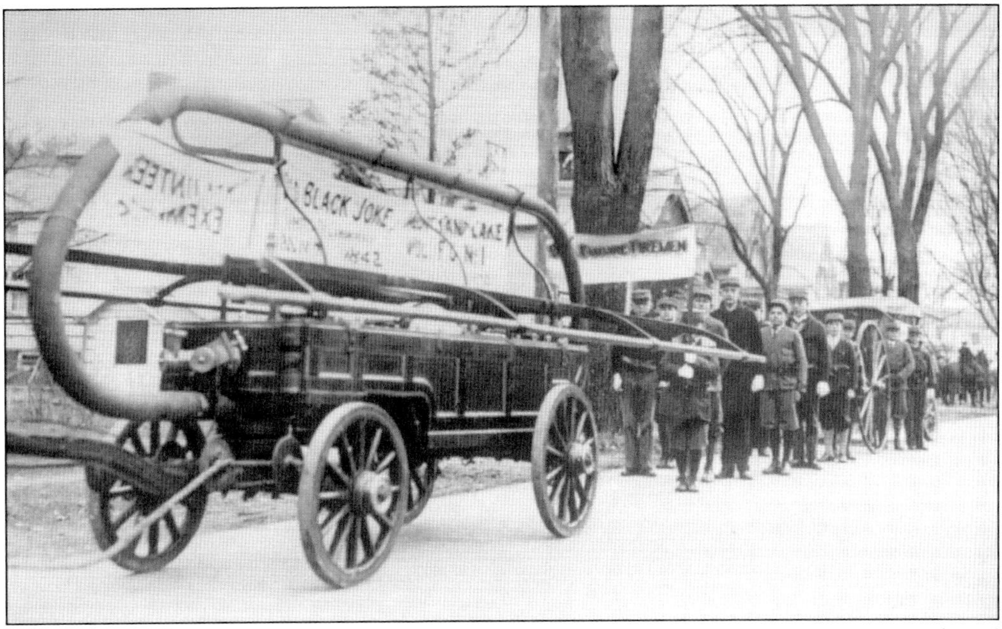

"OLD JOKE" IN 1926 PARADE. This hand pumper was the first piece of fire equipment purchased by the West Sand Lake Fire Company, when the company formed in 1872. John McLaren, founder of the McLaren Mill, was also a founder of the West Sand Lake Fire Company. For this 1926 parade, future firemen dubbed the engine "Old Black Joke." Now completely restored, the engine is affectionately called "Old Joe" and draws much applause when it passes in parades. (Courtesy West Sand Lake Fire Company.)

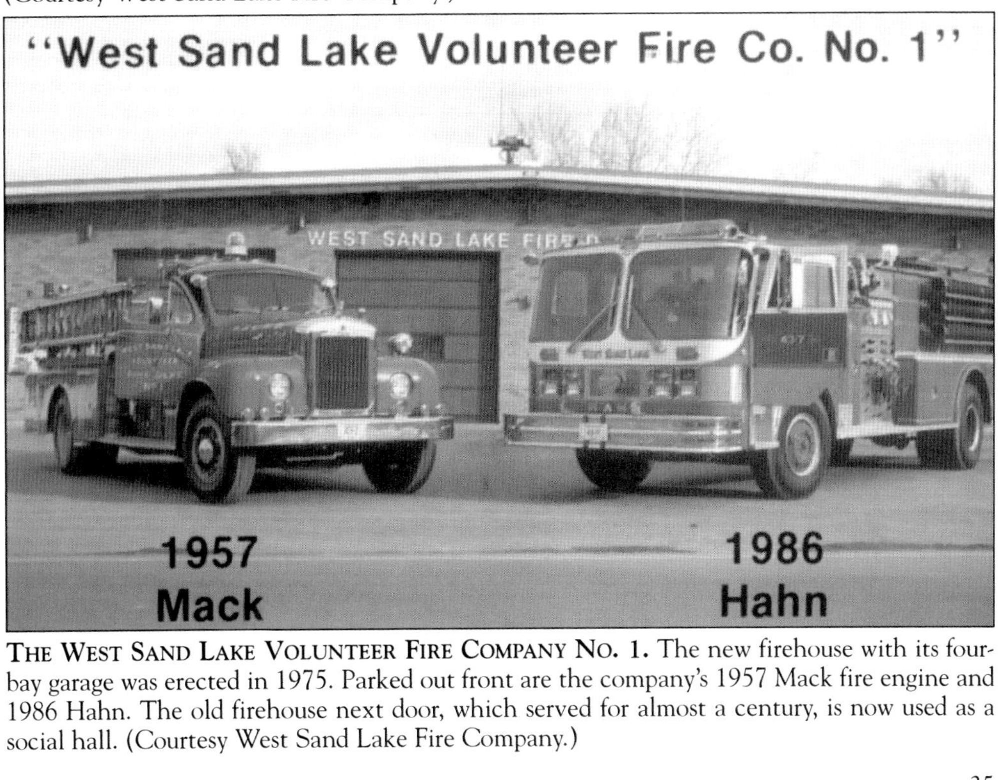

THE WEST SAND LAKE VOLUNTEER FIRE COMPANY NO. 1. The new firehouse with its four-bay garage was erected in 1975. Parked out front are the company's 1957 Mack fire engine and 1986 Hahn. The old firehouse next door, which served for almost a century, is now used as a social hall. (Courtesy West Sand Lake Fire Company.)

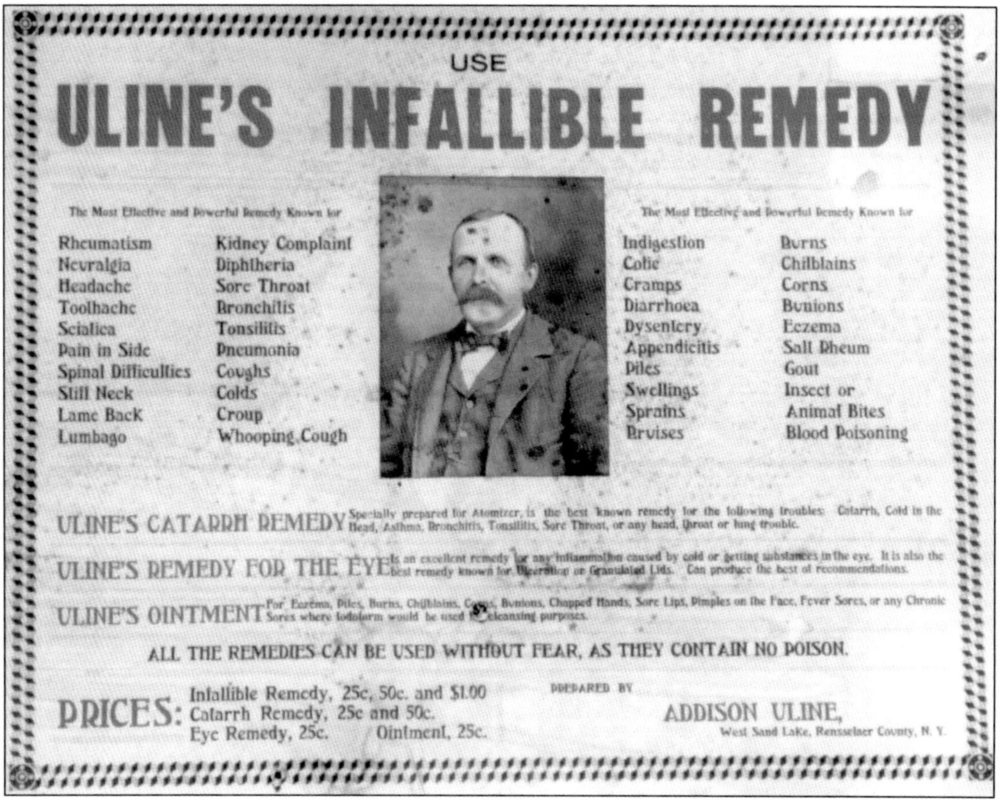

ULINE'S INFALLIBLE REMEDY. The text of the advertisement emphasizes the medicine's name. Addison Uline was a self-appointed healer of many ills. Oral history relates the Infallible Remedy to be a strong-smelling ointment, the recipe for which was a closely guarded secret. The recipe was passed on to son William Garfield Uline, with the stipulation that it be destroyed when it would no longer be used by him. (Courtesy Uline Family Reunion.)

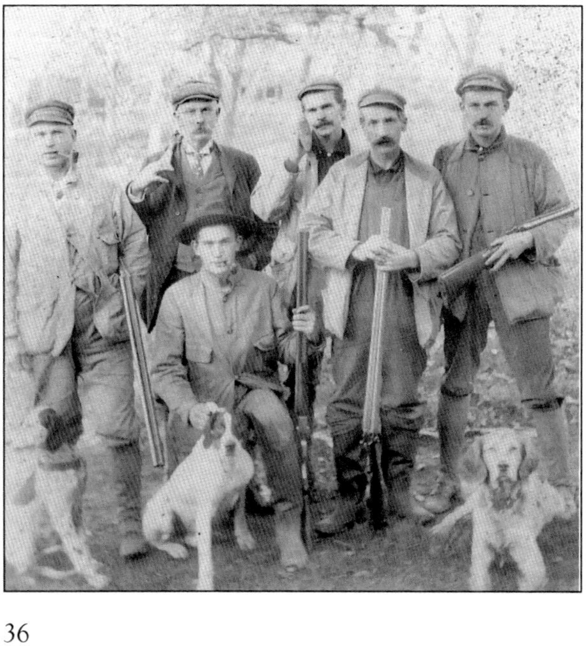

ADDISON ULINE AND HIS SONS. Addison Uline had seven sons and five daughters. In this hunting picture, two persons can be identified. Addison Uline is second from the left, and William Garfield Uline is third from the left. The dogs must have been well disciplined to remain quiet during the time the camera shutter was opened. (Courtesy Betty Uline Engineri, granddaughter of William Garfield Uline.)

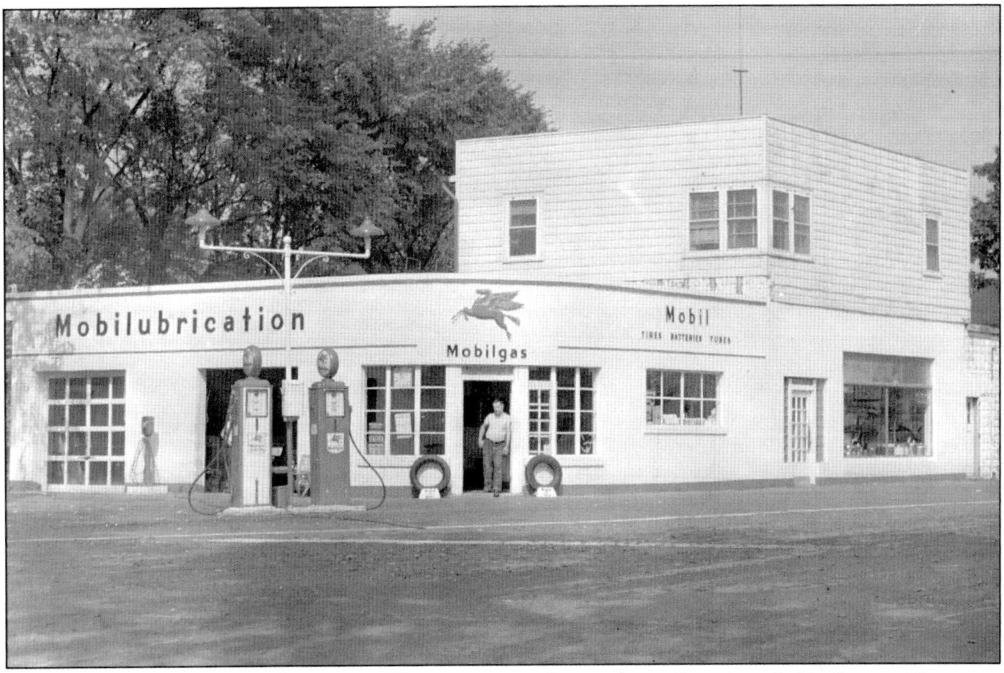

Joseph Werger Mobil Station. This station is located on the site of the former Brewster House. (Courtesy Town of Sand Lake Collection.)

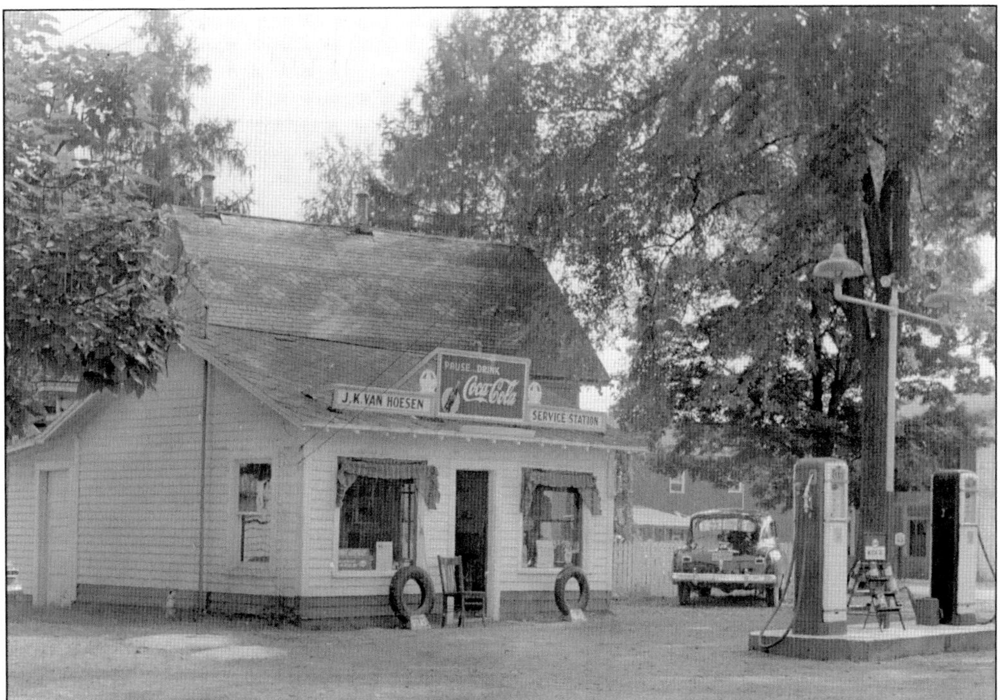

Ken Van Hoesen Gas Station. The Van Hoesen station was located on the northeast corner of Route 43. In the 1990s, a Mobil Station is operated at this site. (Courtesy Town of Sand Lake Collection.)

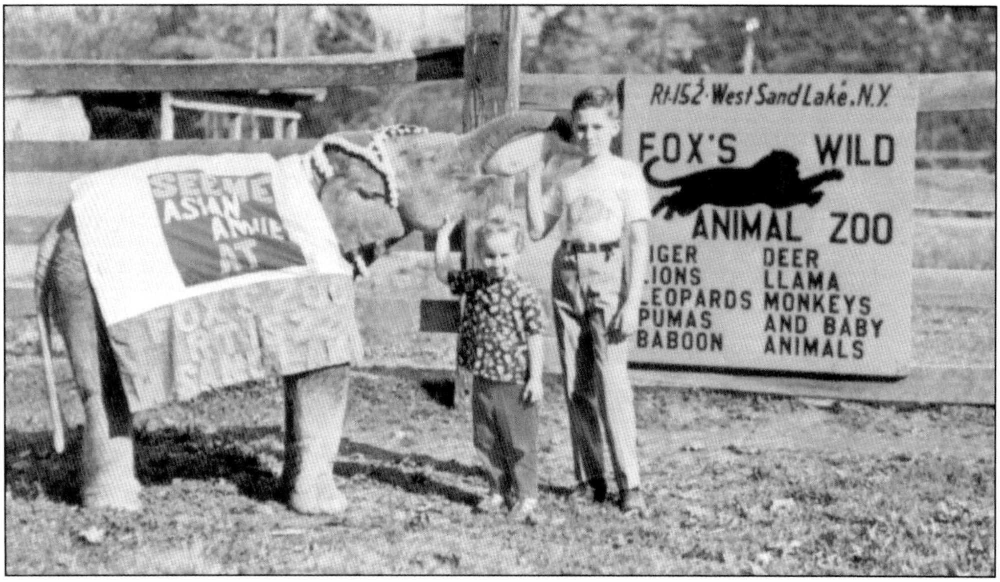

FOX'S WILD ANIMAL ZOO. Located on County Route 55, Fox's Wild Animal Zoo was a favorite attraction from 1959 to 1975. Harold Fox specialized in endangered species and exotic animals, such as the big cats and old world and South American monkeys. Baby elephant Asian Annie enjoys being given a drink. Children were treated to activities with animals when the Zoo Mobile visited their school. Both adults and children also enjoyed their many television appearances. (Courtesy Joseph Connors Jr.)

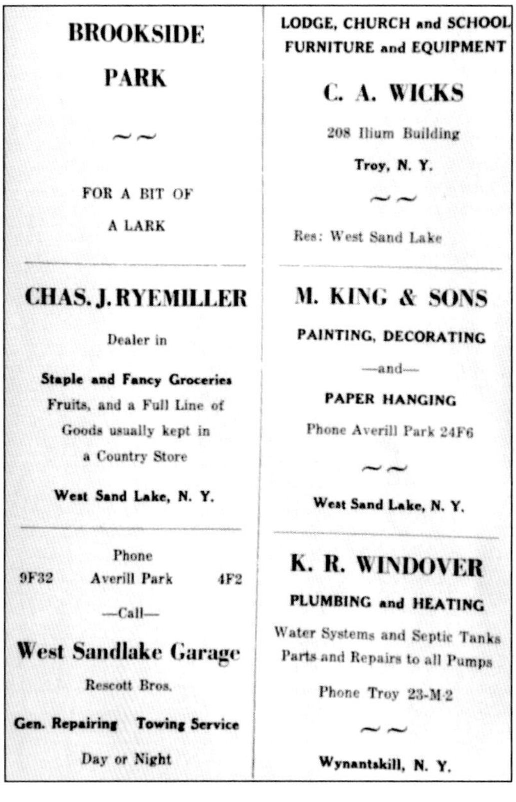

BROOKSIDE PARK

~ ~

FOR A BIT OF A LARK

LODGE, CHURCH and SCHOOL FURNITURE and EQUIPMENT

C. A. WICKS

208 Ilium Building

Troy, N. Y.

~ ~

Res: West Sand Lake

CHAS. J. RYEMILLER

Dealer in

Staple and Fancy Groceries Fruits, and a Full Line of Goods usually kept in a Country Store

West Sand Lake, N. Y.

M. KING & SONS

PAINTING, DECORATING

—and—

PAPER HANGING

Phone Averill Park 24F6

~ ~

West Sand Lake, N. Y.

Phone

9F32 Averill Park 4F2

—Call—

West Sandlake Garage

Rescott Bros.

Gen. Repairing Towing Service

Day or Night

K. R. WINDOVER

PLUMBING and HEATING

Water Systems and Septic Tanks Parts and Repairs to all Pumps

Phone Troy 23-M-2

~ ~

Wynantskill, N. Y.

PROGRAM ADVERTISEMENTS, 1933. A page from the West Sand Lake Minstrels program in 1933 advertises several West Sand Lake businesses. (Courtesy Town of Sand Lake Collection.)

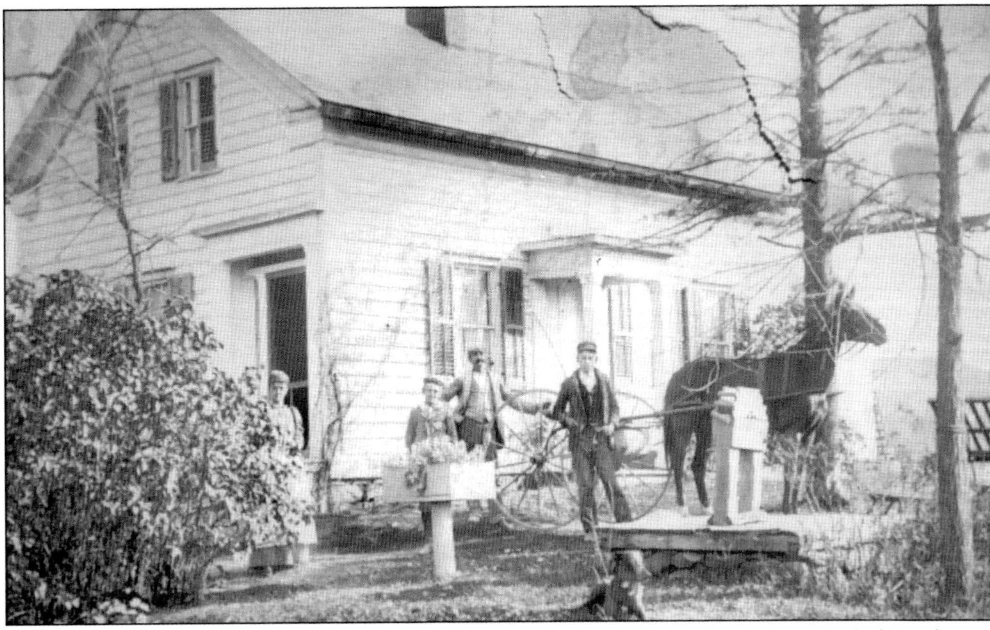

THE HASTINGS FAMILY. Members of the Hastings family pose in front of their home, which still stands on Sand Lake Springs Way. They are, from left to right, Edith Snyder Hastings, the young boy Douglas Hastings, Mr. VanZandt, and unidentified. (Courtesy Beverly Hastings.)

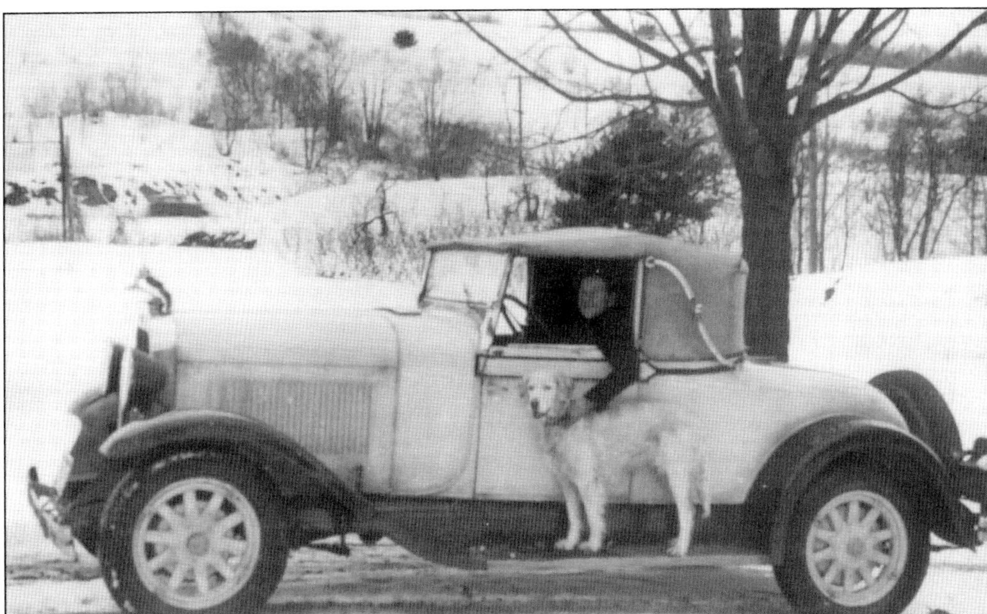

RICHARD HASTINGS. Richard Hastings looks proud in the 1930 Oldsmobile, which his brother gave him. Hastings drove the soda truck and worked in the Sand Lake Springs plant (see page 23), which was run by his father, Douglas Hastings. (Courtesy Beverly Hastings.)

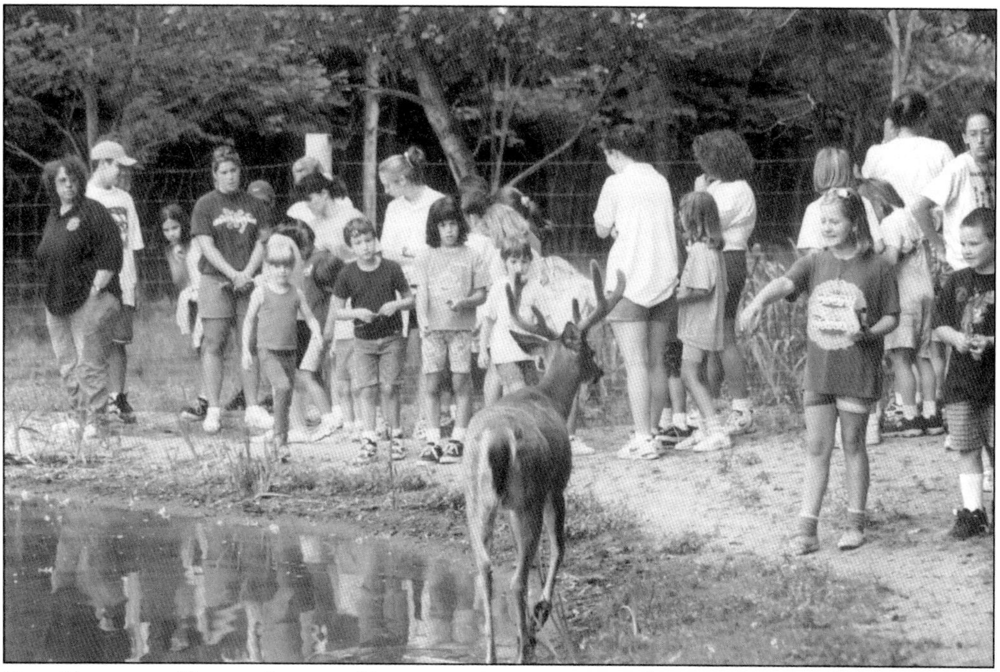

OUR FAVORITE PLACE ANIMAL KINGDOM. Lawrence the deer heads toward children from Sand Lake Day Camp, who are enjoying their field trip to Our Favorite Place Animal Kingdom on Old Best Road. The zoo operates as a not-for-profit charitable organization and encourages visits from school groups and organizations with a special emphasis on including physically or mentally challenged children and adults. (Courtesy Benjamin and Arlie Petrone.)

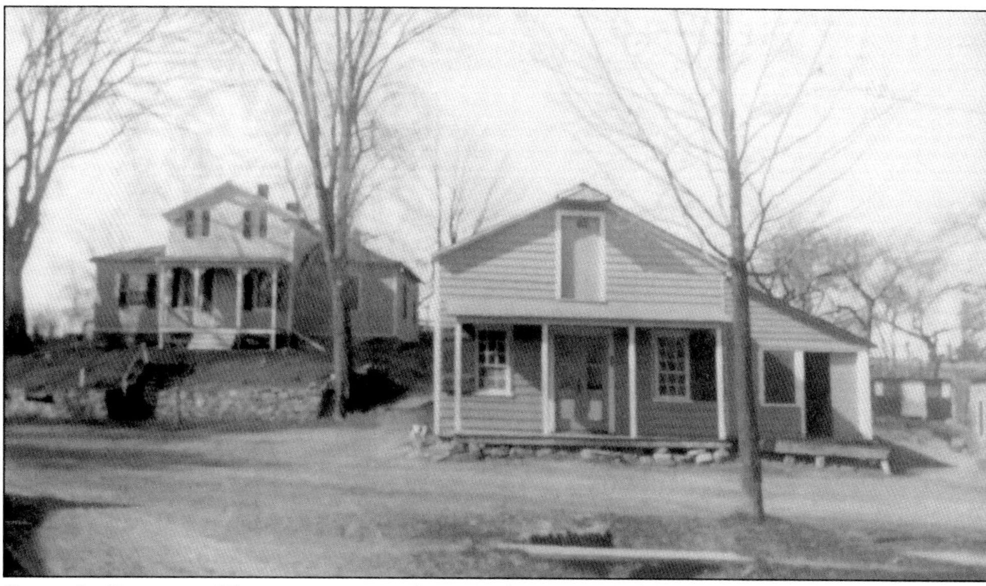

SLITER'S CORNERS. This picture was taken at what is now Sliter's Corners, at the intersection of state Route 150 and county Route 55. The area was previously known as South Sand Lake. The store and post office on the road were established in 1854. The house on the bank was the home of the first postmaster, William Stevens, who served until 1879. He was town supervisor in 1861. (Courtesy Edna DiDomenica Pierce.)

Two

AVERILL PARK AND THE BURDEN LAKES

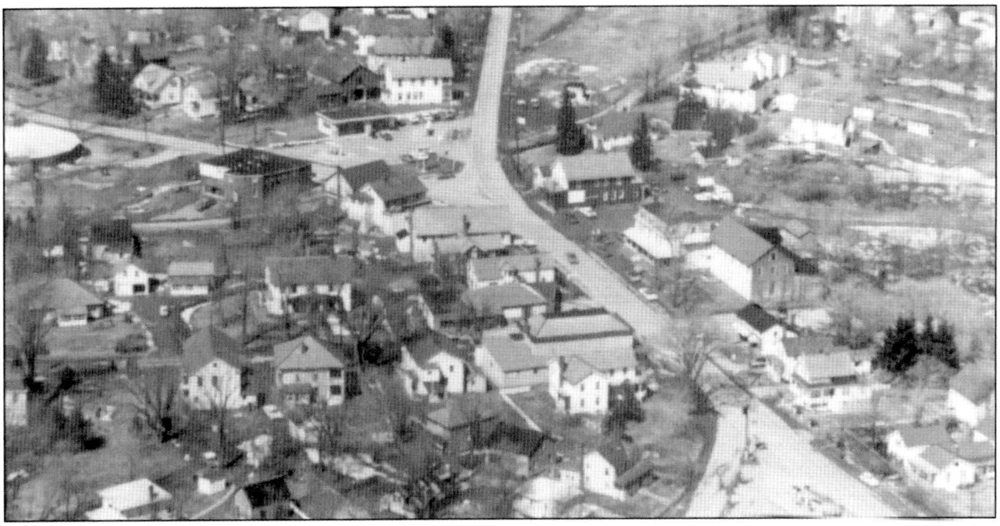

AVERILL PARK. An aerial view of Averill Park shows state Route 43, which was originally the Albany–Sand Lake Plank Road, running diagonally from upper left to right through the hamlet and intersecting county Route 45 first and then Eastern Union Turnpike. The Averills were among the earliest settlers, and members of the family were active in the community as lawyers, store and hotel owners, and real estate promoters. The former "village" of Sand Lake was named Averill on May 3, 1880, and then changed to Averill Park on March 27, 1882, by James K. Averill, a lawyer and promoter in building the Troy & New England Railway. (To interject a bit of Averill trivia, it is recalled that James Averill, a lover of animals, had his favorite horse, Moscow, buried in the family plot in Sand Lake Union Cemetery.) In this aerial picture are roads to sites or former sites of churches, mills, businesses, schools, a trolley station, places of recreation, and hotels. This chapter explores all along Burden Lake Road to the three Burden Lakes. (Courtesy Sand Lake Historical Society Collection.)

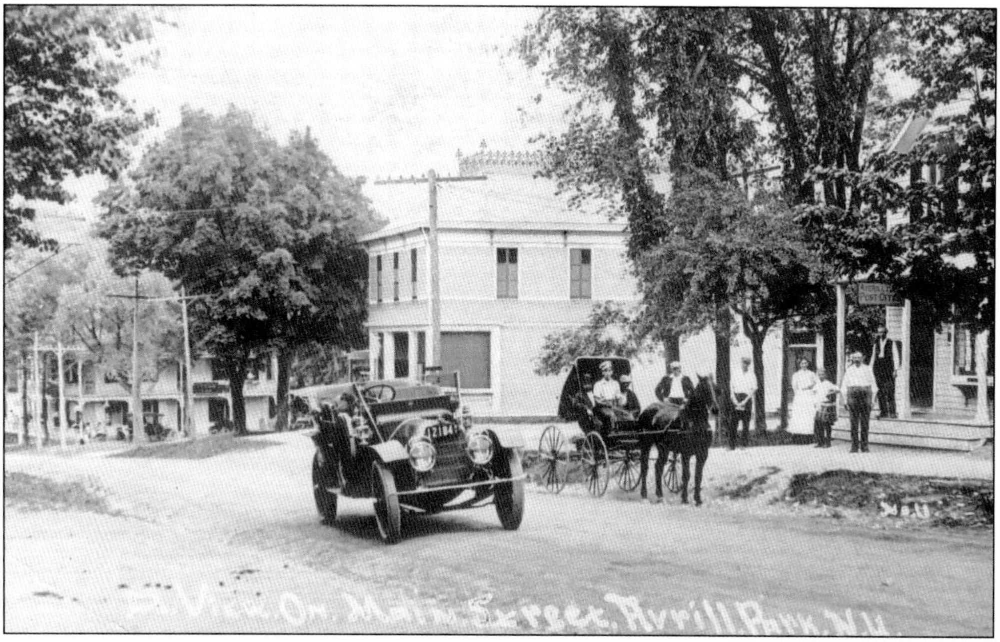

Main Street in Averill Park, Looking East. This 1920s view shows, from left to right, Traveler's Rest Hotel, Jake Warger's Dry Goods Store (which later became Eastman's Variety Store), George Shriner's Store, and the Averill Park Post Office. Which will win the race—the horse-drawn carriage or the horseless carriage? (Courtesy Town of Sand Lake Collection.)

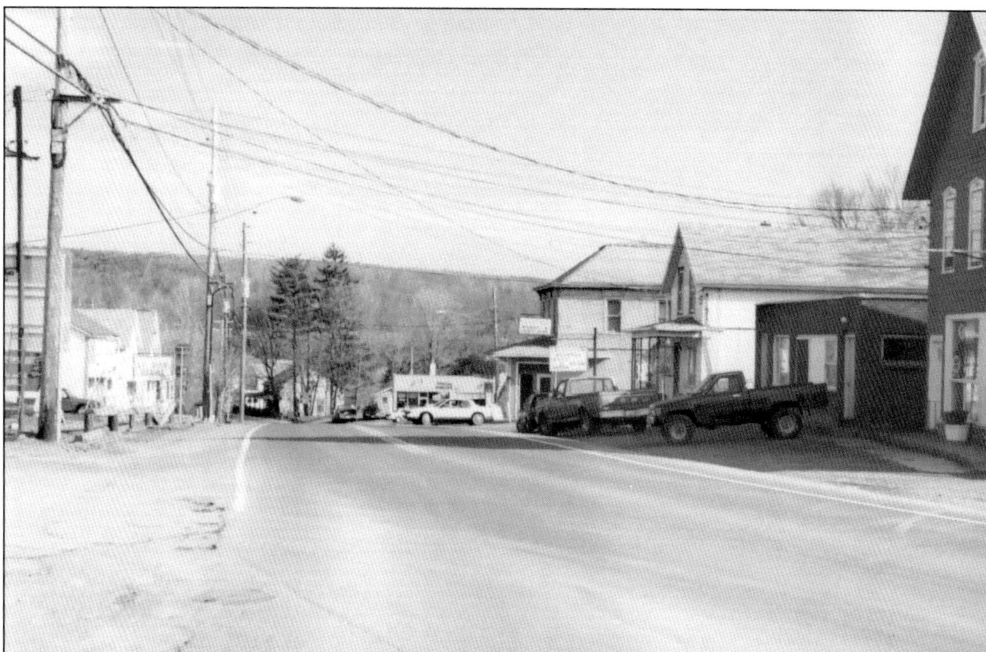

Main Street Averill Park, Looking East, 1999. In 1999, Traveler's Rest is gone, replaced with Miller's Automotive. The Averill Park Variety Store, with new owners, is still prominent. George Shriner's Store is now a residence. (Courtesy Sand Lake Historical Society Collection.)

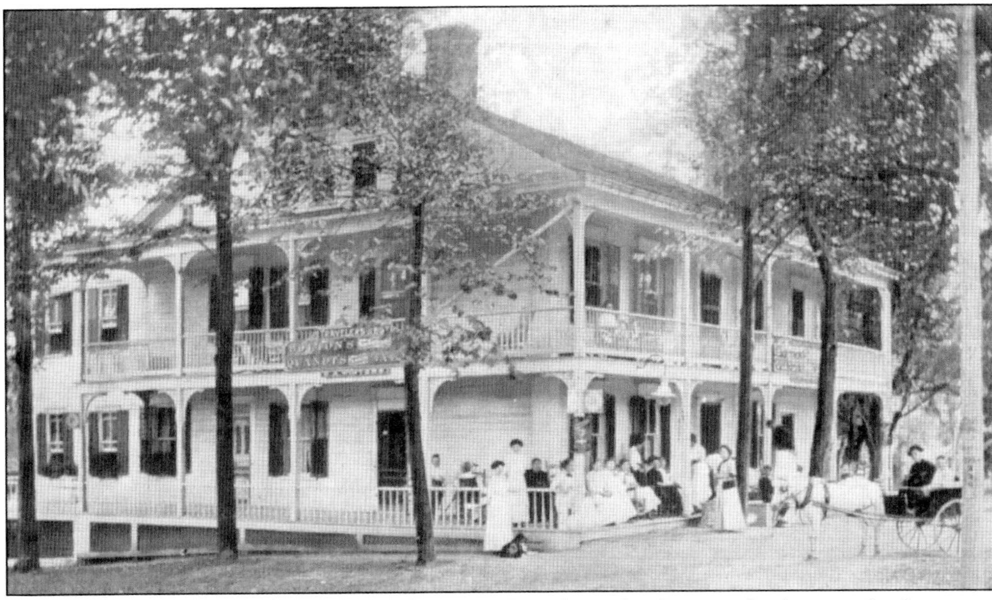

TRAVELER'S REST. Traveler's Rest, with its porches along the front and side, was also known as Sand Lake House, Tillotson's Hotel, and Werger's Hotel. In the 1920s, when it was no longer a hotel, the building housed the Averill Park Post Office. Postmaster Fred Shoemaker and his family lived there. It was destroyed by fire in March 1939. (Courtesy Lawrence Herzog.)

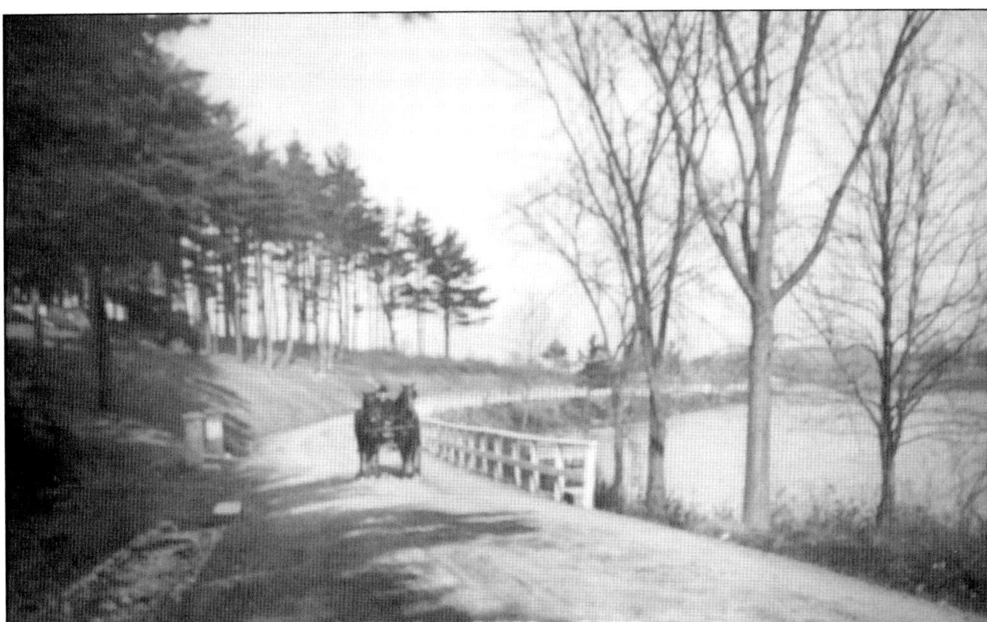

LAKE AVENUE AND THE PINES. Lake Avenue was a quiet road along the north side of Sand Lake, now called Crystal Lake. This road is now county Route 45 or, as some mailboxes state, "Old Route 66." (Courtesy Lawrence Herzog.)

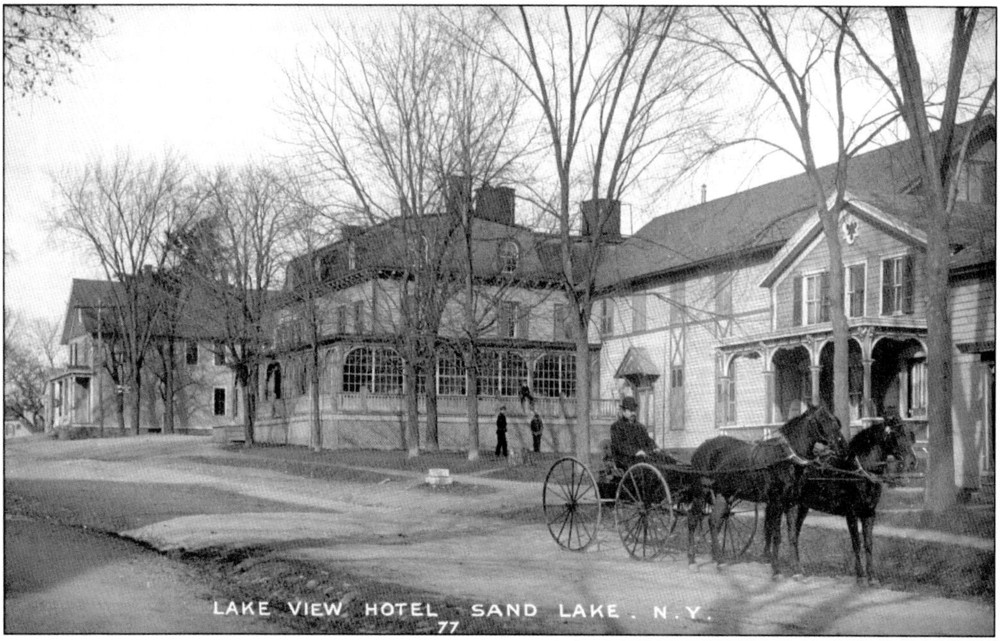

MAIN STREET IN AVERILL PARK, LOOKING WEST. Shown, from left to right, are Stout's Hardware, the Lake View Hotel, and the Griggs home (see book cover), which no longer exists. Notice the sidewalk. You could walk from Averill Park to Glass Lake on the sidewalks. (Courtesy Lawrence Herzog.)

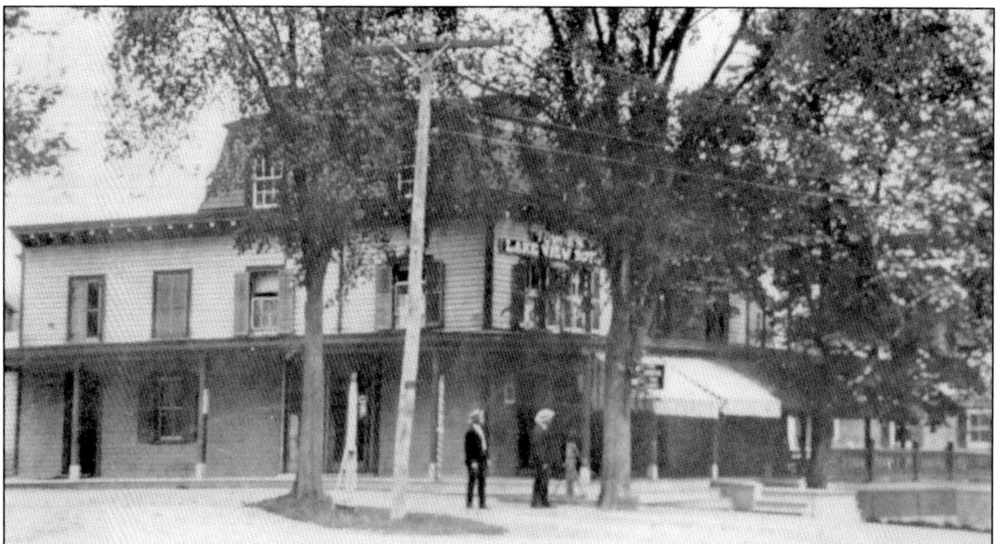

THE LAKE VIEW HOTEL. The Howard family built the Lake View Hotel in 1850. In the late 1880s, the building housed the Averill Park Female Seminary. It was also known as Blake's Lake View and the Gabler Hotel. Many wealthy persons from Troy and the surrounding areas vacationed here for the whole summer. (Courtesy Lawrence Herzog.)

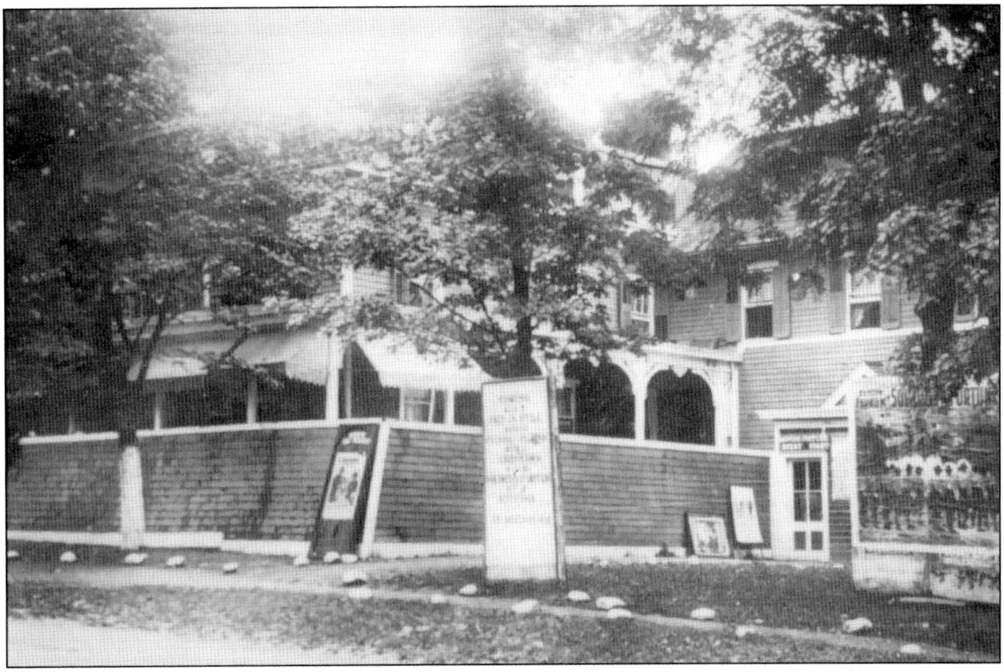

The Lake View Hotel. The Lake View used to have a theater. A stock company of local actors and actresses played there regularly. Movies were also shown. *Soldiers of Fortune* is advertised on the billboard. Later, the theater was replaced with bowling alleys. (Courtesy Alice Tifft.)

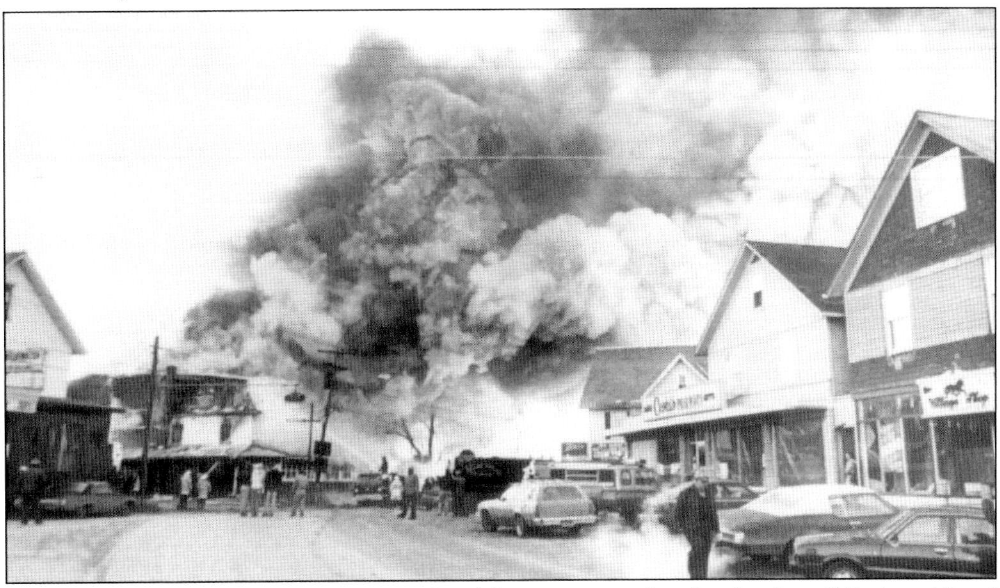

The Lakeview Hotel on Fire. Seven local fire companies besides the Averill Park and Sand Lake Fire Company battled the early morning fire at the Lakeview Hotel in subzero temperatures on March 3, 1980. Although the hotel was lost, heroic efforts saved the other nearby buildings. The Lakeview was rebuilt. Some of the tabletops are made from the bowling lanes, which were buried under the charred ruins. (In later years the name Lakeview was changed to one word). (Courtesy Averill Park and Sand Lake Fire Company.)

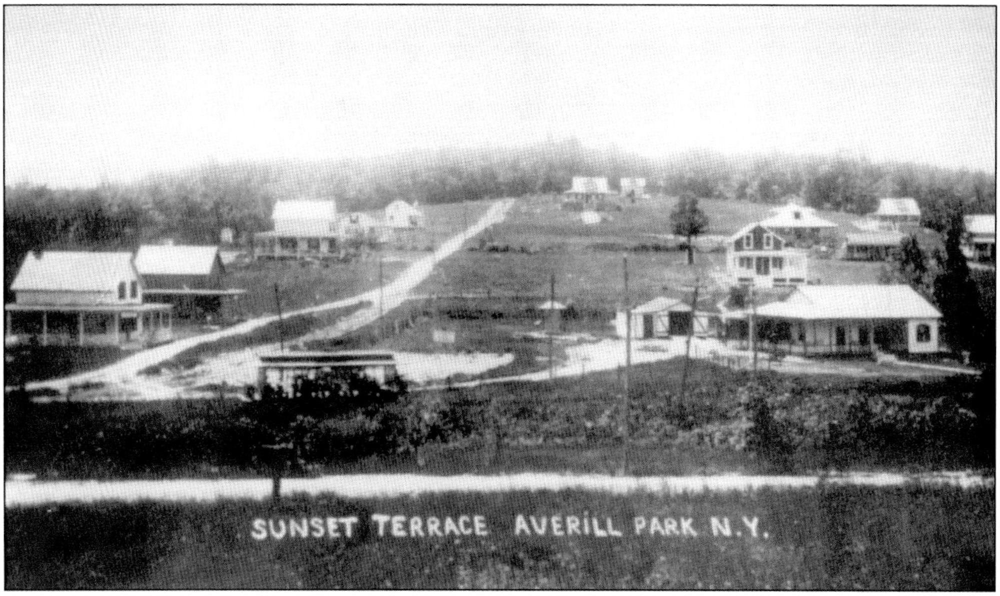

SUNSET TERRACE. Route 43 is in the foreground. The trolley will soon arrive at the Averill Park terminal. What a clear view there used to be with only an occasional tree. Several places were available here for all-summer stays. (Courtesy Sand Lake Historical Society Collection.)

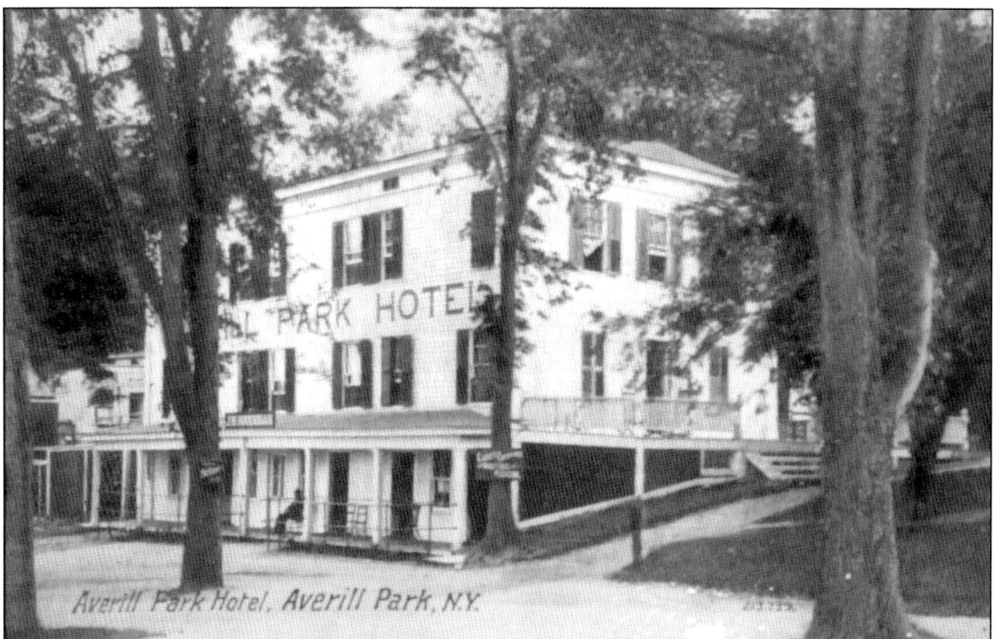

HILKE'S AVERILL PARK HOTEL. This once beautiful old hotel known as Hilke's Averill Park Hotel originally housed the Sand Lake Collegiate Institute. In 1880, Horatio Averill converted it into a hotel. It was destroyed by fire in 1921. The Church of the Covenant is now located on this site. (Courtesy Sand Lake Historical Society Collection.)

G.D. Beebe Receipt. Gilbert Beebe had his blacksmith shop on Johnnycake Lane. This bill shows that Elmer Rendert was charged for work done for the town highway department. Russell "Skip" Patton and family now live on the Beebe property. (Courtesy Town of Sand Lake Collection.)

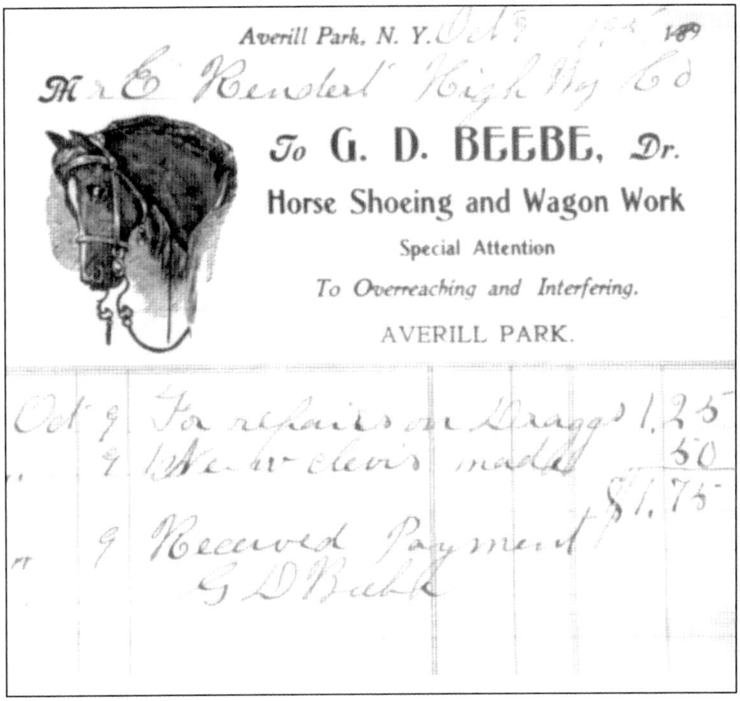

Averill Park, N. Y. Oct 9 189

Mr E Rendert High Way Co

To G. D. BEEBE, Dr.

Horse Shoeing and Wagon Work

Special Attention

To Overreaching and Interfering.

AVERILL PARK.

Oct	9	For repairs on Drags	1.25
"	9	1 New clevis made	.50
			$1.75
"	9	Received Payment G D Beebe	

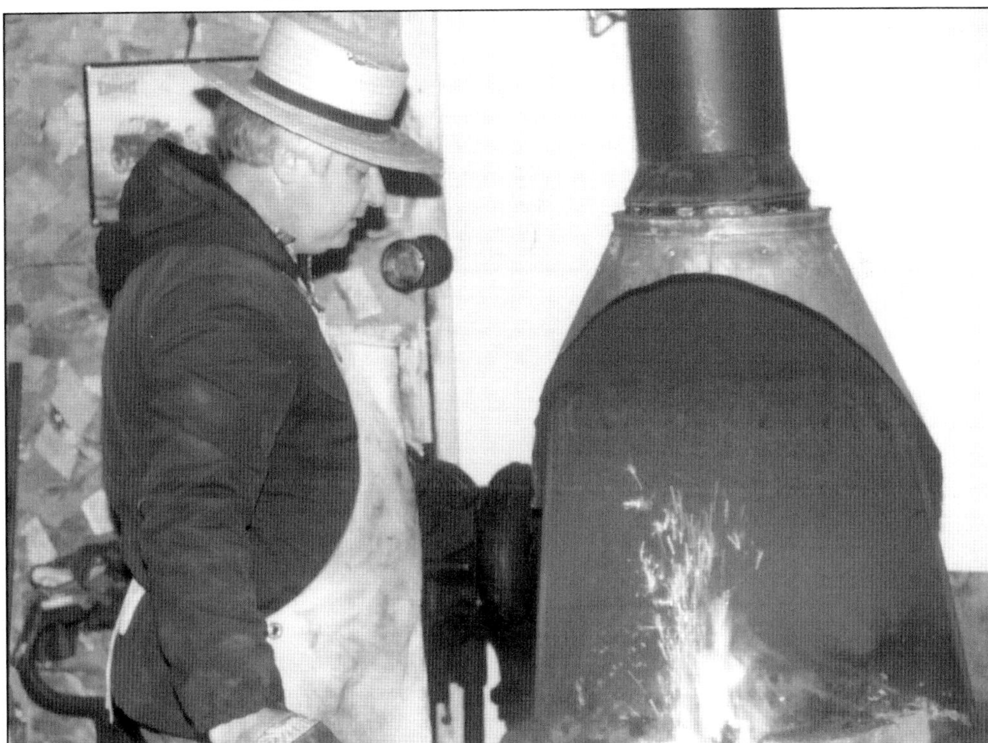

Robert Shuey, Blacksmith. There is still a blacksmith in town. Robert (Bob) Shuey built and outfitted his shop on Eastern Union Turnpike, where he builds and repairs wagons as a hobby. (Courtesy Sand Lake Historical Society Collection.)

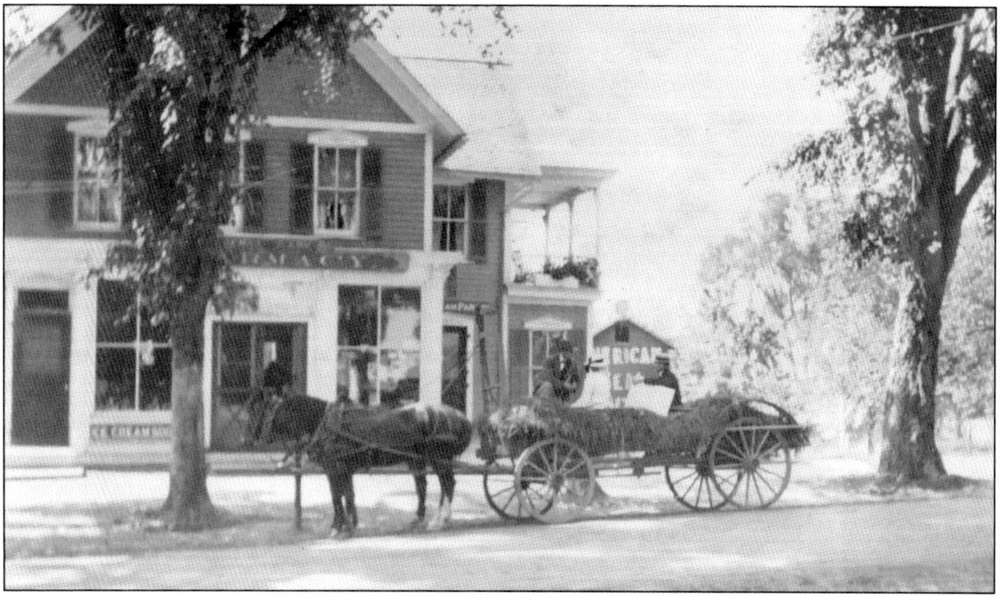

"DR. WRIGHT'S DRUGSTORE." The Averill Park Pharmacy, *c.* 1910, was run by Dr. I.N. Wright, with a grocery store run by Tom Kennedy in the front section. Frank Sowalsky's Ice Cream Parlor was in the building on the side. An A & P store was there from the mid-1930s to the 1950s. Ben and Doris Gauch had a gift shop and appliance store there from 1952 to 1986 (see pages 121 and 127). Currently, the building houses Dillenbeck's American Karate. (Courtesy Town of Sand Lake Collection.)

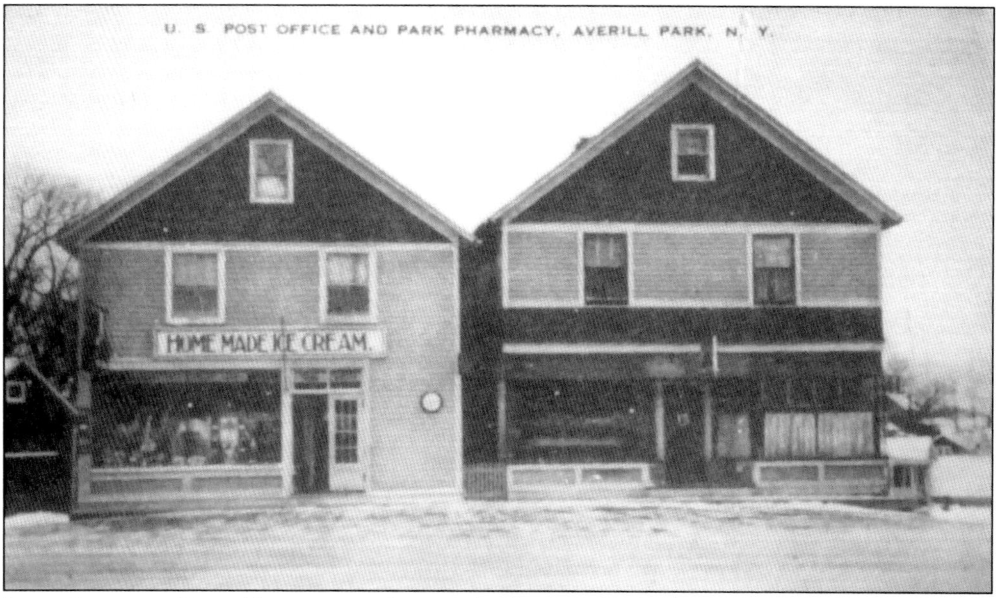

JERRY LEWIS AT PARK PHARMACY. As seen by the sign, Park Pharmacy was also noted for its homemade ice cream. Its other claim to fame was that Jerry Lewis worked here as a soda jerk in 1942, when his father was a superintendent in the Faith Mills. Lewis, one of the best-known comedians, returned to the area in 1971 and opened at the Colonie Coliseum Theater. At a press conference, his greeting to former pharmacy owner Benjamin Silberg was "Hello, Boss." (Courtesy Sand Lake Historical Society Collection.)

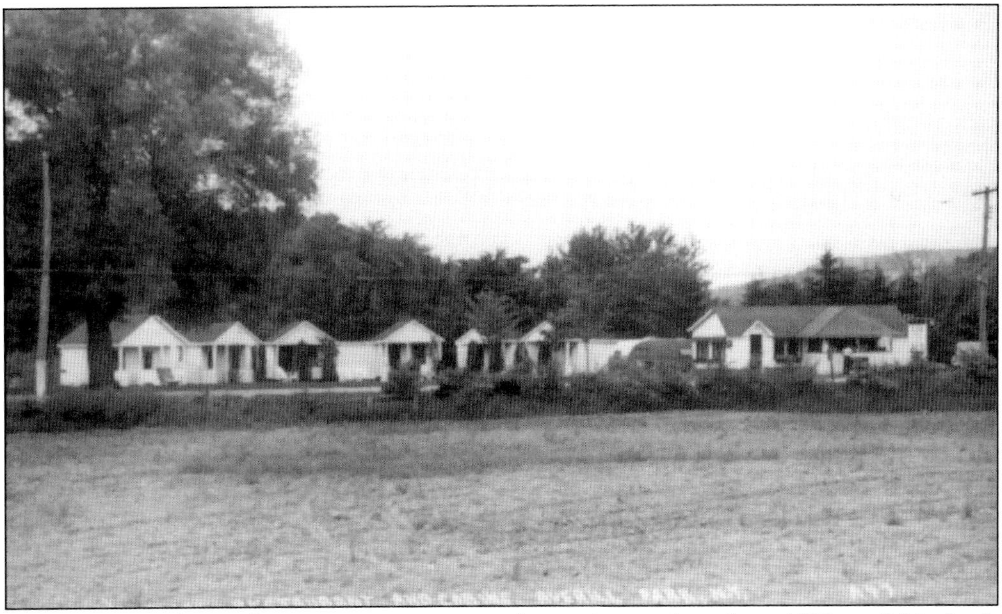

AL'S PLACE. Albert Kilmer ran a restaurant and rented out cabins from 1938 until his death in 1960. The children from nearby Averill Park Central School frequented Al's Place, as did persons who came back year after year. The cabins were razed, but the restaurant housed various businesses over the years, the most recent being Engwer's Coffee & Creame. (Courtesy Helen Crape Guy.)

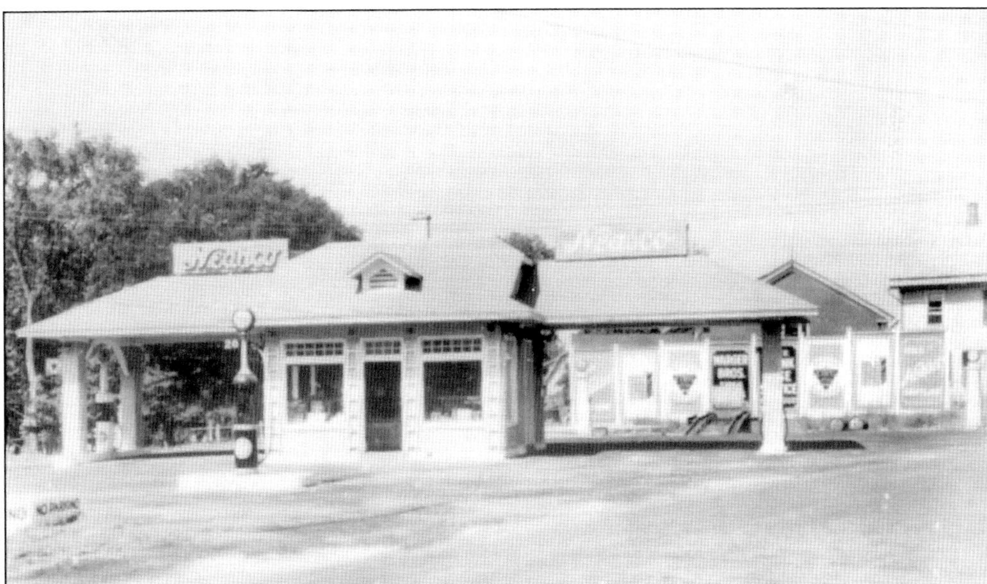

NEASCO GAS STATION. This gas station was at the intersection of Routes 43 and 66, now county Route 45. North End Auto Supply Company (Neasco) was begun in Troy in 1916. The Jiff-E-Mart is on the same location. (Courtesy Robert Moore.)

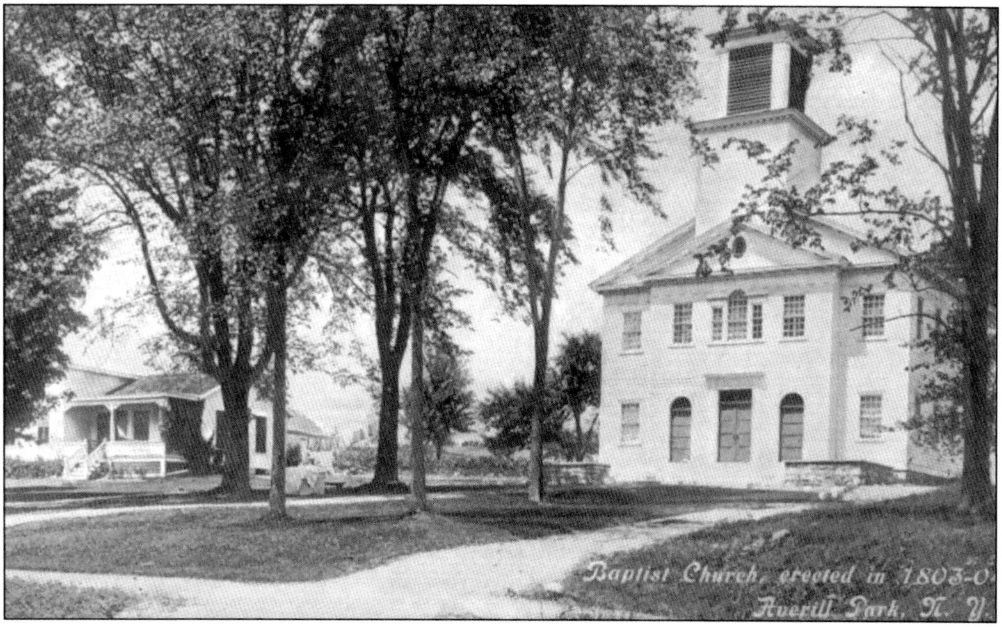

THE SAND LAKE BAPTIST CHURCH. The Sand Lake Baptist Church, the oldest public building in the town of Sand Lake, was erected in 1805 as a meetinghouse for Baptists, Methodists, and Presbyterians. The Methodists sold their meetinghouse rights to the Presbyterians in 1831 and built their church at Glass Lake (see page 92). In 1835, the Presbyterians sold their portion of the church to the Baptists and erected a church at the corners of Routes 43 and 66 in Sand Lake (see page 82). (Courtesy Lawrence Herzog.)

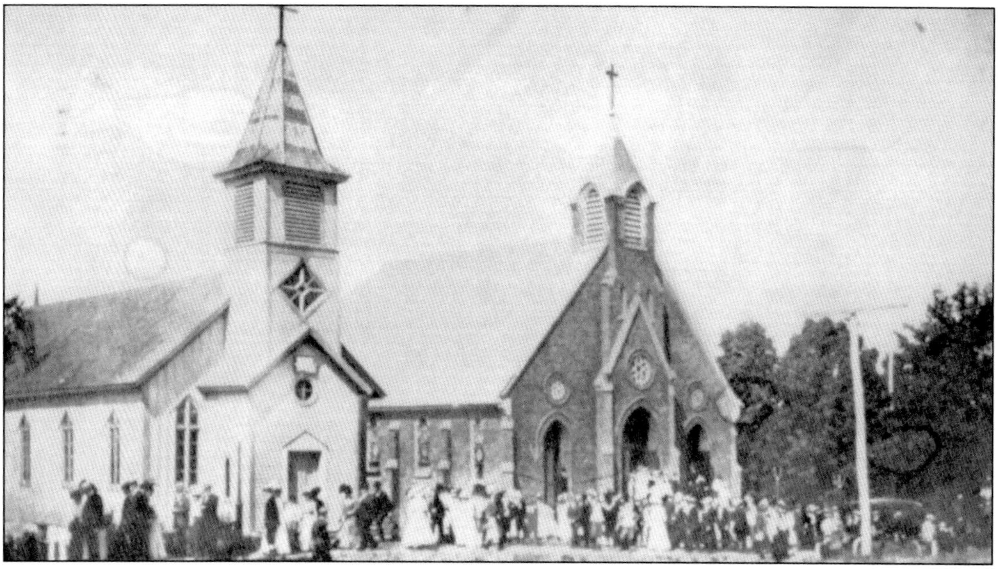

ST. HENRY'S CHURCH. Spiritual guidance was first given to area German Catholics in private homes in Poestenkill. St. Mary of the Woods Chapel was built c. 1860 in Poestenkill. The original wooden structure of St. Henry's Church was dedicated on April 17, 1870, in Averill Park, on land donated by John Aken, a well-known mill owner. In 1977, the building was sold and moved to be reassembled. The brick church was built in 1902 and was renovated in 1982. (Courtesy Sand Lake Historical Society Collection.)

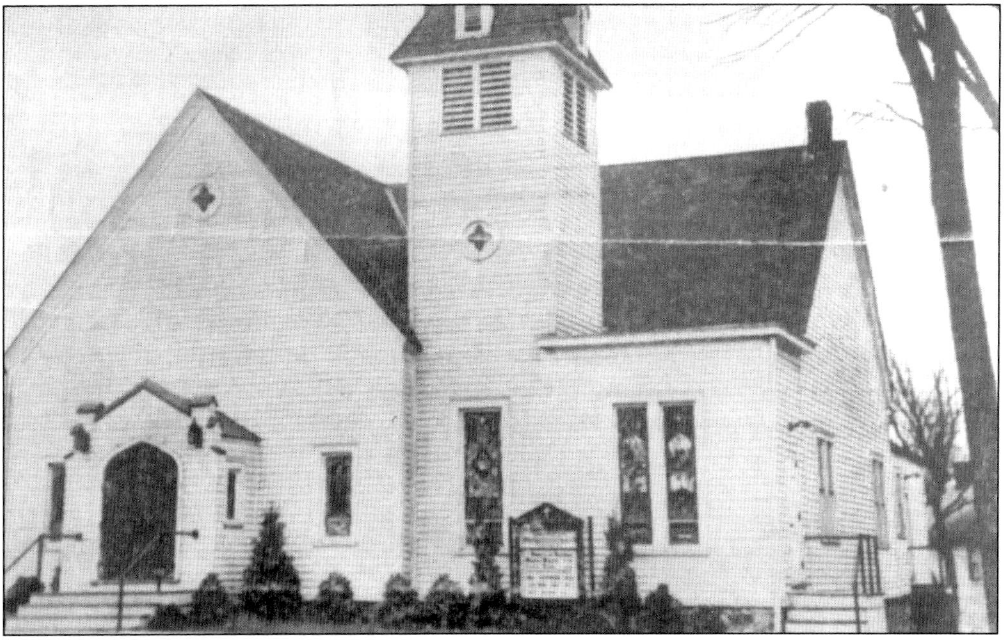

THE AVERILL PARK METHODIST CHURCH. The Averill Park Methodist Church was dedicated on December 31, 1874. It was known as the Olive Chapel Methodist Episcopal Society until 1926, when it was named Averill Park Methodist Church. Located on Burden Lake Road, it was rebuilt after the fire of 1936 and repaired after the fire of 1937. It burned again in 1959 and was rebuilt on the site of the Averill Park Hotel (see pages 46 and 92). (Courtesy Sand Lake Historical Society Collection.)

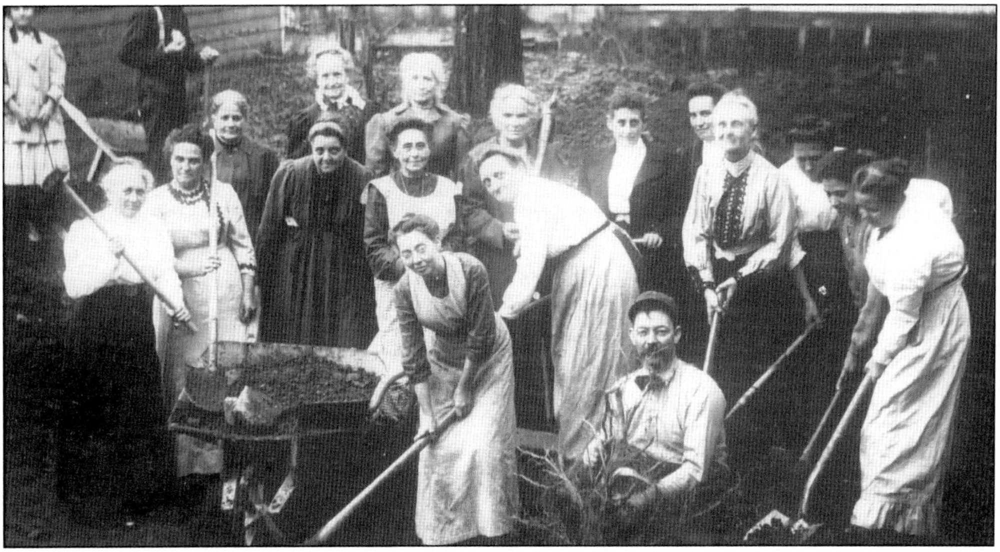

THE LADIES' AID SOCIETY TAKES ACTION. Averill Park Methodist Ladies' Aid Society breaks ground for the new parsonage on October 24, 1912. The group includes Mrs. Wilford Amadon, president, holding the wheelbarrow; Mrs. W.H. Pohl, in front with the pick; and Rev. G.E. Straight, holding the root of a tree. Since the church was the only one in the Troy Methodist District without a parsonage, the ladies decided to assume the debt for erecting the parsonage. (Courtesy Dorothy Leitgeb; the *Troy Times*, November 9, 1912.)

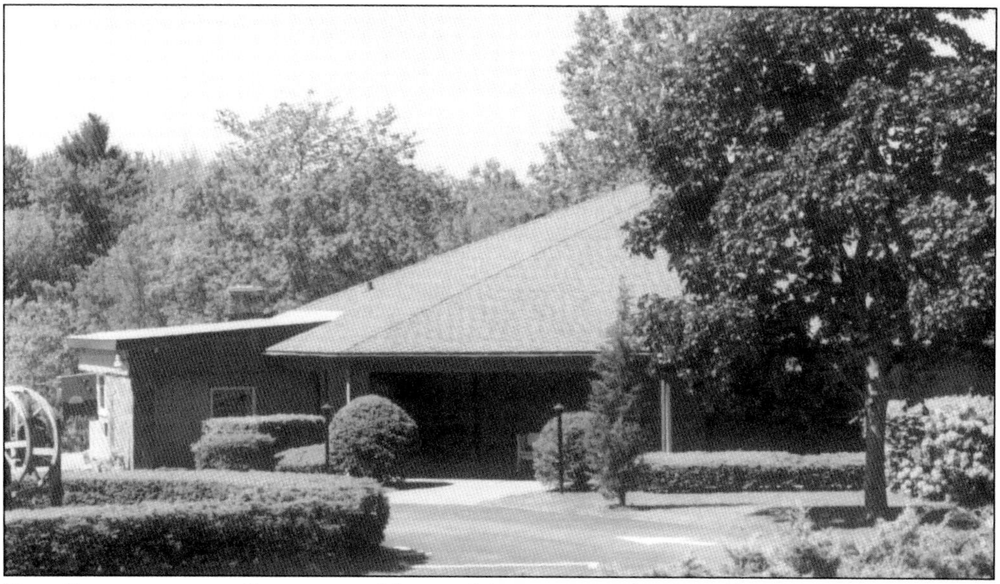

THE CHURCH OF THE COVENANT, UNITED METHODIST. The Averill Park Methodist Church was rebuilt on the site of the Averill Park Hotel and was dedicated on May 28, 1961 (see page 46). A merger between the First Presbyterian Church of Sand Lake and the Averill Park Methodist Church occurred in 1967, resulting in the Church of the Covenant. The building is often called the "Round Church" in keeping with its circular architectural construction. (Courtesy Sand Lake Historical Society Collection.)

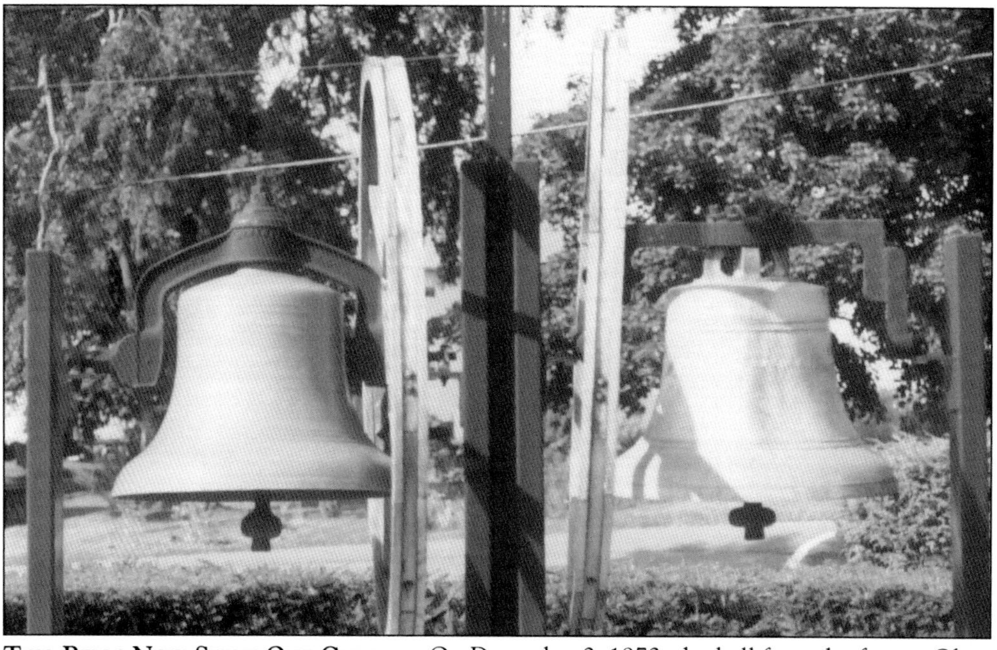

TWO BELLS NOW SERVE ONE CHURCH. On December 2, 1973, the bell from the former Olive Methodist Episcopal Chapel, *c.* 1886, and the bell from the First Presbyterian Church of Sand Lake, *c.* 1840, were rung in concert as both were rededicated at a side-by-side location in front of the Church of the Covenant. This symbolized the merger of the two previous churches into the present church. (Courtesy Sand Lake Historical Society Collection.)

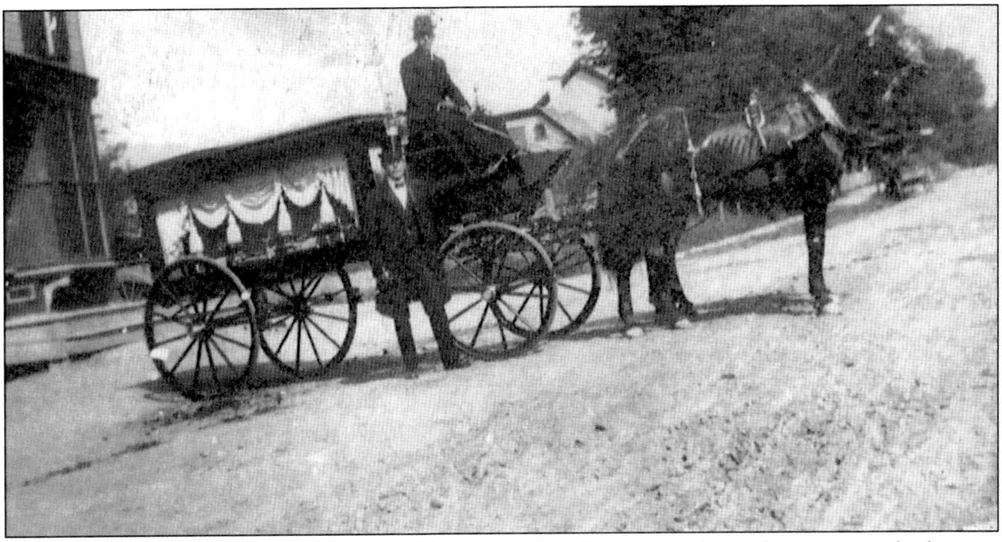

THE WILLIS D. LARKIN SR. HEARSE. Willis D. Larkin Sr., pictured standing next to the hearse, sent this postcard to a friend in 1903 (see page 61). On the card he wrote, "Just started on our first trip with our new hearse. How do you like it?" (Courtesy Willis D. Larkin Jr.)

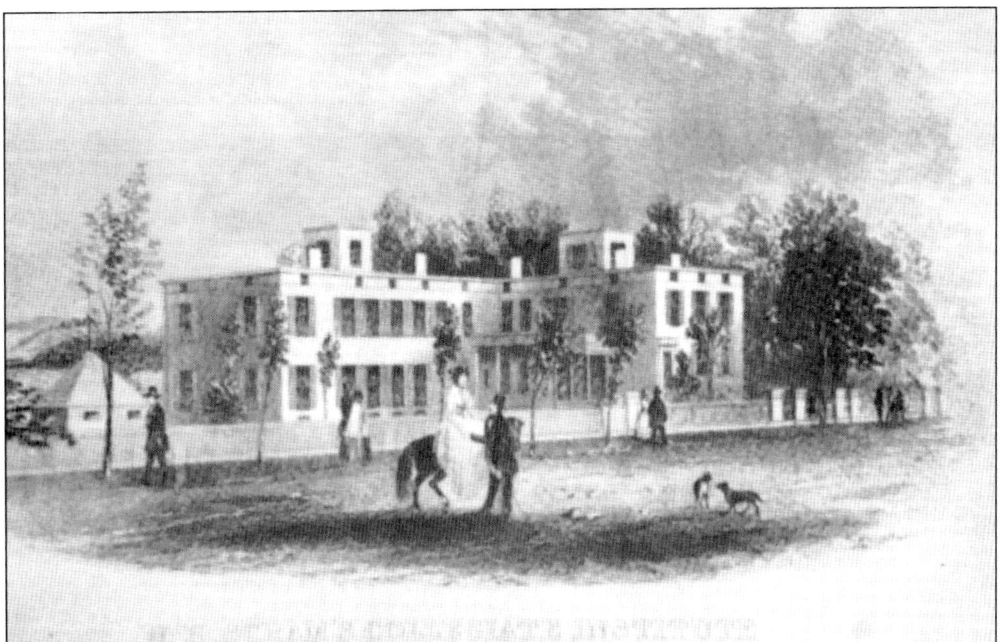

W.H. SCRAM'S COLLEGIATE INSTITUTE. This boarding school was established by William Scram in 1852 and continued until his death in 1875. As stated in an advertisement, its purpose was to "prepare young men and lads for college, the counting-room or for general business." Some pupils came from as far away as Cuba and South America. After William Scram died, Horatio Averill converted the school to Hilke's Averill Park Hotel (see page 46). The Church of the Covenant is now located there. (Courtesy Sand Lake Historical Society Collection.)

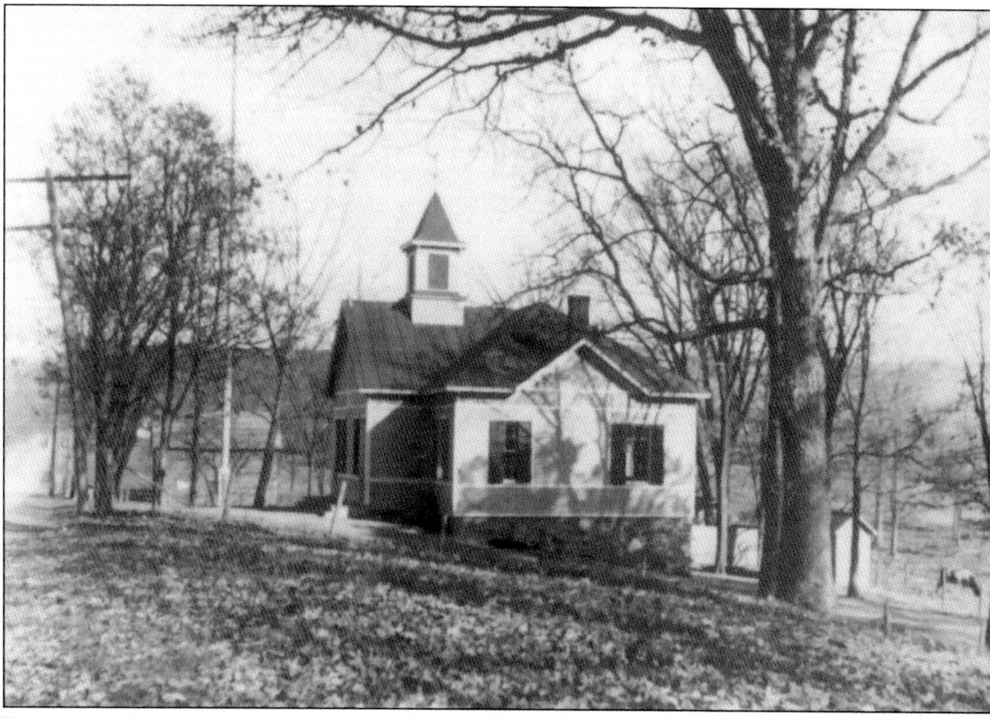

District No. 7 School, Averill Park. This school, located on Route 43, could boast having two rooms. The school was one of the original ones that consolidated into Averill Park Central School District. It is the present Sgt. Walter Adams American Legion Post No. 1021. (Courtesy Town of Sand Lake Collection.)

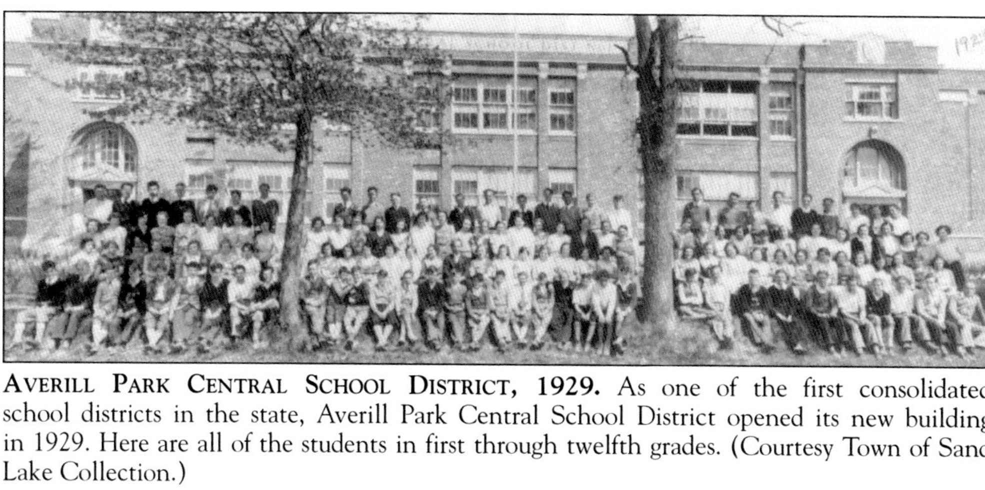

Averill Park Central School District, 1929. As one of the first consolidated school districts in the state, Averill Park Central School District opened its new building in 1929. Here are all of the students in first through twelfth grades. (Courtesy Town of Sand Lake Collection.)

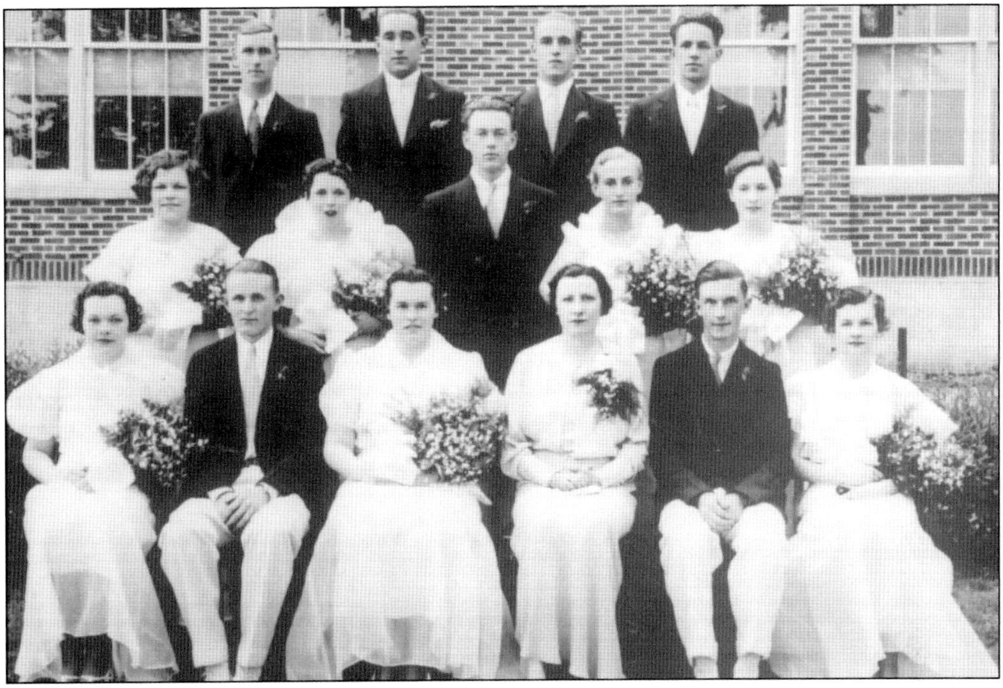

THE AVERILL PARK HIGH SCHOOL CLASS OF 1935. Graduates, from left to right, are as follows: (front row) Doris Tifft, Robert Goldie, Helen Kane, Miss Harrington, Raymond Geerholt, and Katherine Sowalsky; (middle row) Ruth Shoemaker, Agnes Olbert, John Basolt, Margaret Smith, and Lois Wallace; (back row) Clifford Robertson, Charles Hack, Robert Smith, and Michael Setne. (Courtesy Town of Sand Lake Collection.)

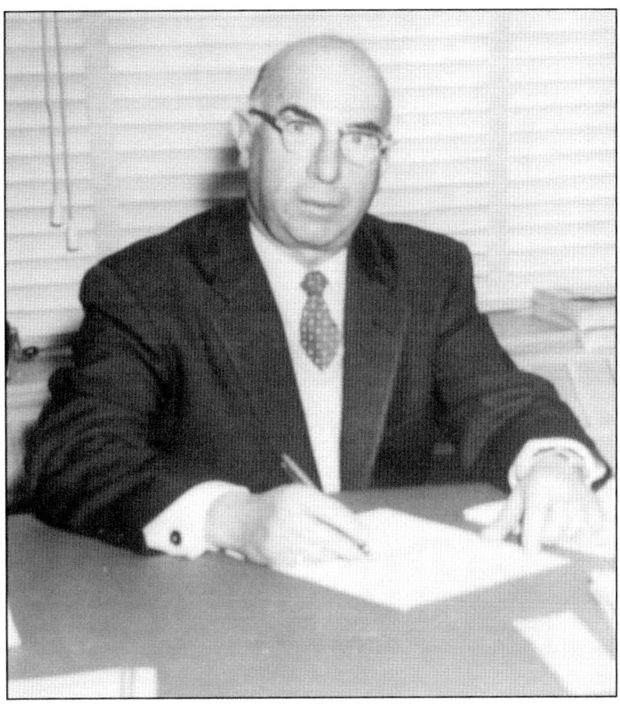

ELMER E. STAHLMAN. Elmer E. Stahlman served as a high school principal and then as the supervising principal of the Averill Park School District from 1929 to 1959. In 1946, during his tenure, District No. 3 School of Poestenkill was annexed. Miller Hill Elementary School was built in 1950, and Averill Park High School was built in 1957. Always interested in sports, Stahlman coached the championship baseball team of 1945. (Courtesy Averill Park Central School District.)

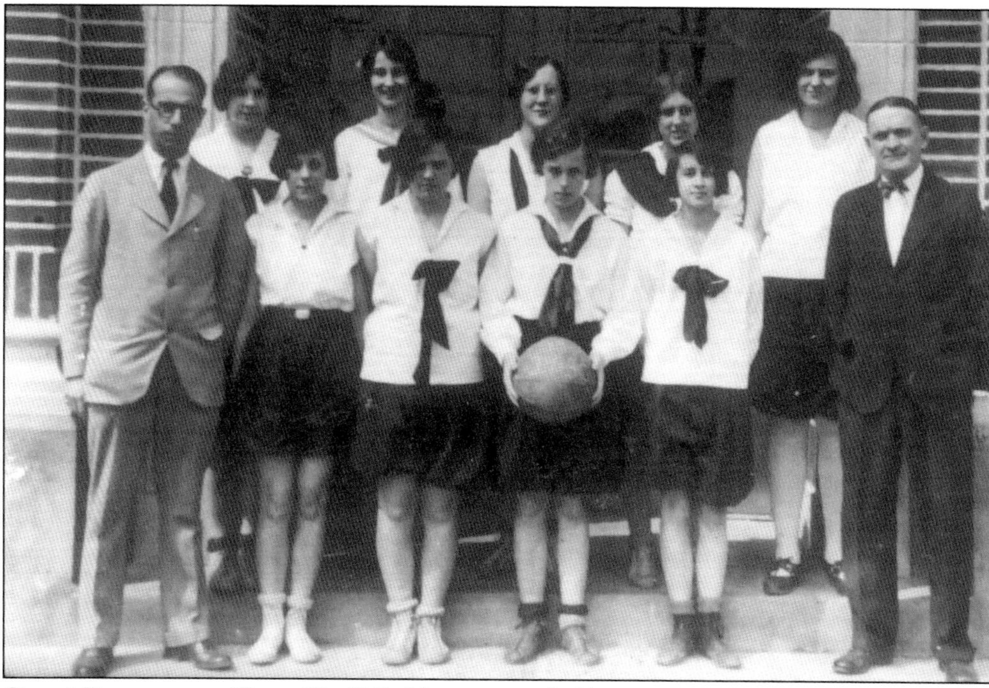

GIRLS' BASKETBALL. Elmer "Prof" Stahlman extended his interest in sports to the organizing of a girls' basketball team. Shown, from left to right, are the following: (front row) Elmer Stahlman (principal), Dorothy Hack (McChesney), Mildred Sicily, Elsie Robinson, Esther Kirchner, and Mr. Hubbard; (back row) Betty Hubbard, Grace Teal, Catherine Beck, Evelyn Miller, and Mary Feathers (Monch). (Courtesy Town of Sand Lake Collection.)

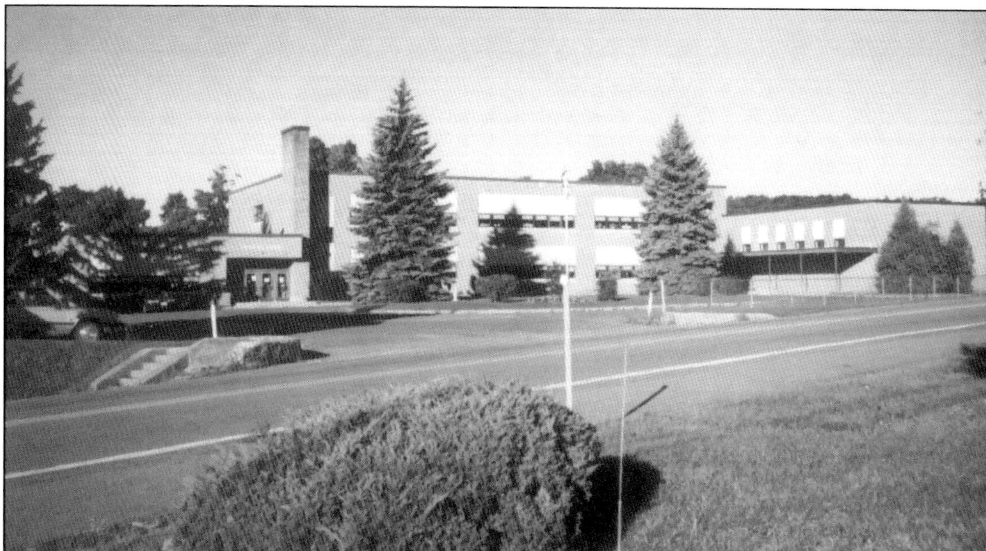

MILLER HILL ELEMENTARY SCHOOL. Miller Hill Elementary School was built in 1950 and was closed in 1980. Due to the town population change, the school reopened in 1990. Since then, the building has had renovations and an addition, which was constructed in 1996 under the enhanced state aid package that paid for 95 percent of the cost. (Courtesy Sand Lake Historical Society Collection.)

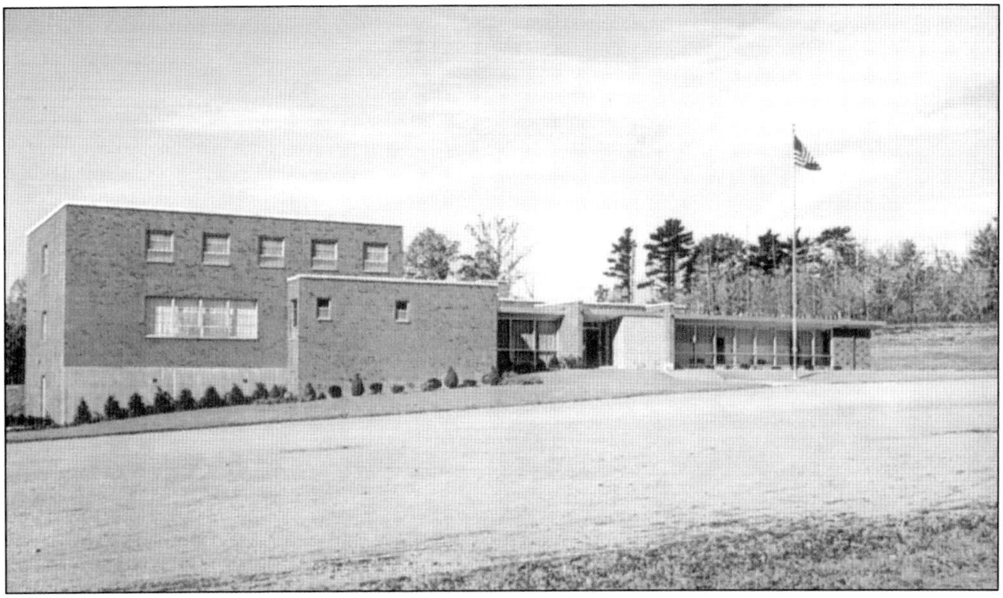

St. Henry's School (William D. Mahony Memorial School). William D. Mahony (see page 66) gave funds to build St. Henry's School. The parochial school opened with kindergarten through grade four in 1959 and was operated by the Sisters of St. Francis of Allegheny until June 1971. From the fall of 1971 to 1975, an all lay staff operated it, with Ann Lilly as principal. Lake Avenue Community Church is now located on the site. (Courtesy Sand Lake Historical Society Collection.)

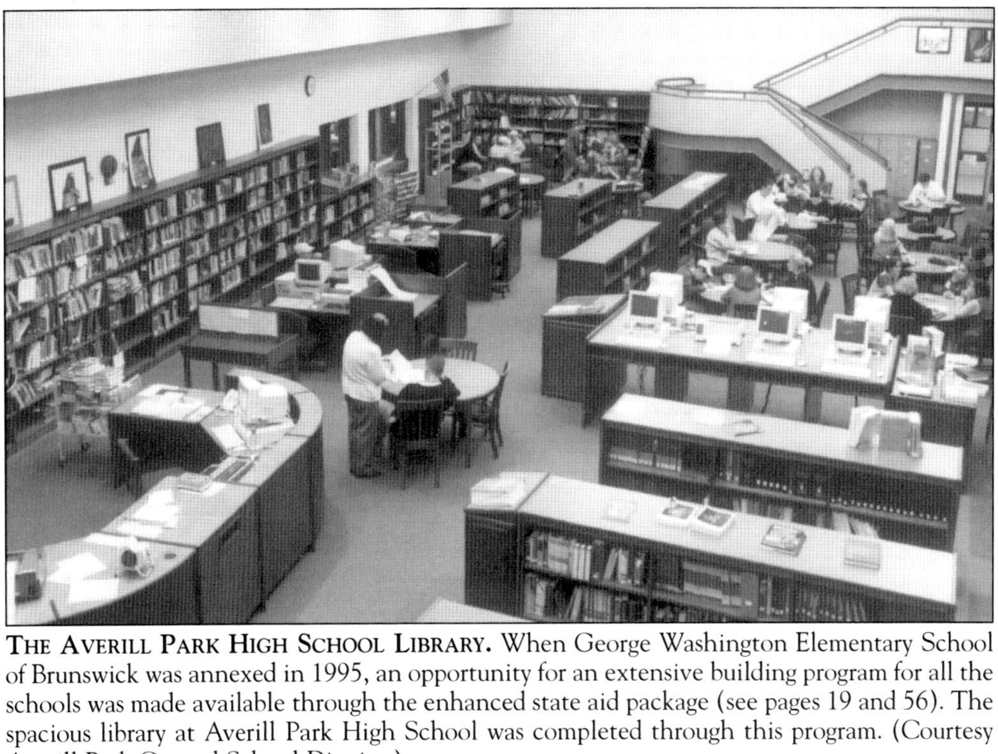

The Averill Park High School Library. When George Washington Elementary School of Brunswick was annexed in 1995, an opportunity for an extensive building program for all the schools was made available through the enhanced state aid package (see pages 19 and 56). The spacious library at Averill Park High School was completed through this program. (Courtesy Averill Park Central School District.)

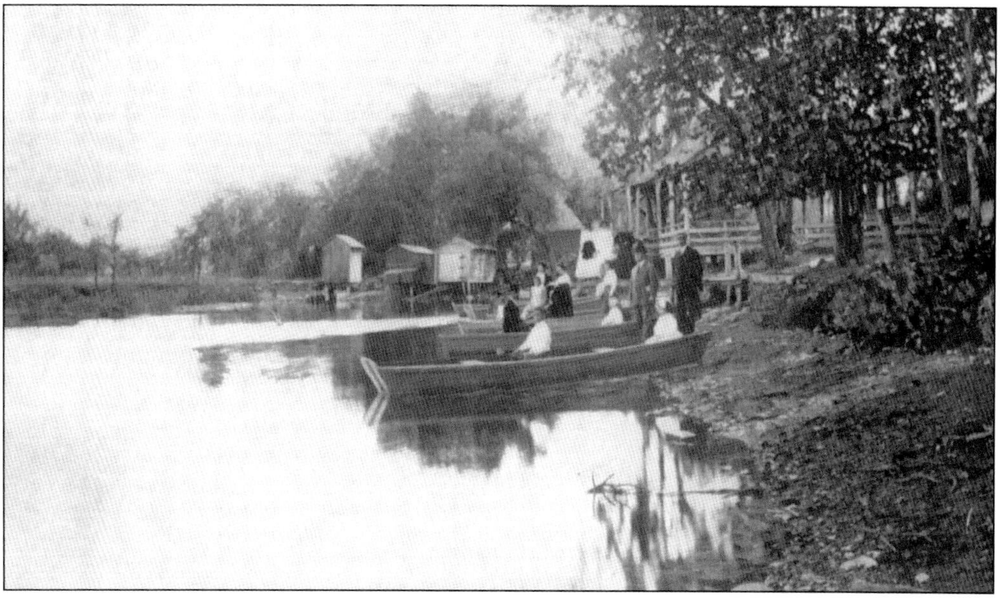

The Lake View Boat Landing on Crystal Lake. At the boat dock behind the Lake View Hotel began an opportunity to explore Crystal Lake. The first building on the left is the gatehouse that contained the valve used to regulate the water supply for the Wynantskill Improvement Association. (Courtesy Lawrence Herzog.)

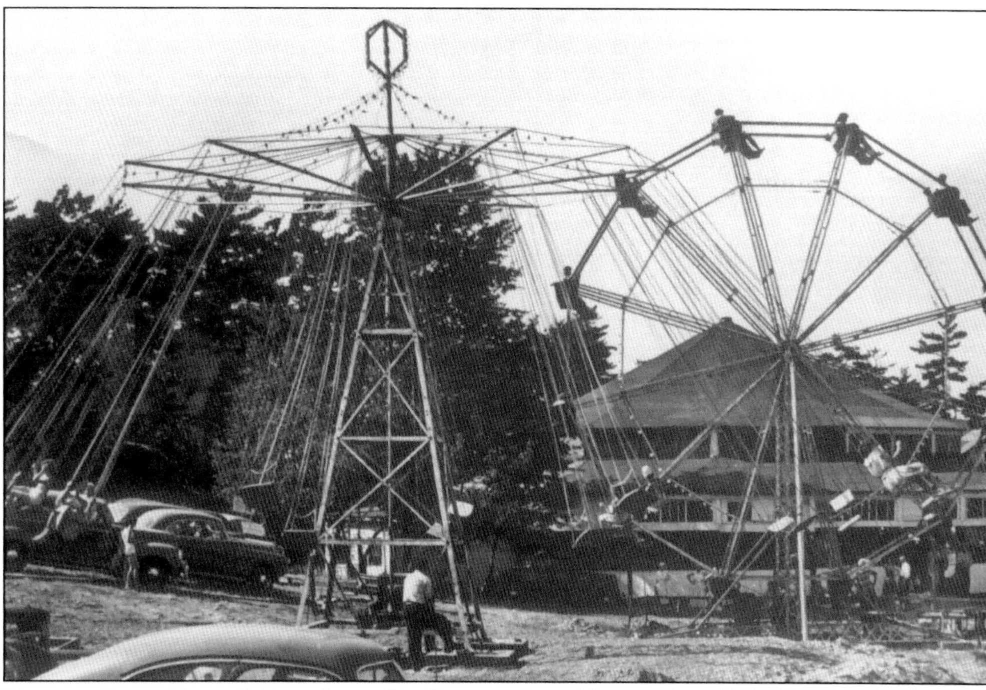

Crystal Lake Park. When the trolley line ran from Troy to Averill Park, Crystal Lake Park was referred to as "the Upstate Coney Island" with its swing, Ferris wheel, and merry-go-round. (Courtesy Charles Viens.)

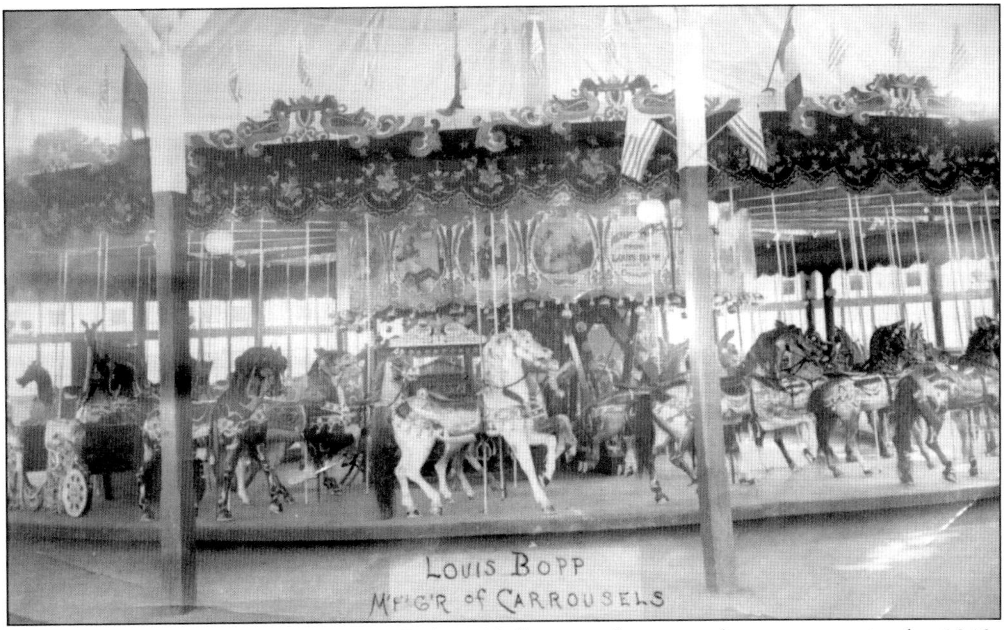

THE CAROUSEL AT CRYSTAL LAKE. Robert Kolb remembers spending summers in the 1940s with his grandfather Edward Henry Kolb, who owned the carousel at Crystal Lake Park. Many persons recount stories of working on the carousel, of picking their favorite animal, and of winning a free ride after catching the brass ring. (Courtesy Robert Kolb.)

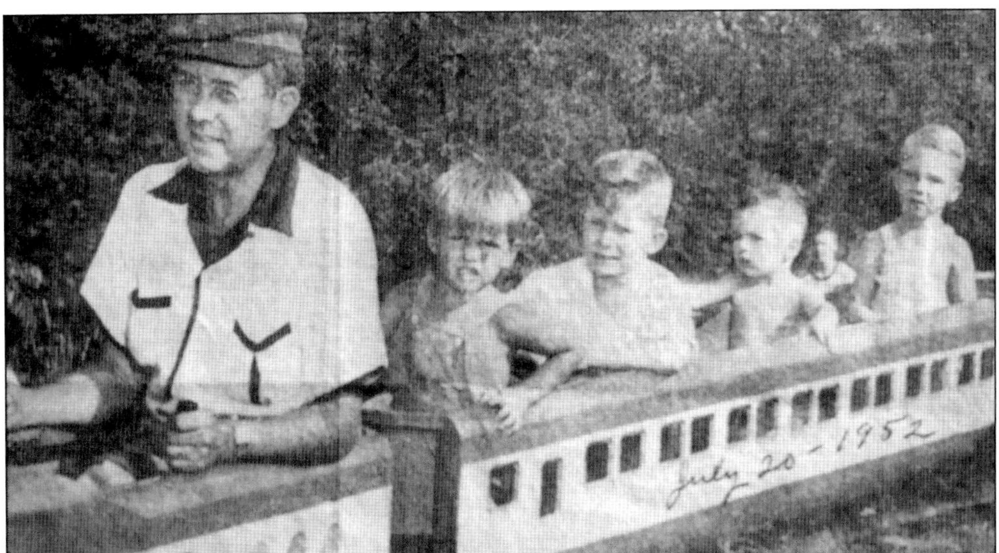

MINIATURE TRAIN RIDE AT CRYSTAL LAKE PARK. Off for a ride on the miniature train on July 20, 1952, are, from left to right, Bernard Mantha, Bruce Layman, Larry Burdock, Michael Esposito, and Frank Mantha. (Courtesy Sand Lake Historical Society Collection.)

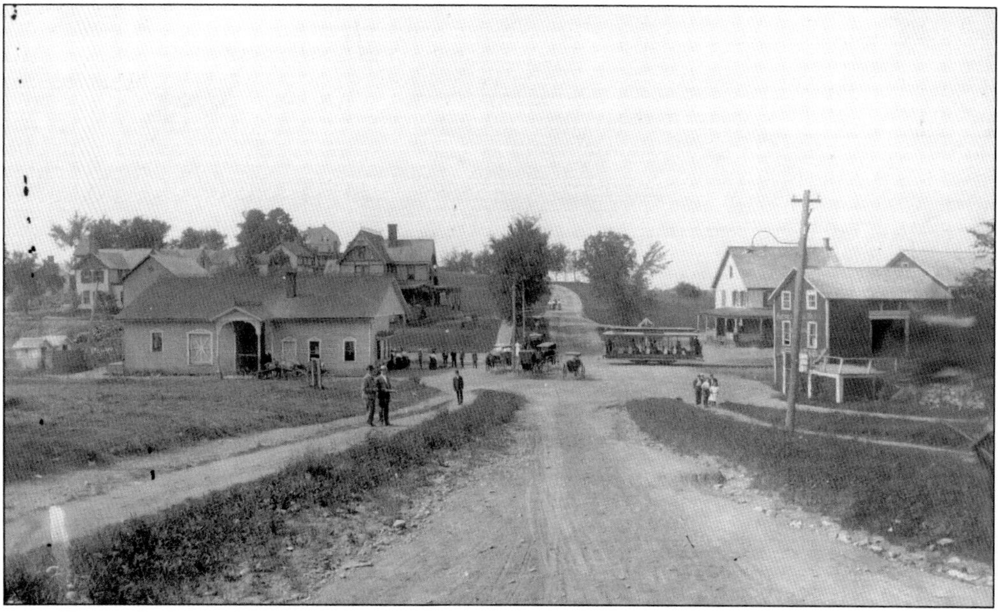

THE TROY & NEW ENGLAND RAILWAY COMPANY. This trolley line began on September 30, 1885, and ceased operation on March 31, 1925. The trolley in this picture is entering the terminal building in Averill Park. Note the taxis waiting to take the passengers to local hotels and beaches. Above the station is the Gabler House. Across the street are Clum's Hotel and the barn of the Averill Park Hotel. (Courtesy Charles Viens.)

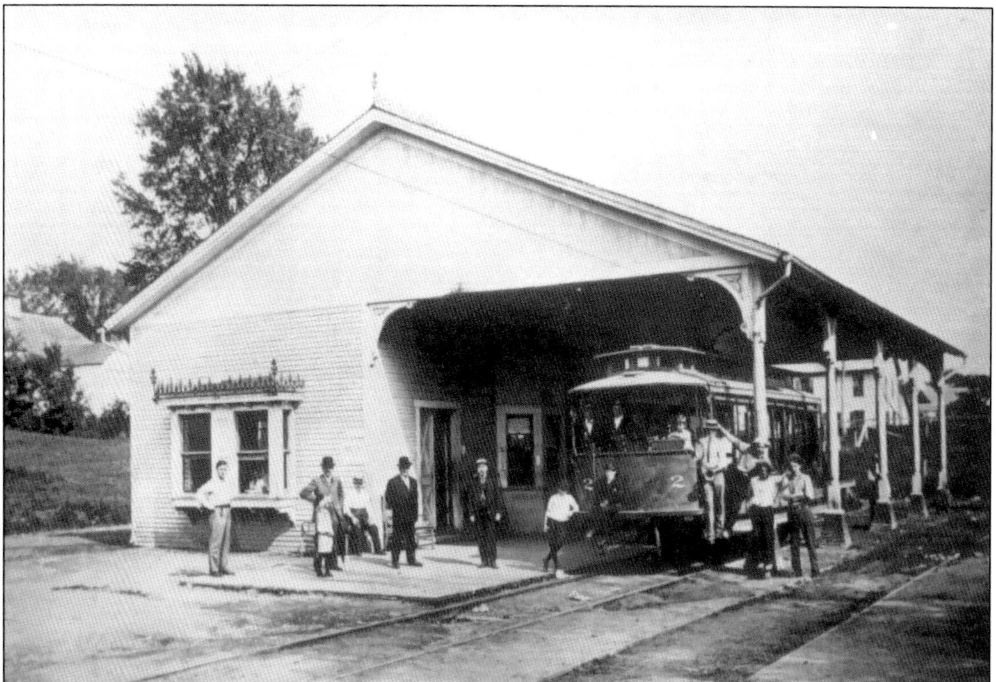

THE TROY & NEW ENGLAND RAILWAY, AVERILL PARK TERMINAL. A close-up of the station shows the trolley next to the loading platform. The building was used by the Tremont Lumber Company from 1958 to 1985. (Courtesy Charles Viens.)

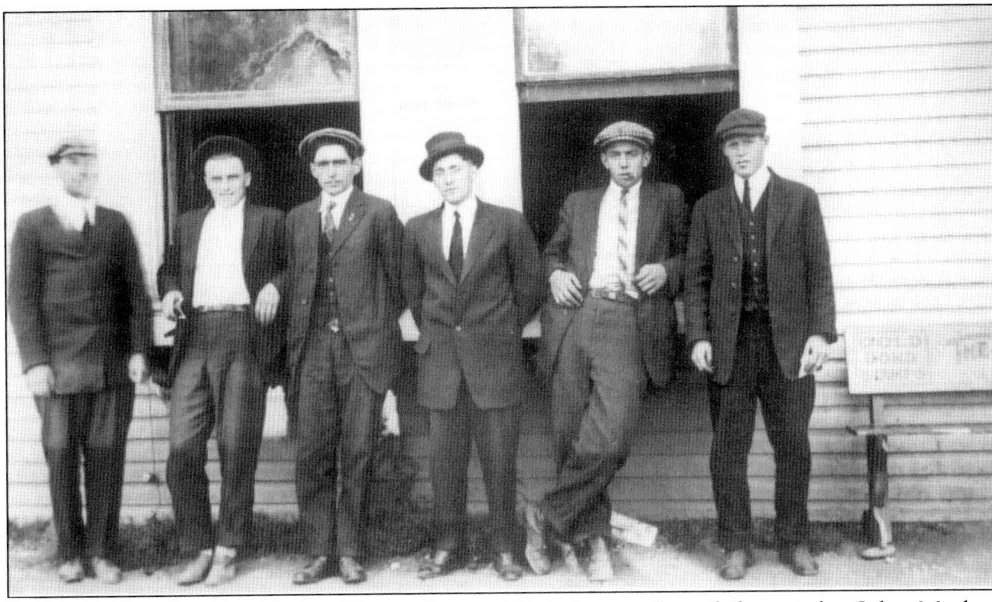

Taxi Drivers Waiting for Their Fares. Taxi drivers, from left to right, John Mosher, William Karl, Samuel McNary, Edwin Harrington, Edward Knapp, and John Abel, relax until the trolley comes. Then, they will take their passengers to the chosen destinations of Crooked Lake, Glass Lake, Burden Lake, or wherever it is too far to walk. (Courtesy Charles Viens.)

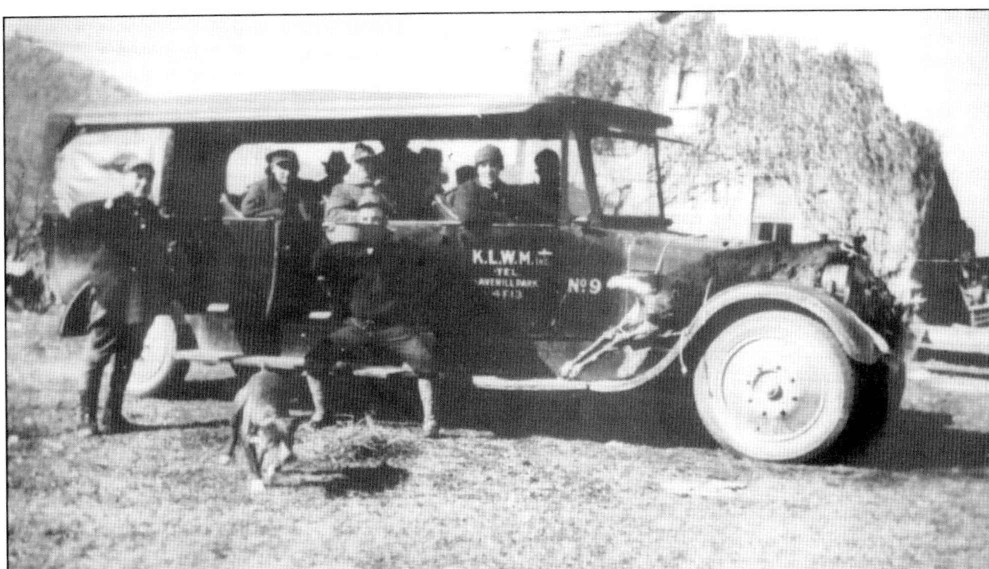

KLWM Bus Service. After the trolley stopped operation in 1925, Edward Knapp, Willis Larkin Sr. (see page 53), Chester Wendell, and Samuel McNary (see pages 93 and 125) began the KLWM Bus Company. The route ran from Troy to Glass Lake. Hunters hired this bus, and the hunting was good. The bus company was later sold to the United Traction Company. (Courtesy Willis Larkin Jr.)

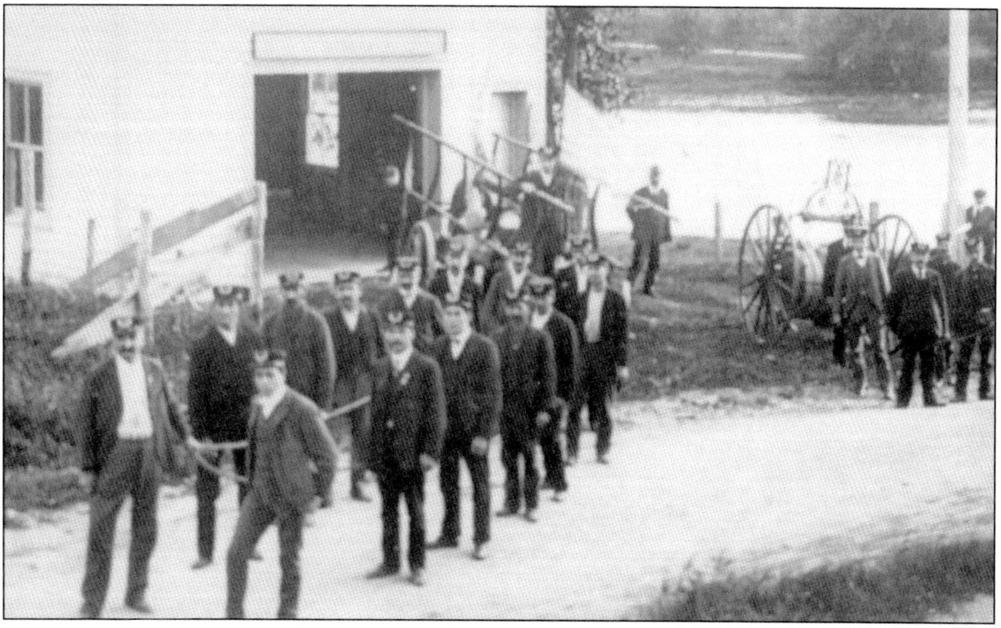

THE AVERILL PARK AND SAND LAKE FIRE COMPANY, C. 1905. Firemen are pulling the hand-pumped fire engine affectionately called "Nickwackett," meaning "river horse," out of the original firehouse on Route 43, halfway between the hamlets of Averill Park and Sand Lake. On the right is the two-wheeled hand-drawn hose cart. (Courtesy Alice Tifft.)

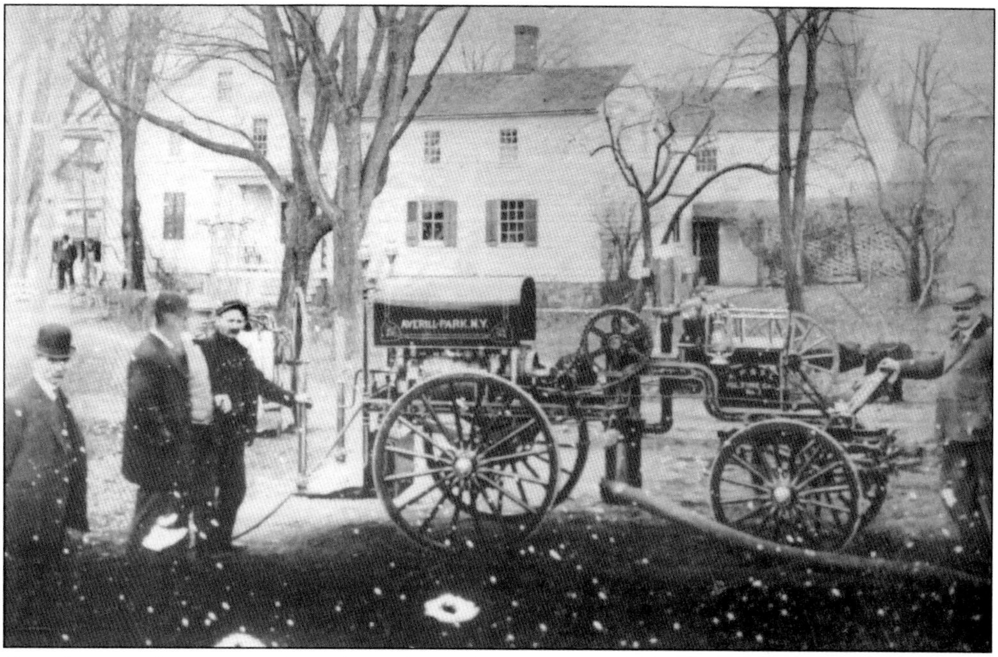

THE AVERILL PARK AND SAND LAKE FIRE COMPANY, C. 1912. At a drill using the fire engine purchased in 1911, Dr. Elmer Reichard stands to the right of the pumper. This horse-drawn pumper, with a 45-horsepower gasoline motor, could throw a stream of water over the tallest church steeple in the town. The introduction of gasoline power was a major advancement in firefighting for the town. (Courtesy Town of Sand Lake Collection.)

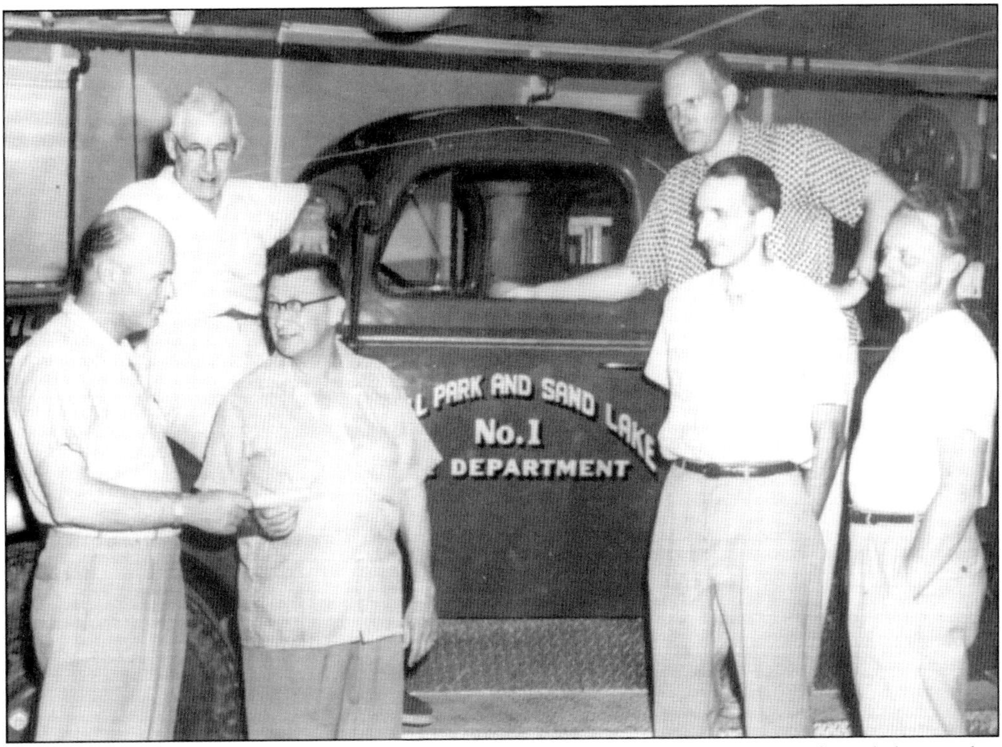

AVERILL PARK AND SAND LAKE FIREMEN. Gathered by the fire truck are, from left to right, Wally Dickinson, Frank Hack, Edward Guy, an unidentified man, Ernest Hoffman, and Richard Seufert. (Courtesy Averill Park and Sand Lake Fire Company.)

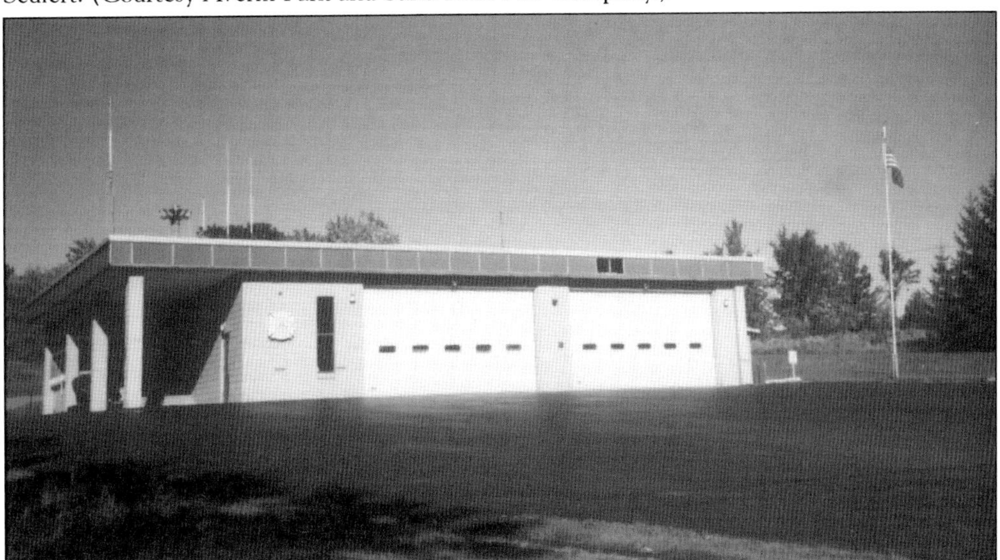

THE NEW FIRE STATION ON EASTERN UNION TURNPIKE. The new fire station was occupied in 1968. It has four bays and a large community hall in the back. Cooperative emergency medical services with the Sand Lake Ambulance and the Taborton and West Sand Lake Fire Companies began in the 1970s. Over the years, the volunteers have worked and held fund-raisers to secure state-of-the-art equipment for the town. (Courtesy Sand Lake Historical Society Collection.)

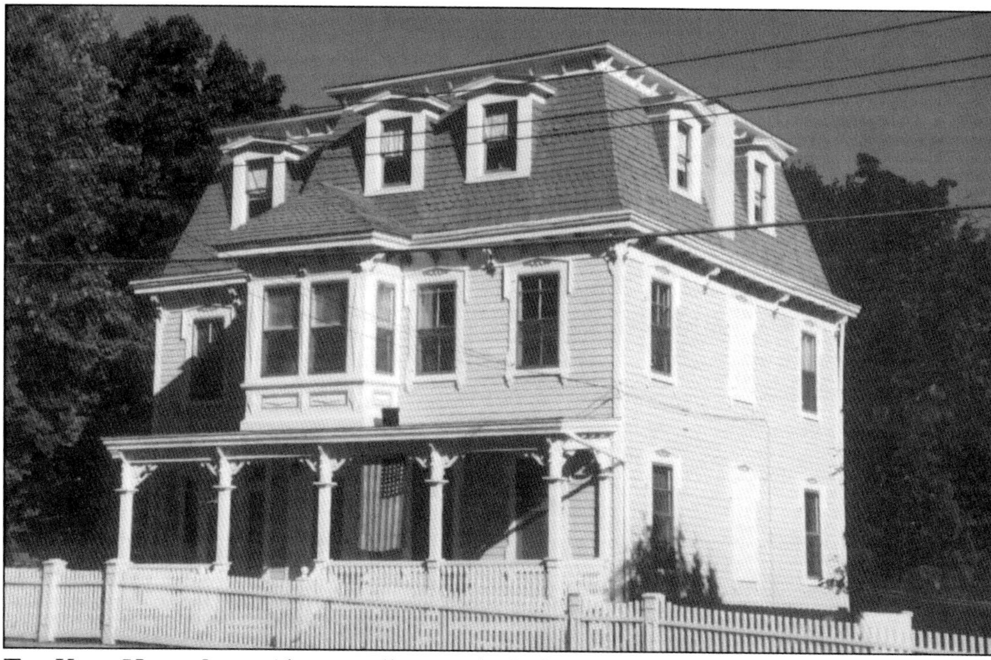

THE KANE HOME. James Aken, a mill owner, built the Kane home in the 1850s. It was acquired by Nicholas and Pierce Kane *c.* 1870 and was in the Kane family until 1992. It is on the corner of Burden Lake Road and Tin Can Alley. (Oral history gives the number of tin cans thrown in the area as the reason for the name.) (Courtesy Sand Lake Historical Society Collection.)

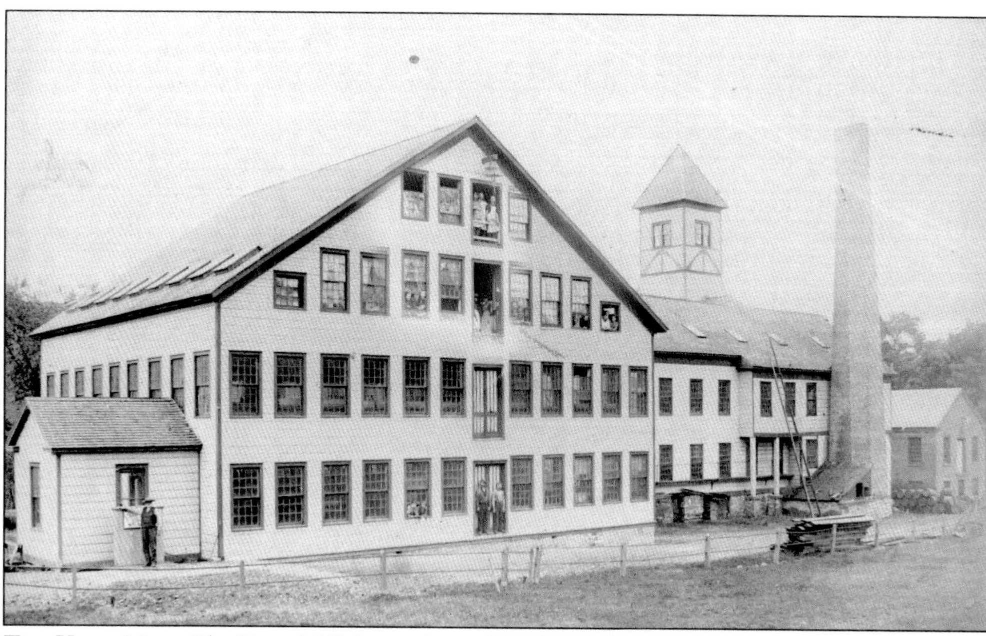

THE KANE MILL. The Kane Mill, located near Tin Can Alley, was built in 1862 by James Aken and sold to Nicholas Kane in 1875. A completely water-operated hosiery mill, it employed 85 persons and produced 30,000 dozen pairs of hosiery annually. Note the mill girls standing by the hoist doors, posing for the picture. (Courtesy Charles Viens.)

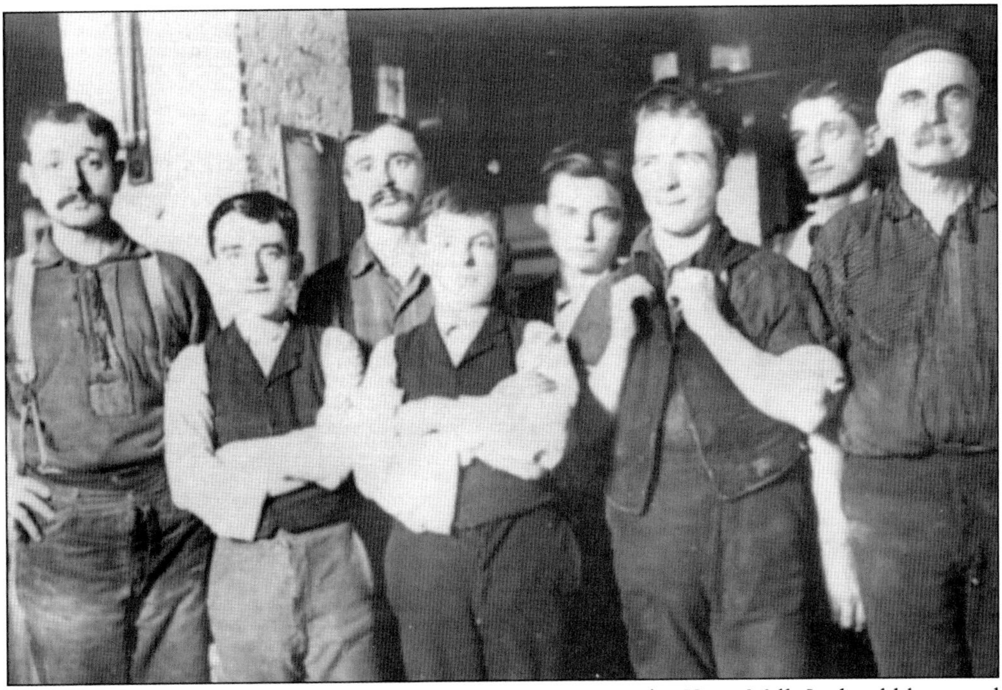

KANE MILL WORKERS. Some workers pose for a picture at the Kane Mill. It should be noted that the mill also employed large numbers of women and children. (Courtesy Town of Sand Lake Collection.)

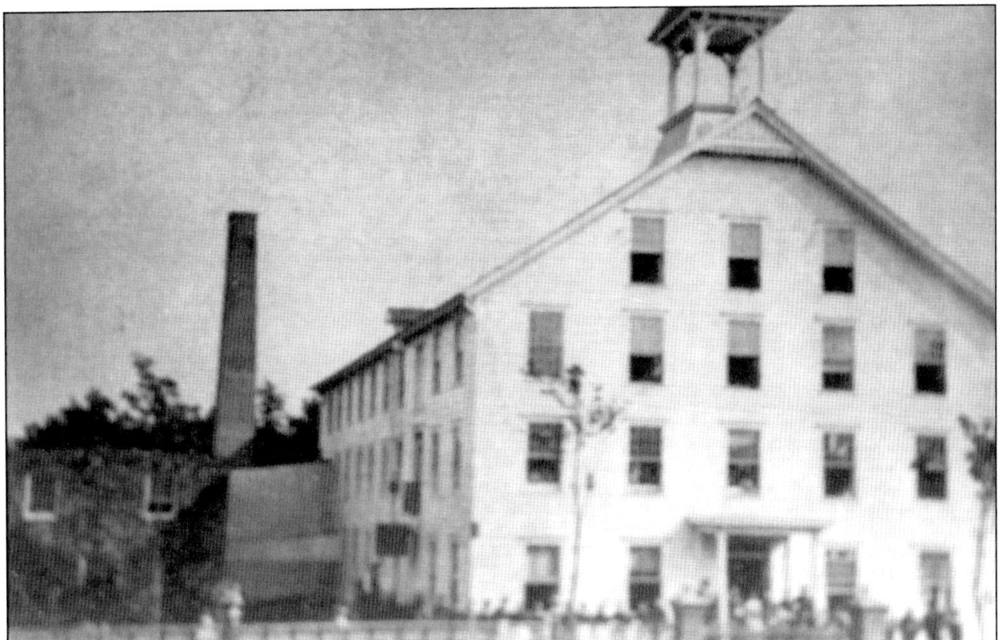

KNOWLSON'S BEVERWYCK HOSIERY MILL. This mill was built in 1875 after fire destroyed an older mill. Andrew Knowlson manufactured men's, ladies', and children's Beverwyck hosiery, as well as knit shirts and drawers. The mill closed in 1896 and was taken over by Faith Knitting Company in 1897. It burned down in 1906. (Courtesy Town of Sand Lake Collection.)

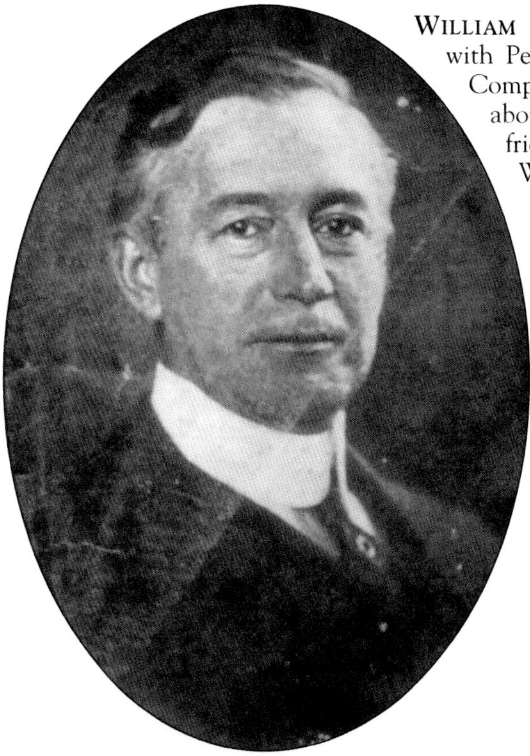

WILLIAM D. MAHONY. William D. Mahony, with Peter McCarthy, founded the Faith Knitting Company in 1897. At first he was hesitant about the new venture. His wife and friends encouraged him saying, "Have faith, Will. Have faith." This resulted in the naming of the Faith Knitting Company. As well as being president of the company, Mahony was president of the board of education that was instrumental in forming the Averill Park Central School District. (Courtesy Town of Sand Lake Collection.)

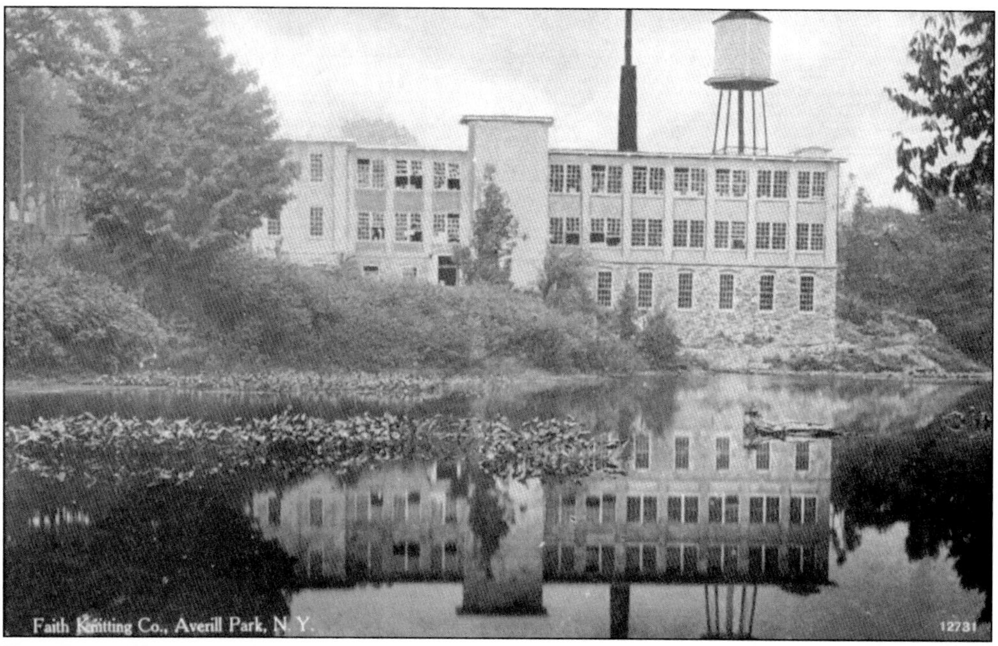

THE FAITH KNITTING COMPANY. After fire destroyed the Knowlson's former wooden building (see page 65), the Faith Knitting Company erected a new masonry building in 1906 on the same site. The new mill was powered by a 100-horsepower steam engine and had electric incandescent lighting. In 1929, the name was changed to Faith Mills. It was the last operating mill in the town of Sand Lake, closing in 1962. (Courtesy Ada and Wesley Miller.)

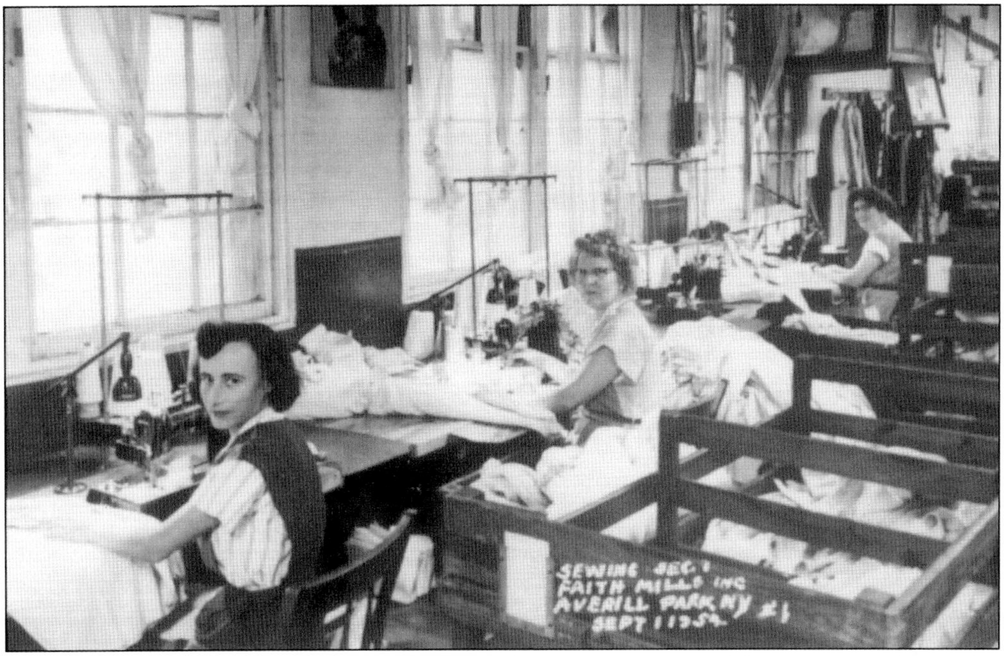

THE FAITH MILLS SEWING ROOM. At work in the sewing room in 1953 are, from left to right, Ida Zipkin, Jennie Cann, and Florence Shaw sewing on knit wool shirts or drawers. Faith Mills was the major employer of workers in Averill Park. (Courtesy Ida Zipkin Schips.)

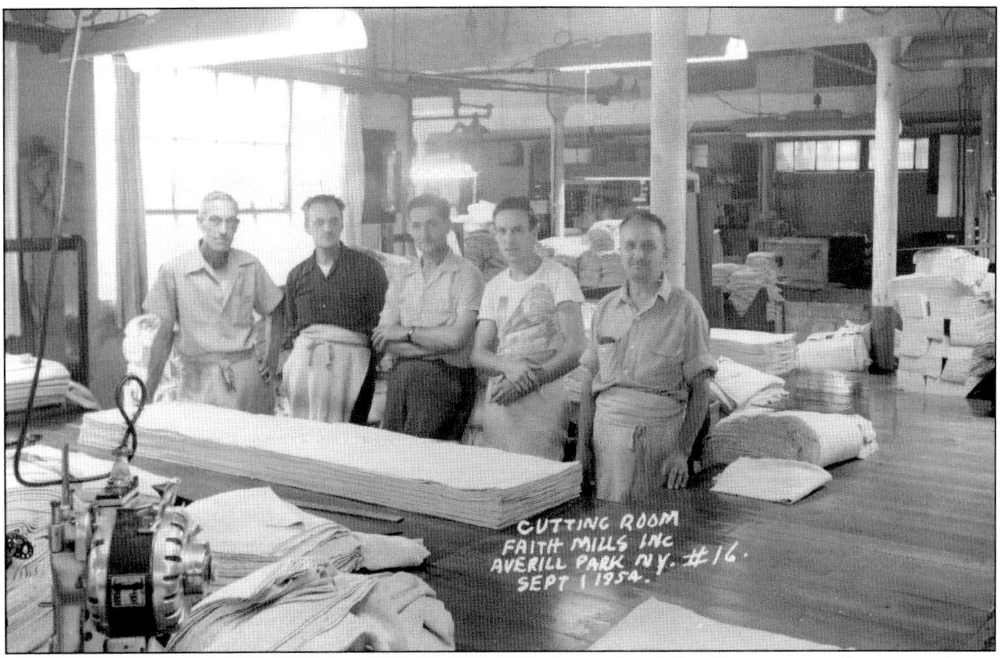

THE CUTTING ROOM AT FAITH MILLS, SEPTEMBER 1954. This knitting mill received raw wool and cotton, spun the thread, knit the cloth, cut the cloth to patterns, assembled the finished garments, and folded and packed the garments for shipping. In the cutting room are, from left to right, Clayton Barnum, Charles Dawson, Fred "Snick" Shoemaker, an unidentified man, and Leslie French. (Courtesy Ross French, son of Leslie French.)

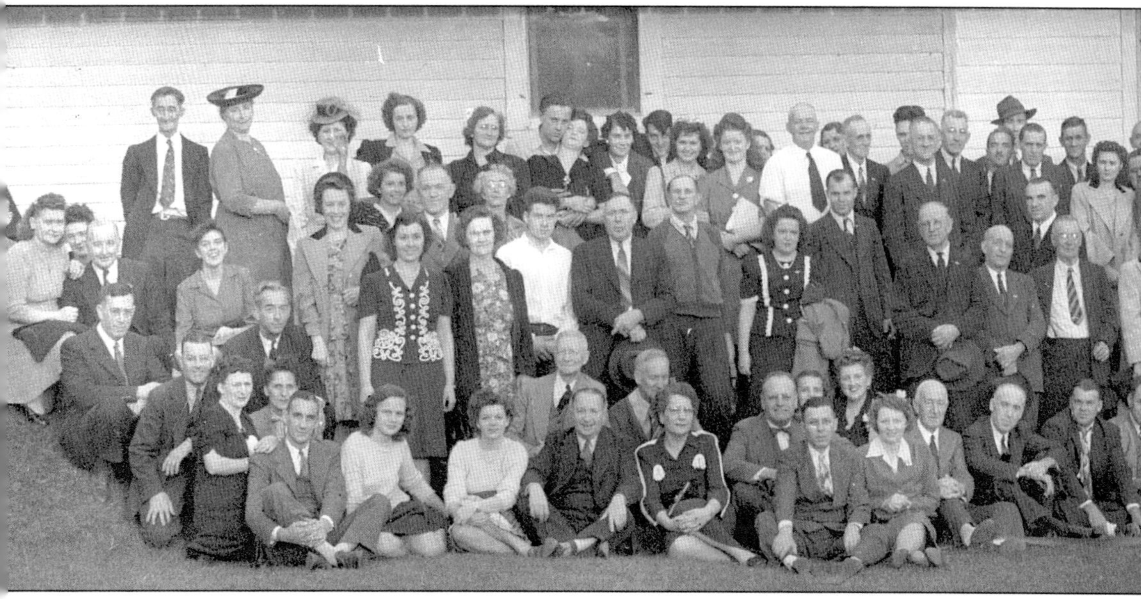

EMPLOYEES POSING FOR E AWARD , 1943. The work force of Faith Mills in 1943 is shown when the mill and each of the employees received the E Award for providing long woolen underwear and blankets for the war effort. The award dinner was held at the Burden Lake Casino. At the ceremony Dr. Ray Palmer Baker, dean of students at Rensselaer Polytechnic

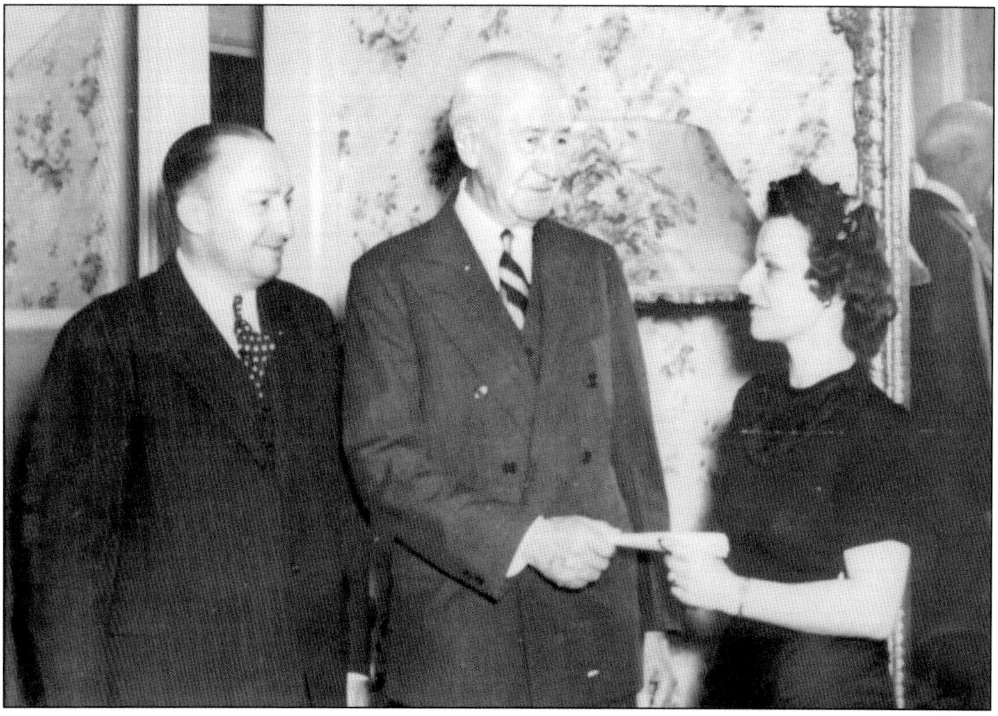

MABEL STANLEY RECEIVING AWARD FOR EMPLOYEES. At the presentation, from left to right, are George Wentworth, supervisor in the finishing room; William D. Mahony, president of Faith Mills; and Mabel Stanley, representative of the employees receiving the E Award. (Courtesy Annamae Leavenworth Hebert.)

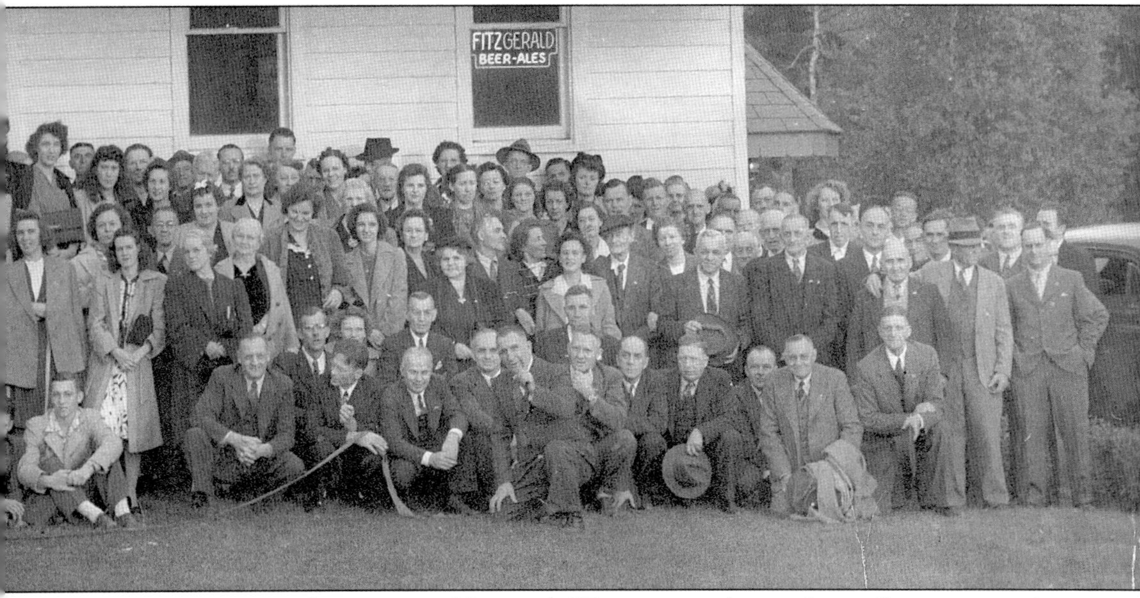

Institute, was master of ceremonies. He noted, "To represent the employees [by accepting the award], the management and employees have jointly selected Miss Mabel Stanley, who will be aided by Miss Mary Brown, Hiram G. Smyth, and Aaron Dibble." (Courtesy Linda Ormsby.)

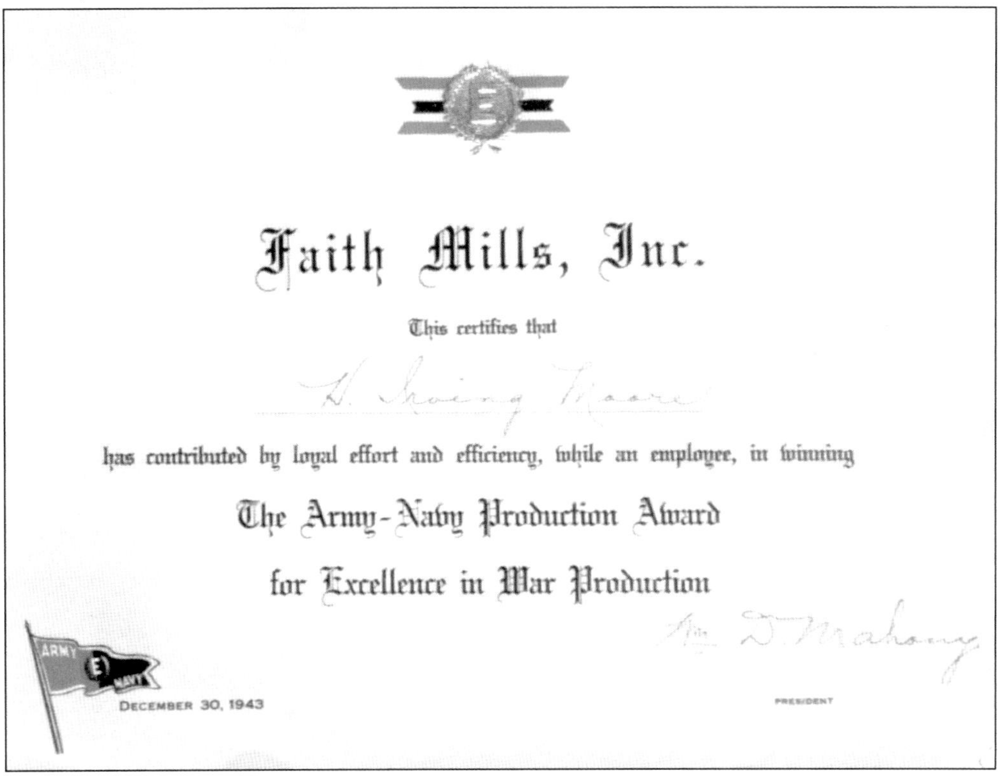

AN E AWARD CERTIFICATE. H. Irving Moore and the other Faith Mills employees were each given an Army-Navy Production Award certificate along with an E Award pin in recognition of their part in the war effort. (Courtesy Robert Moore, son of H. Irving Moore.)

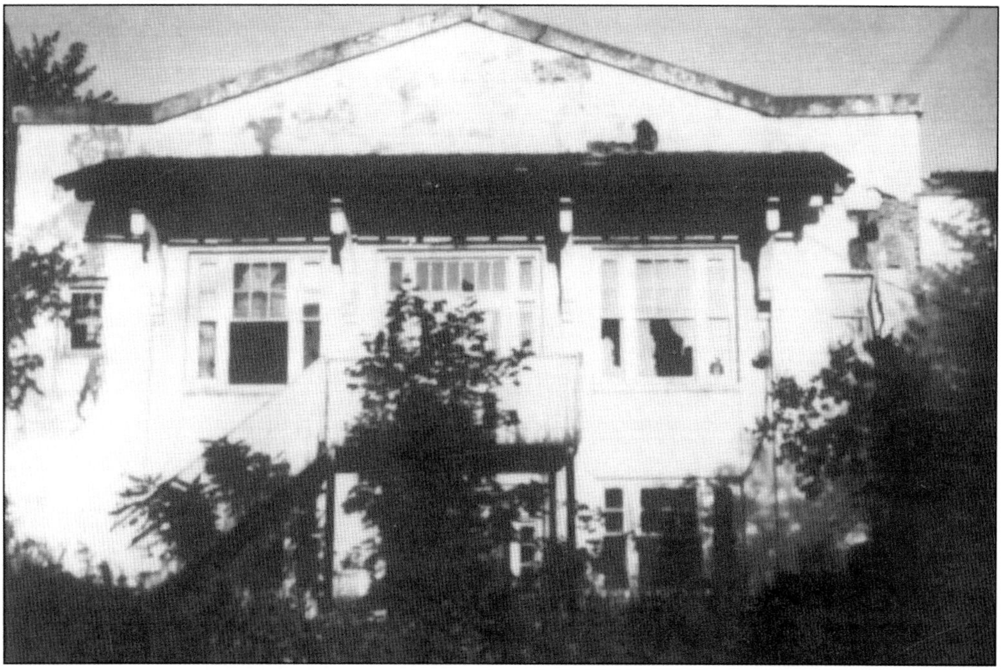

The Community Clubhouse. The Faith Mills Community Clubhouse provided after-hours social activities for mill workers and townspeople. It had a movie theater, four bowling lanes, a cafeteria, and a large meeting hall with a stage. It was the entertainment center of the town for many years. (Courtesy Robert Moore.)

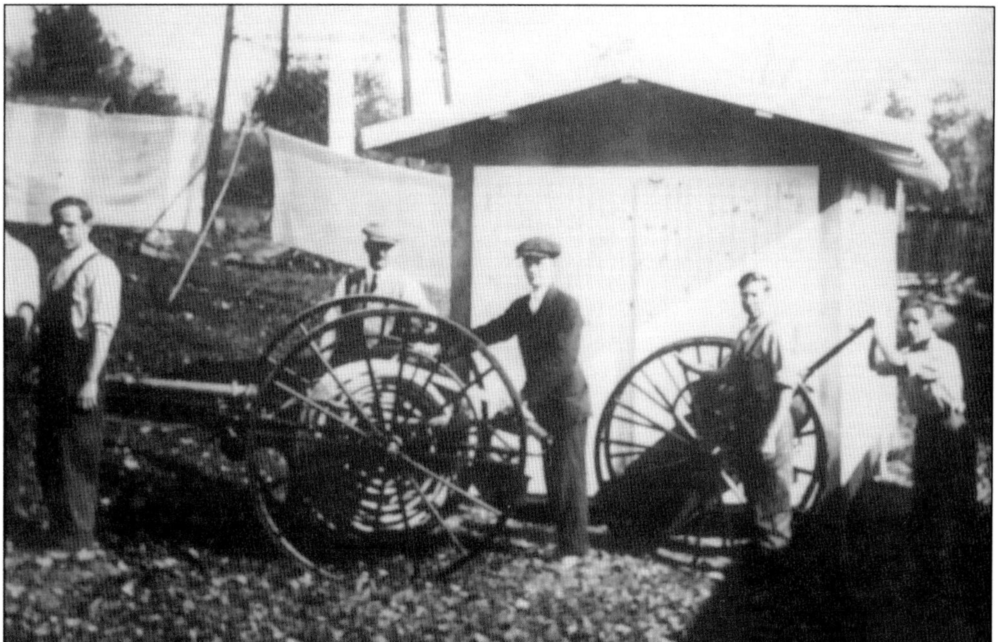

Faith Mills Fire Brigade. Fire was a constant threat in a knitting mill, due to the dust and lint in the air. Each mill had its own fire brigade. Here, Faith Mills workers practice with a hand-drawn cart. (Courtesy Town of Sand Lake Collection.)

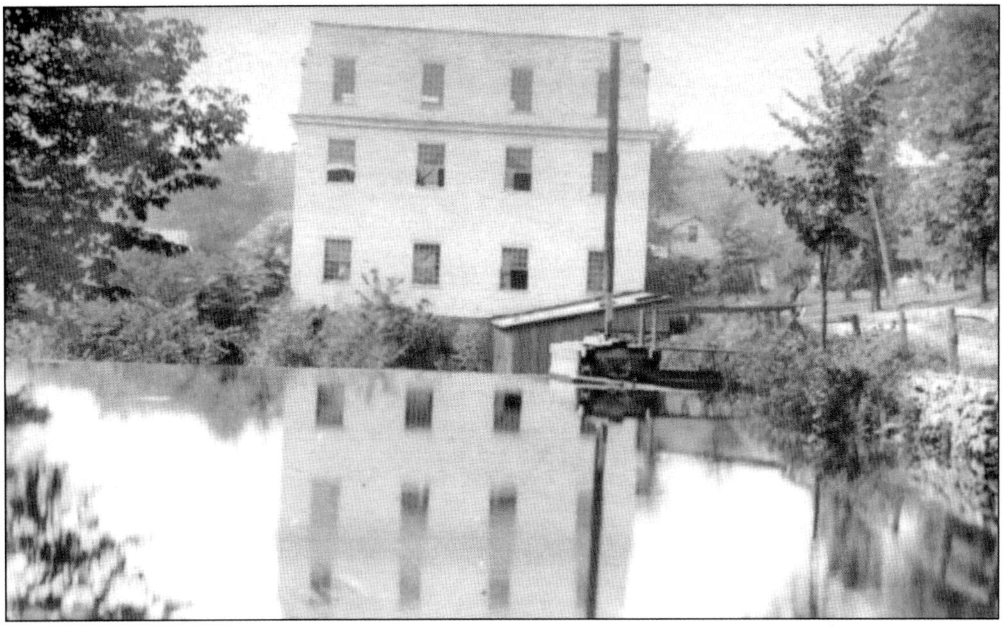

JOHN ALBERTSON'S CLOTH-DRESSING FACTORY. This was a mill site as early as 1820, when John Albertson operated a cloth-dressing factory here. The building was last occupied by the McConihe Warp Mill, which manufactured both white and colored cotton warp until 1886. The mill then was idle until *c.* 1900. (Courtesy Alice Tifft.)

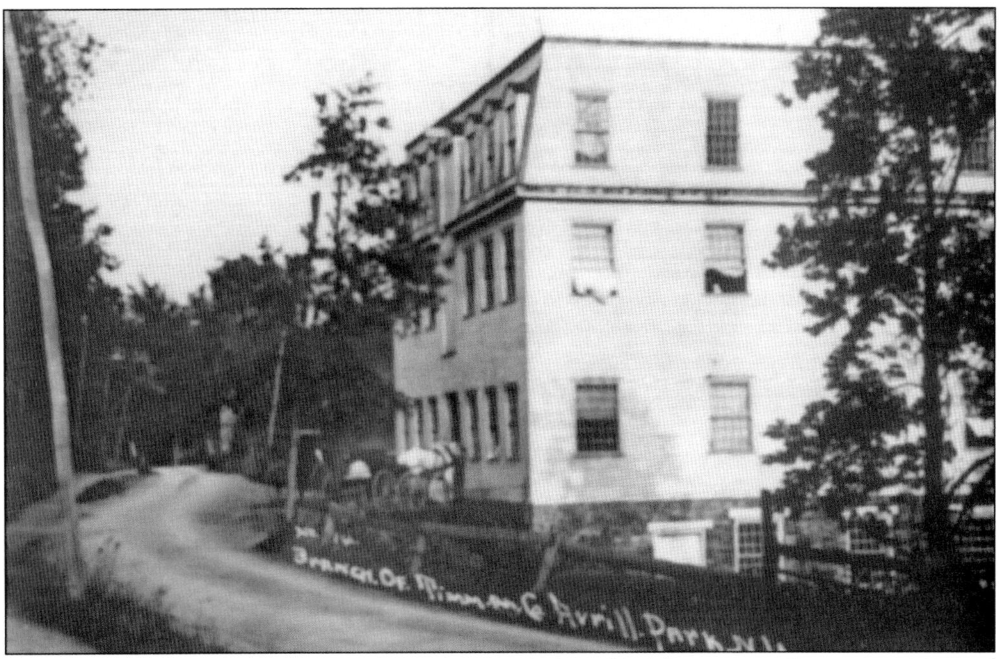

TIMM & COMPANY. Timm & Company rented the old Albertson mill site *c.* 1900 and manufactured the Troy shirt here until 1914. The structure then became part of the Faith Mills complex. (Courtesy Helen Crape Guy.)

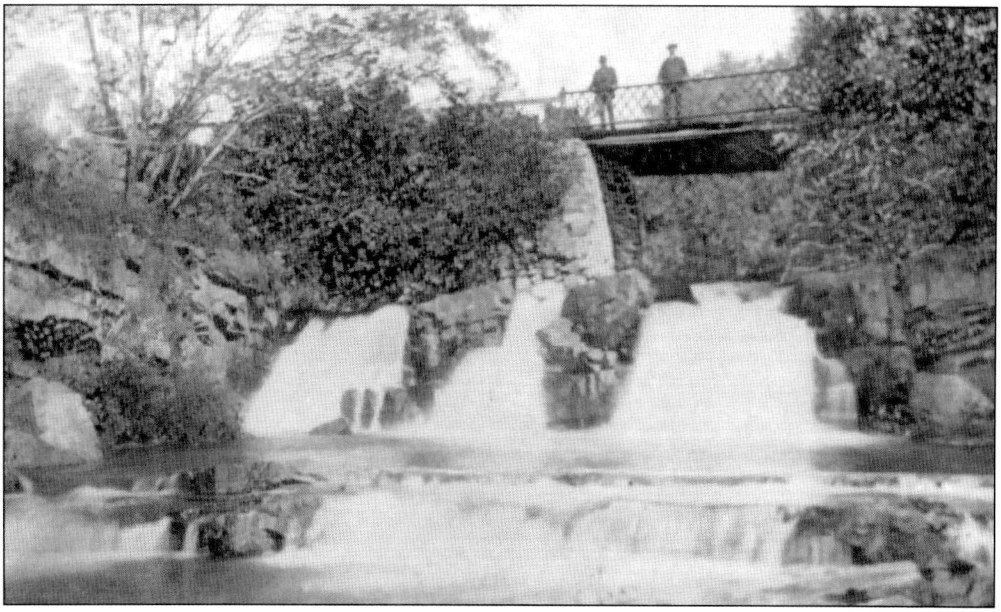

THE FALLS, AVERILL PARK. At the bridge on Burden Lake Road—county Route 51, just before the first Burden Lake—is a scenic falls on the Wynantskill Creek. Staats Tompkins's Paper Mill, once located on the left bank, is long gone. (Courtesy Lawrence Herzog.)

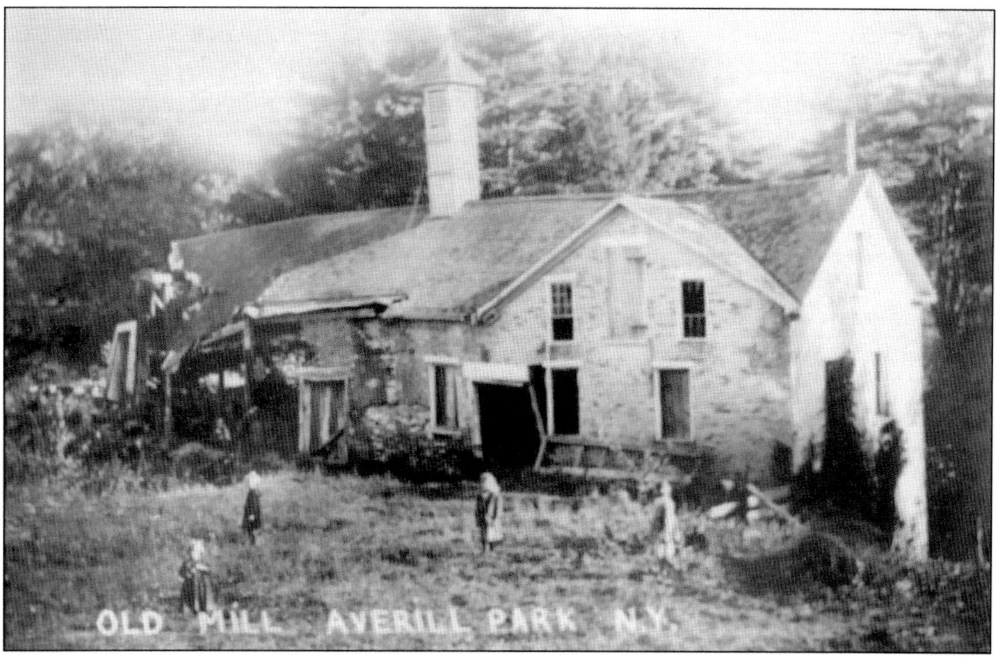

STAATS TOMPKINS'S PAPER MILL. Staats D. Tompkins built a paper mill on the Wynantskill across from Garner Road c. 1854. In 1865, it became the E. & J. Merwin Paper Company and was sold in 1875 to Andrew Smart, a manufacturer of straw wrapping paper. The flood of 1891 caused heavy damage, and the mill never reopened (see page 117). Only parts of the foundation remain, but Tompkins house remains and is currently the home of William Kennedy, author and 1984 Pulitzer Prize winner. (Courtesy Sand Lake Historical Society Collection.)

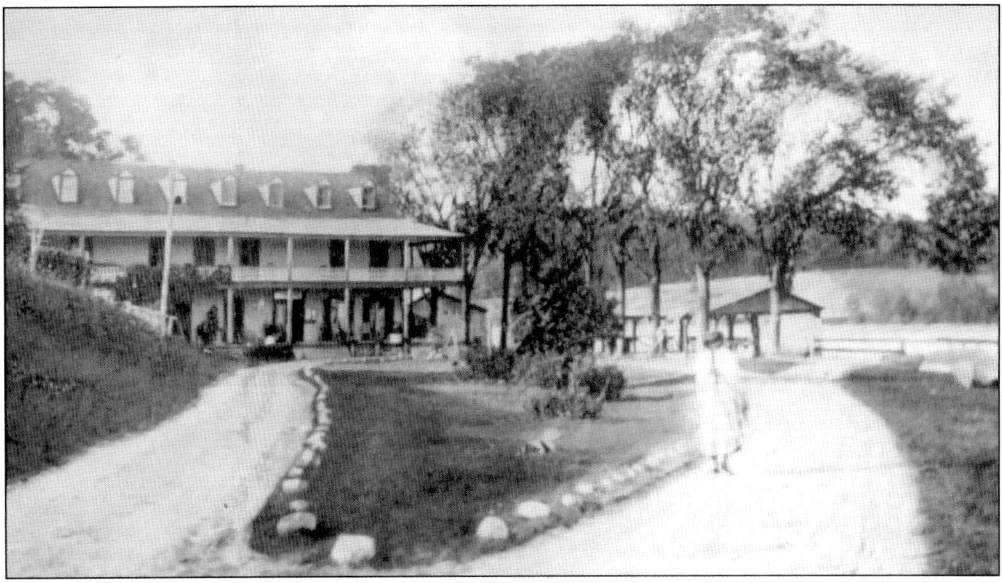

THE BURDEN LAKE HOUSE. The Calkins family established this well-known resort hotel in the 1840s and ran it for about 100 years. The hotel is now Kay's Burden Lake Restaurant on the second Burden Lake. Most people refer to it by its informal name, Kay's Pizza. (Courtesy Joseph Connors Jr.)

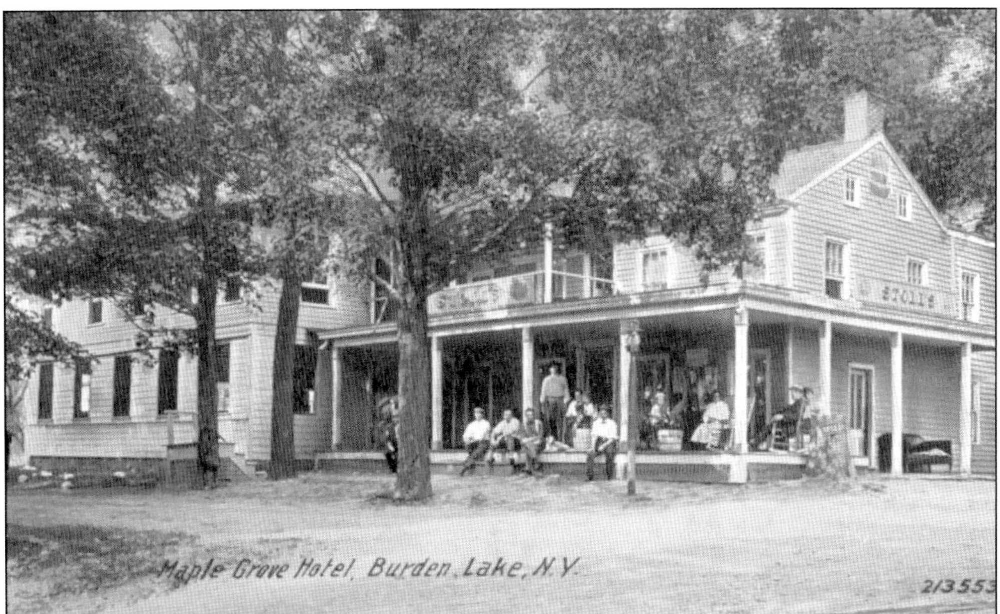

THE MAPLE GROVE HOTEL. The Maple Grove Hotel shown in this picture was torn down. The Stackrows of First Dyke Road operated the rebuilt hotel. In later years, it was Irish's Maple Grove Hotel. It burned January 1968 and again in 1986. (Courtesy Sand Lake Historical Society Collection.)

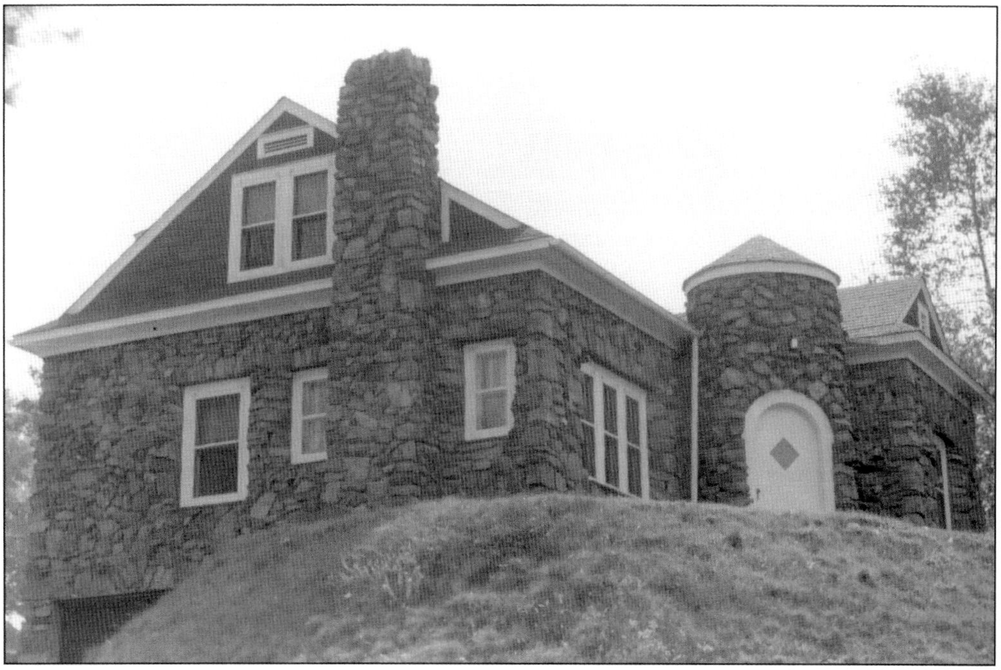

A STONE HOUSE ON THAIS ROAD. James Clinton Baxter, a master stonemason, built this house for the late Joseph Connors Sr. and Arthea Connors Gibbs. He also constructed the other stone houses on Thais Road and did the stone work on Crooked Lake Hotel and Motel (see page 96). He named Thais Road for his wife. (Courtesy Joseph Connors Jr.)

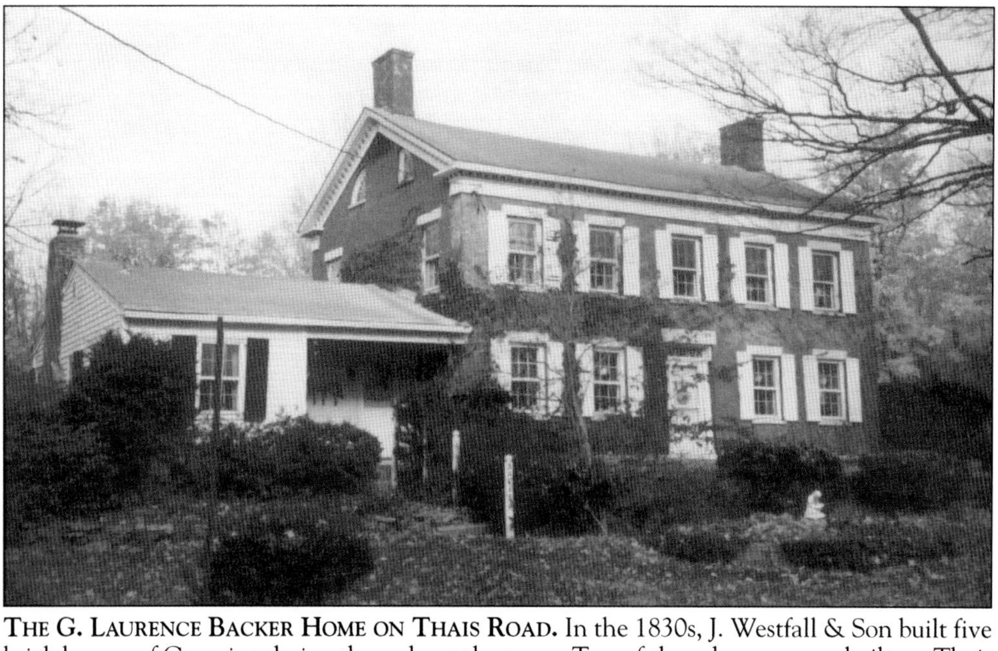

THE G. LAURENCE BACKER HOME ON THAIS ROAD. In the 1830s, J. Westfall & Son built five brick houses of Georgian design throughout the town. Two of these houses were built on Thais Road. The others are located on Biittig Road and at Bon Acre Trailer Park on Route 43. The fifth house has been torn down. The Westfalls also built the brick section of Cedarhurst (see page 30). (Courtesy Sand Lake Historical Society Collection.)

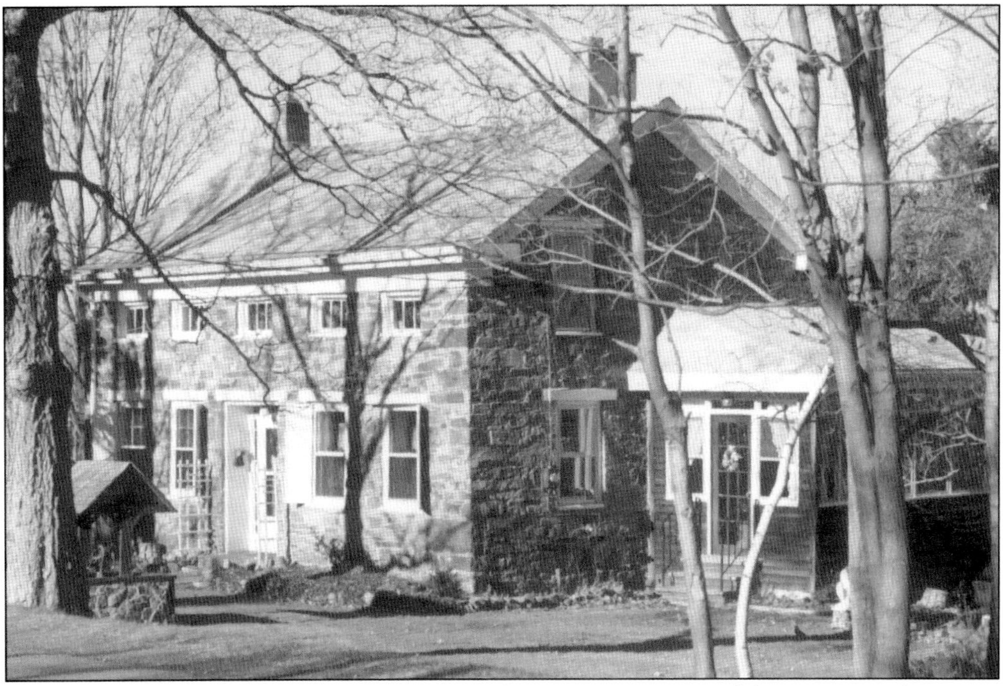

The Hogle House. Edward Hogle built this house in 1801, one of the two stone houses in town. It has been in the family for seven generations. Stones used in the building are from the nearby fields. The walls above ground are 26 inches thick and below ground are 36 inches thick. (Courtesy Sand Lake Historical Society Collection.)

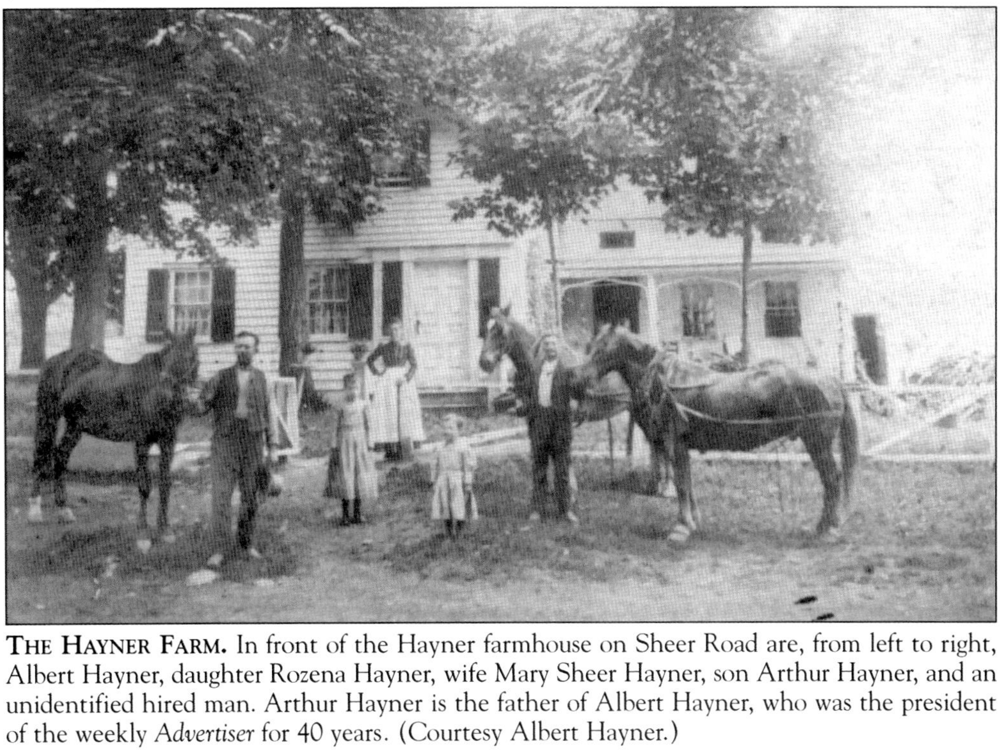

The Hayner Farm. In front of the Hayner farmhouse on Sheer Road are, from left to right, Albert Hayner, daughter Rozena Hayner, wife Mary Sheer Hayner, son Arthur Hayner, and an unidentified hired man. Arthur Hayner is the father of Albert Hayner, who was the president of the weekly *Advertiser* for 40 years. (Courtesy Albert Hayner.)

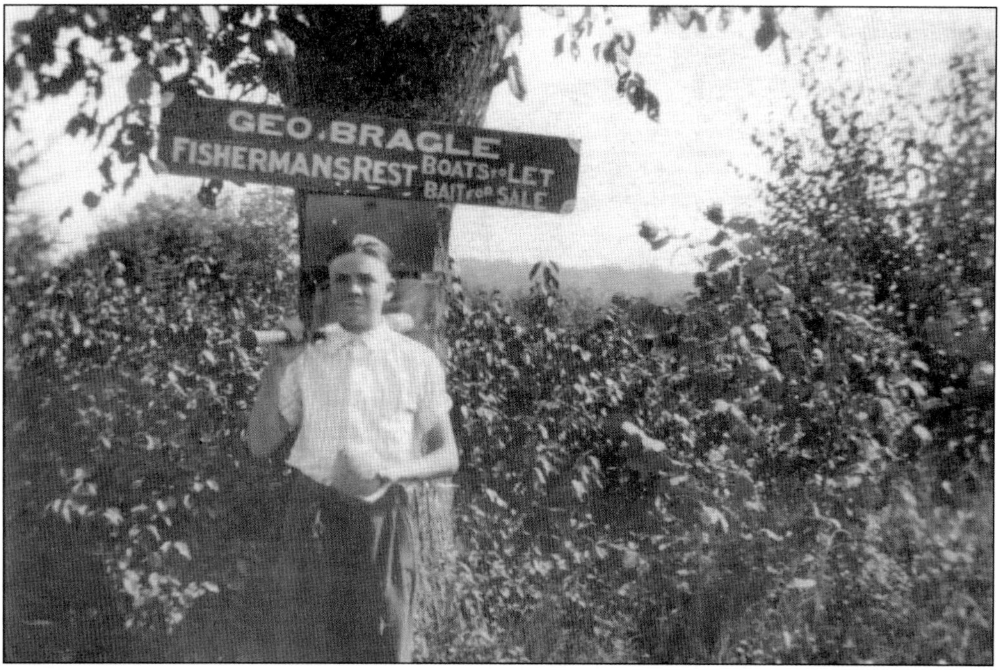

Fisherman's Rest. Joseph Bragle (also spelled Breigle) shows off his day's catch. In the early 1900s, his father, George ran this hideaway on second Burden Lake, providing accommodations for up to 18 men who wished to spend a few days fishing. He would meet his boarders at the trolley station with his wagon and transport them to the lodge. Later, Fisherman's Rest became Burden Lake Hotel and Burden Lake Casino. It burned in 1959. (Courtesy George Breigle.)

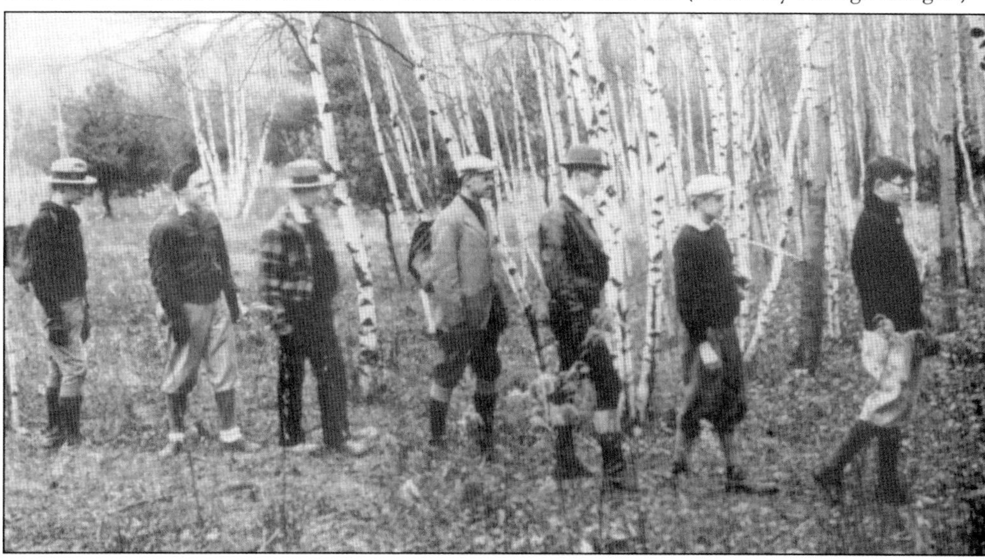

Camp Van Schoonhoven. The YMCA operated Camp Van Schoonhoven on the third Burden Lake from the late 1920s to 1970s. This picture from the book, *Taconic Trails*, by Edward T. Heald, c. 1929, shows a group in full hiking attire beginning their trek over Intercamp Trail in 1928. In the 1940s, campers would be brought by canoe to the Maple Grove Hotel beach. Then they would go to Hayner's Store for ice cream and candy. (Courtesy Judy Rowe, from *Taconic Trails*.)

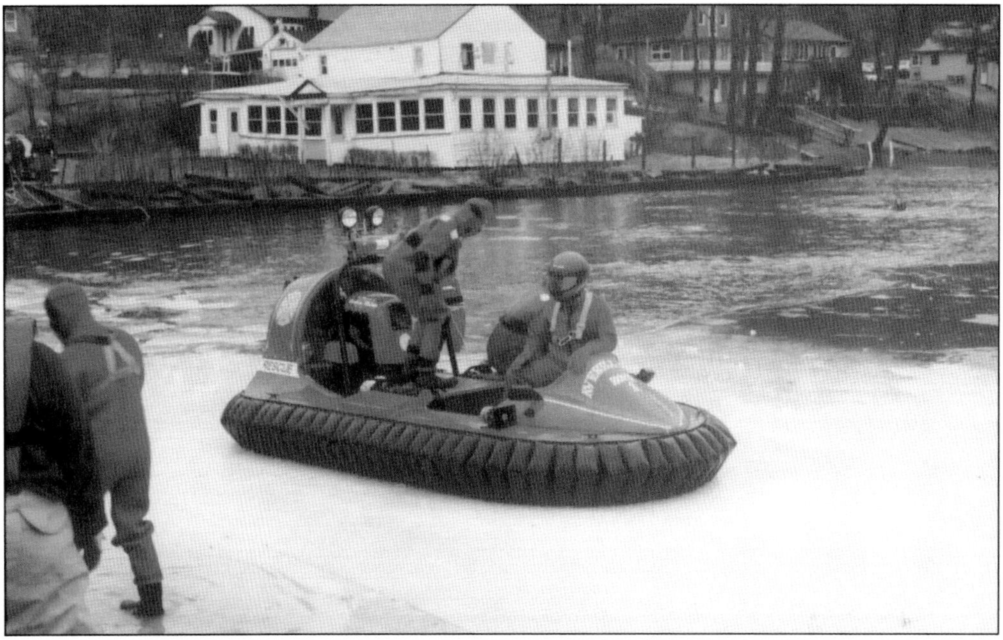

HOVERCRAFT ON BURDEN LAKE. Seen here is the hovercraft that was purchased in 1994 through the efforts of the Molitor family after Barbara Molitor went through the ice on the second Burden Lake and died from exposure. It is being given a practice session near Kay's Burden Lake Restaurant (see page 73). (Courtesy Averill Park and Sand Lake Fire Company.)

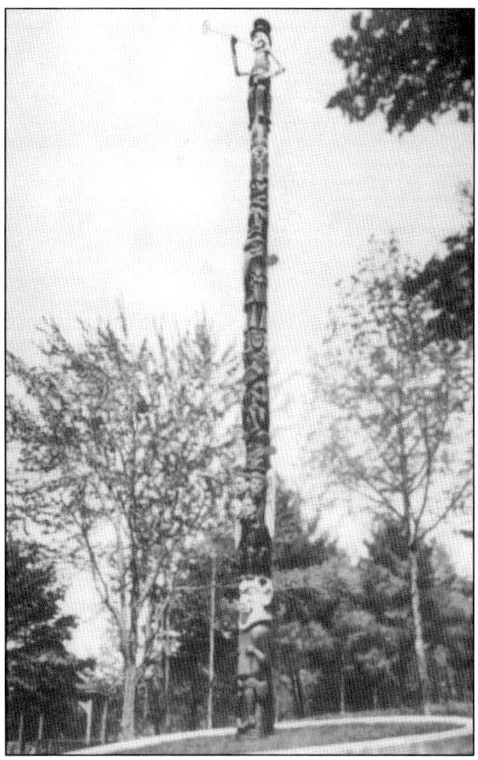

TOTEM LODGE. Summer clientele from the New York City area arrived at Averill Park and were taxied to Totem Lodge, located on the third Burden Lake. This summer adult camp was named for its prominently erected totem pole. Henry Tobias, who was social director for many years, featured the lodge in his book, *The Borscht Belt*, and booked such notable entertainers as Beverly Sills, Eddie Cantor, Martha Raye, and Roy Rogers. The lodge was torn down in 1985. (Courtesy Sand Lake Historical Society Collection.)

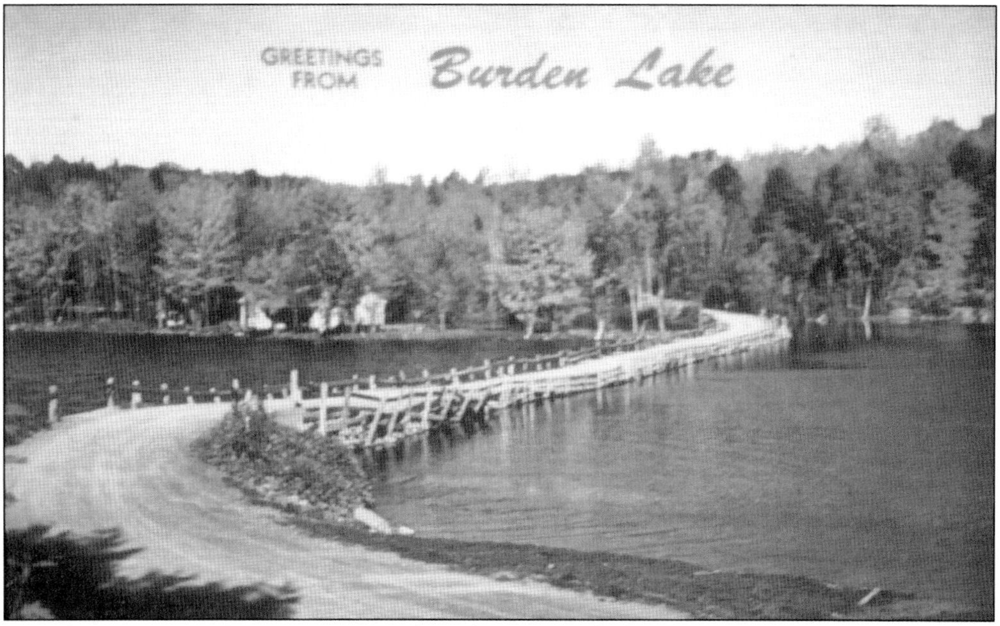

The First Dyke at Burden Lake. When the Wynantskill Improvement Association flooded the valley and stream from Martins Lake, later named Burden Lake, two roads had to be raised above the new water level. They are today First Dyke Road and Second Dyke Road. Water was supplied to mills along the banks of the Wynantskill. (Courtesy Joseph Connors Jr.)

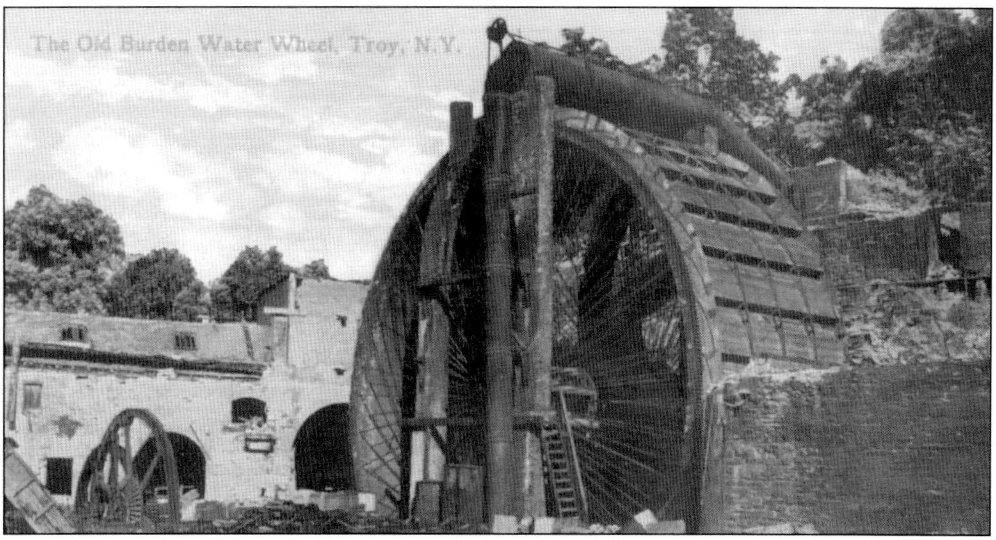

The Burden Waterwheel. Water continued down the Wynantskill through Albia and Troy until it reached its final destination and furnished waterpower for the largest waterwheel in North America at the Burden Iron Works in Troy. (Courtesy Robert J. Lilly.)

Three

Sand Lake, Glass Lake, and Crooked Lake

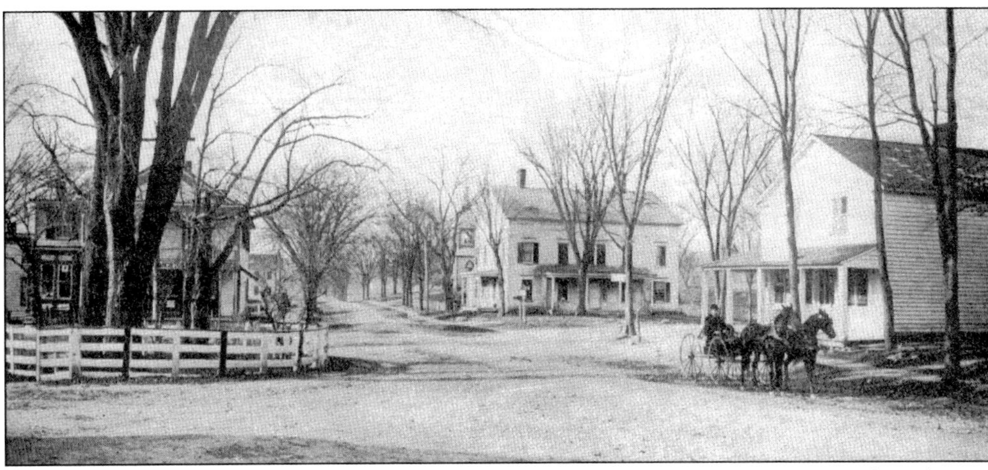

Sand Lake Corners. The hamlet of Sand Lake was named Sliter's Corners for Clement Sliter, a pioneer settler, and then was changed to Sand Lake *c.* 1880. The "Beauty Spot of Sand Lake," or Sand Lake Corners, was at the present intersection of Routes 43 and 66. In this view looking west, the building that housed Nash's Store and the Sand Lake Post Office is on the left. It was turned and moved back from the road *c.* 1929, when Route 43 was widened. Next is the Butts house also called the "Beehive." The house on the right was Nash's Store prior to its relocation on the southwest corner. The steeple of the First Presbyterian Church of Sand Lake is visible to the left of the Butts house. The horses and wagon are heading east on Taborton Road and have a steep climb ahead of them. The yard of Crape's Hotel is in the foreground. South on current Routes 43 and 66 is the hamlet of Glass House, later called Glass Lake. It was established to meet the needs of the Rensselaer Glass Factory and included workers' and owners' homes, stores, church, school, and boardinghouse. Farther south on Routes 43 and 66 is Crooked Lake. The hotel is its most prominent feature, with development along the lakeshore following. (Courtesy Lawrence Herzog.)

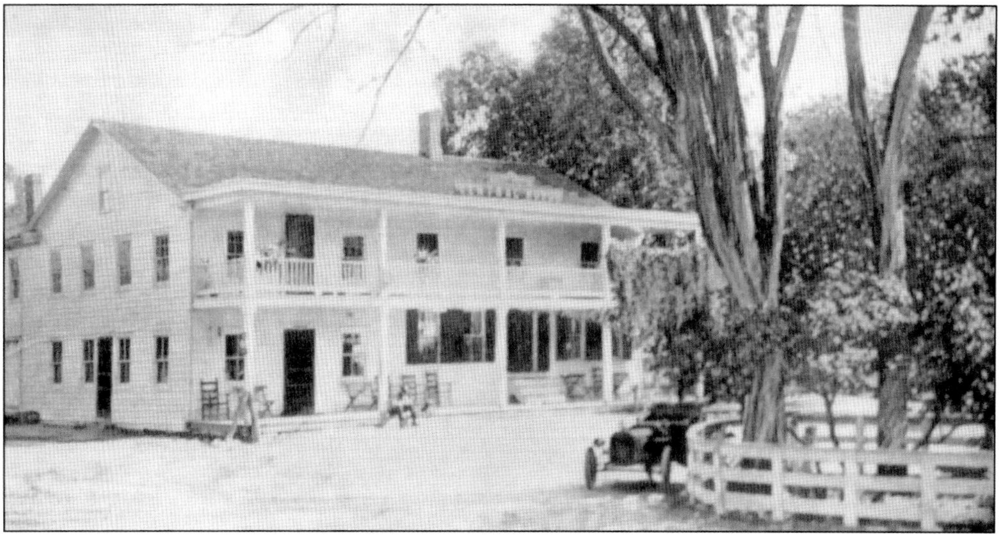

CRIST CRAPE'S CENTRAL HOTEL. This hotel was built *c.* 1800 by Clement Sliter and had various owners before it became Crist Crape's Central Hotel. It was located on the southeast corner of Taborton Road and Routes 43 and 66. The Crape family raised much of the meat, poultry, and produce to serve to persons traveling from Albany to Boston by stagecoach and from Troy by horse and buggy or trolley. The hotel had a beautiful mahogany bar and ballroom upstairs, both notable attractions. It was razed in 1957. (Courtesy Lawrence Herzog.)

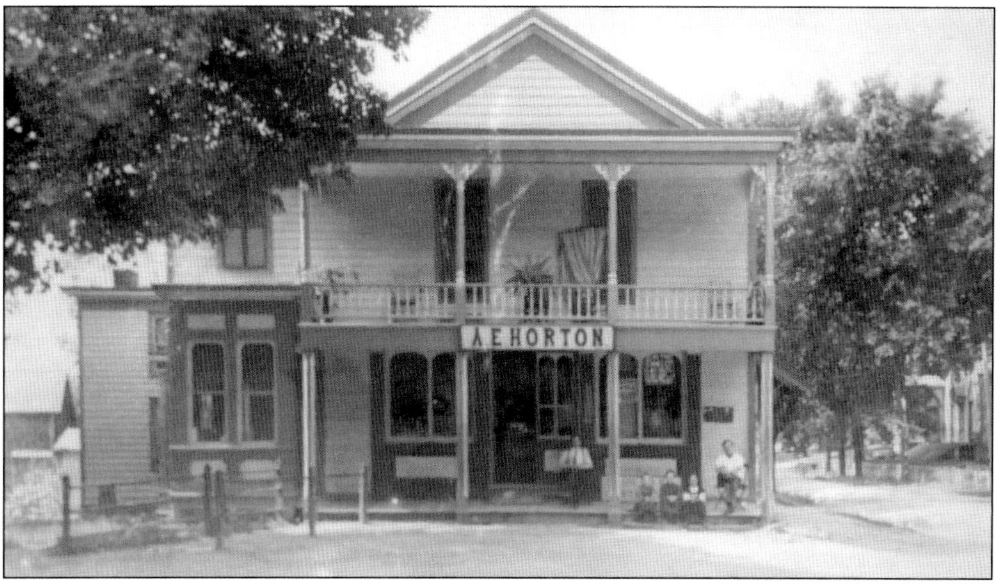

A.E. HORTON'S STORE. Franklin Averill ran the first store here *c.* 1830. The post office was located in the store from 1907 to 1978, with Albert Horton as postmaster from 1907 to 1914. Chester Nash acquired it in 1911 and was postmaster from 1914 until his death in 1949. His sons, Raymond and Walter Nash, ran it until Raymond's death in 1965, and then Walter Nash and his sister-in-law, Lillian Nash, ran the store and post office until 1978 (see page 81). (Courtesy Alice Tifft.)

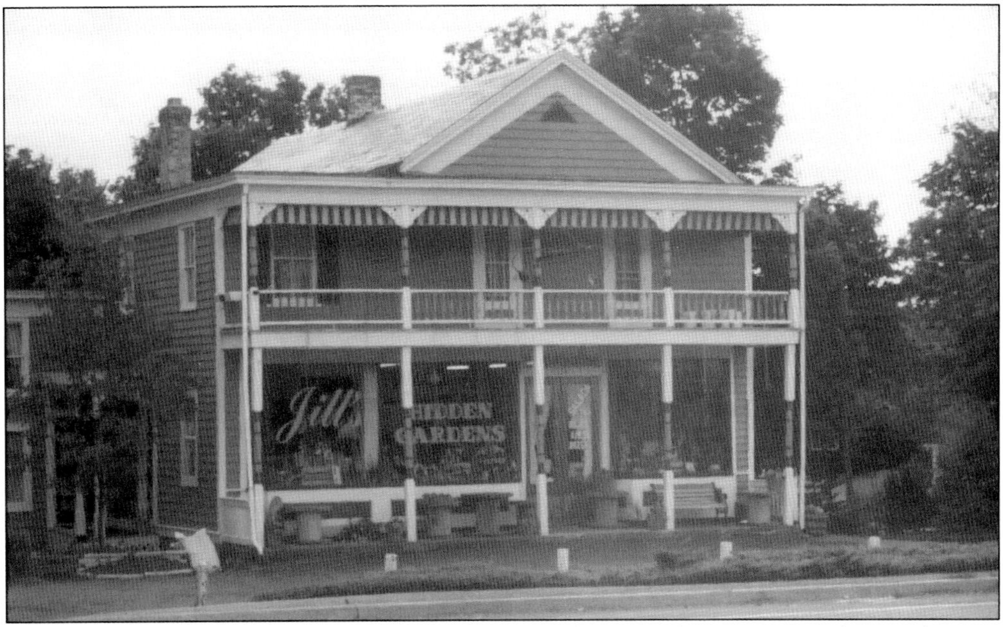

NASH'S STORE, 1998. In the 1980s, Nash's Store became the Country Token, a favorite old country store and gift shop. It now houses Jill's Hidden Gardens. (Courtesy Sand Lake Historical Society Collection.)

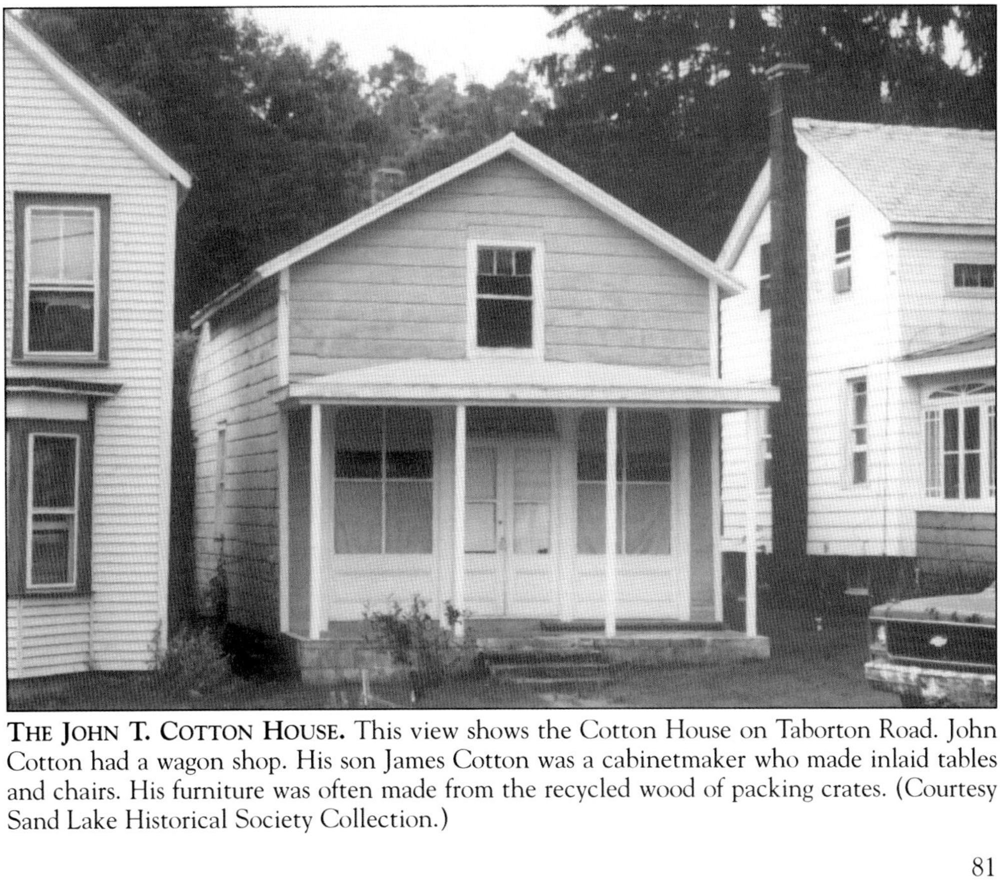

THE JOHN T. COTTON HOUSE. This view shows the Cotton House on Taborton Road. John Cotton had a wagon shop. His son James Cotton was a cabinetmaker who made inlaid tables and chairs. His furniture was often made from the recycled wood of packing crates. (Courtesy Sand Lake Historical Society Collection.)

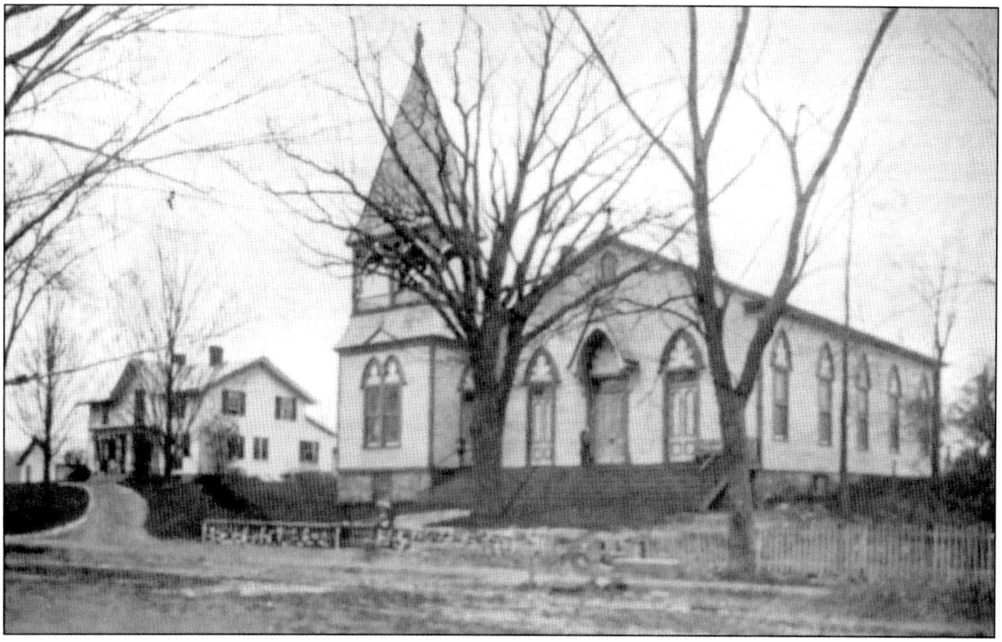

The First Presbyterian Church of Sand Lake. From 1808 until 1835, the Presbyterians worshiped at the meetinghouse (see page 50), which is now Sand Lake Baptist Church. The First Presbyterian Church of Sand Lake was dedicated October 28, 1835. In 1967, it merged with the Averill Park Methodist Church and formed the Church of the Covenant. The town of Sand Lake purchased the church, remodeled it, added offices, and used it as the town hall from 1972 to 1999. (Courtesy Sand Lake Historical Society Collection.)

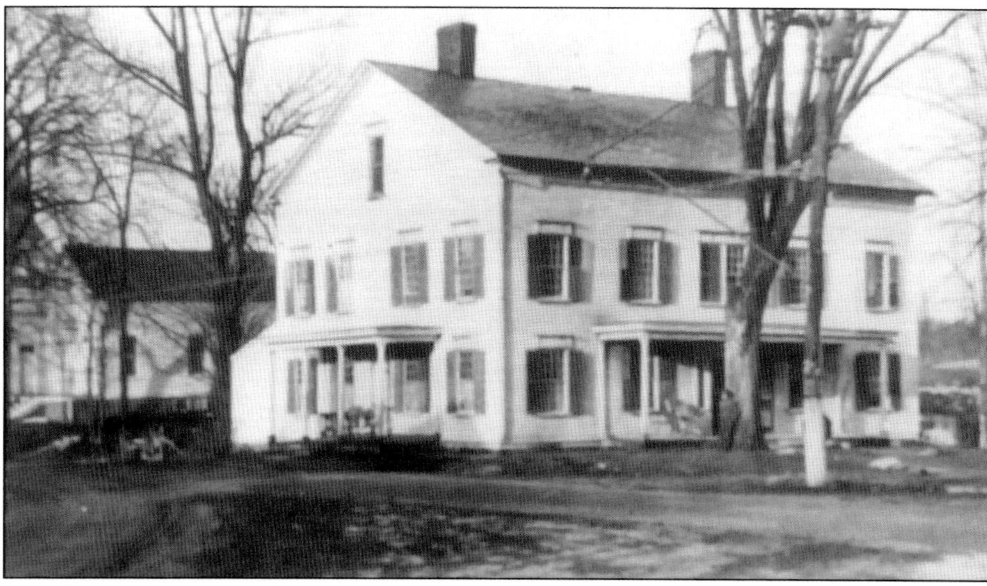

The Butts House at Four Corners in Sand Lake. This house was built by Gideon Butts, a lumber pioneer, in 1824. It had a huge fireplace with a Dutch oven in the cellar. The house, which was nicknamed the "Beehive," was torn down in 1956. Cumberland Farms is now located on this site. The post office moved from Nash's Store to this site in 1978 (see page 80). (Courtesy Town of Sand Lake Collection.)

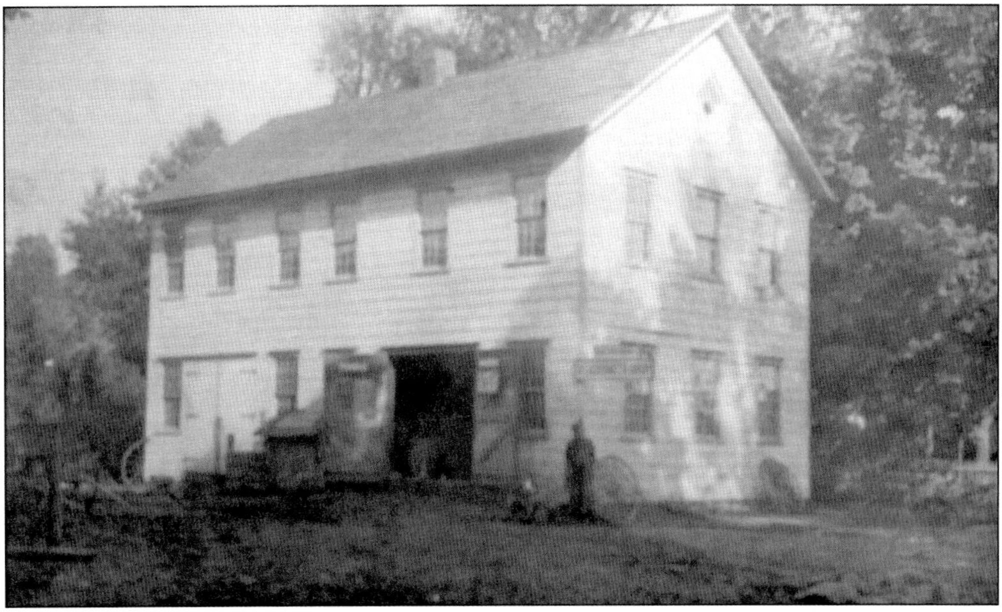

Bart Warren's Blacksmith Shop. The sign on this building reads "George Hoffman, Jr. Blacksmith Shop." The building was heavily damaged in the flood of 1891. Bart Warren (see page 24) opened a blacksmith shop near the bridge at this Route 43 and 66 location. (Courtesy Town of Sand Lake Collection.)

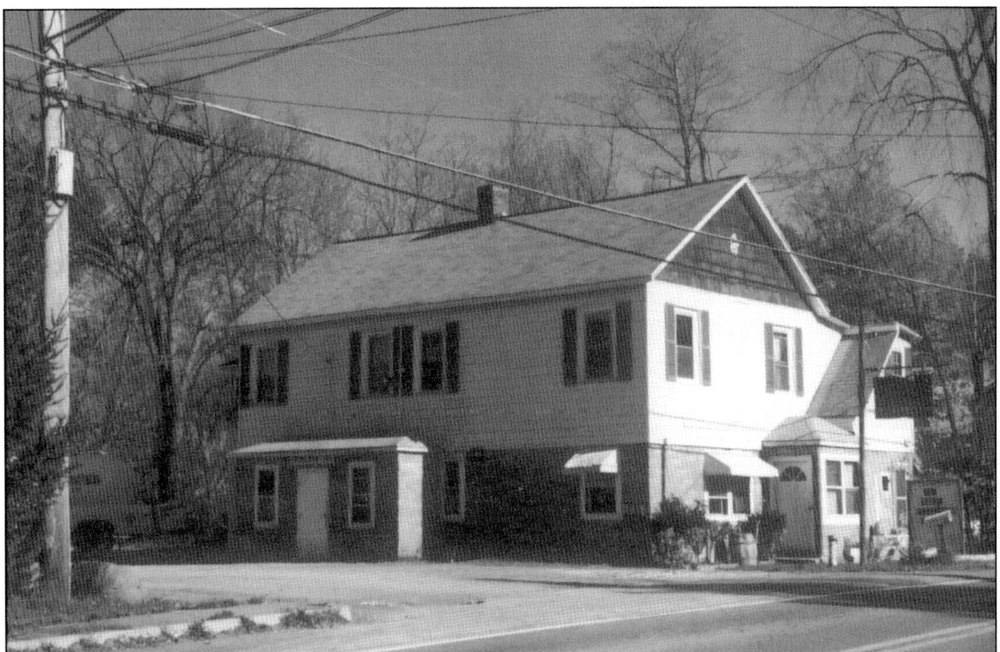

The Park Restaurant. The Park Restaurant is an example of reuse of the former Bart Warren Blacksmith Shop. During hunting season a sign is displayed, "Open 6 AM for hunters." (Courtesy Sand Lake Historical Society Collection.)

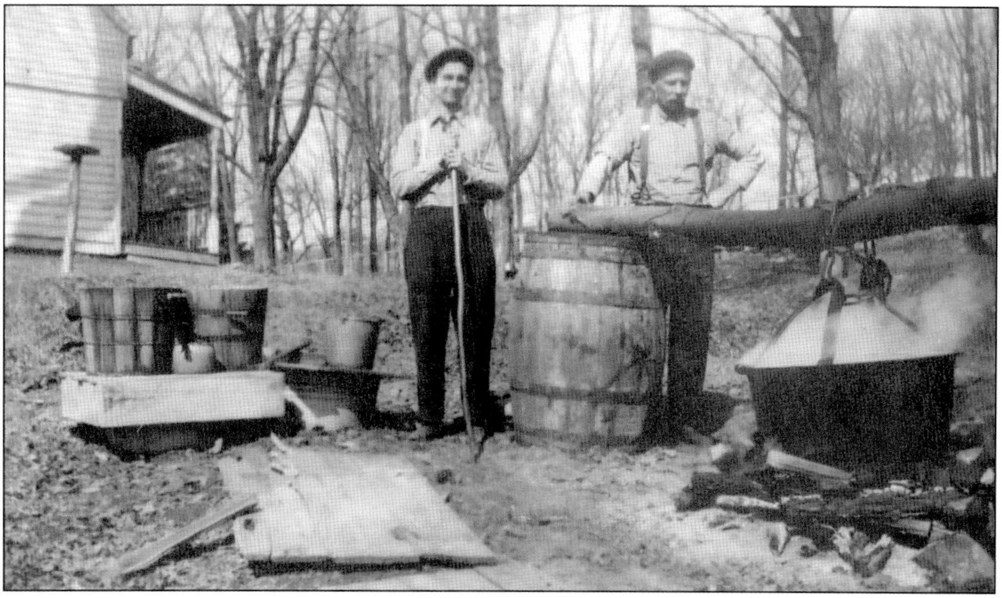

BOILING MAPLE SYRUP. On the side lawn at the French home on Schumann Road, Leslie French and George Leavenworth boil sap to make maple syrup. (Courtesy Ross French, son of Leslie French and grandson of George Leavenworth.)

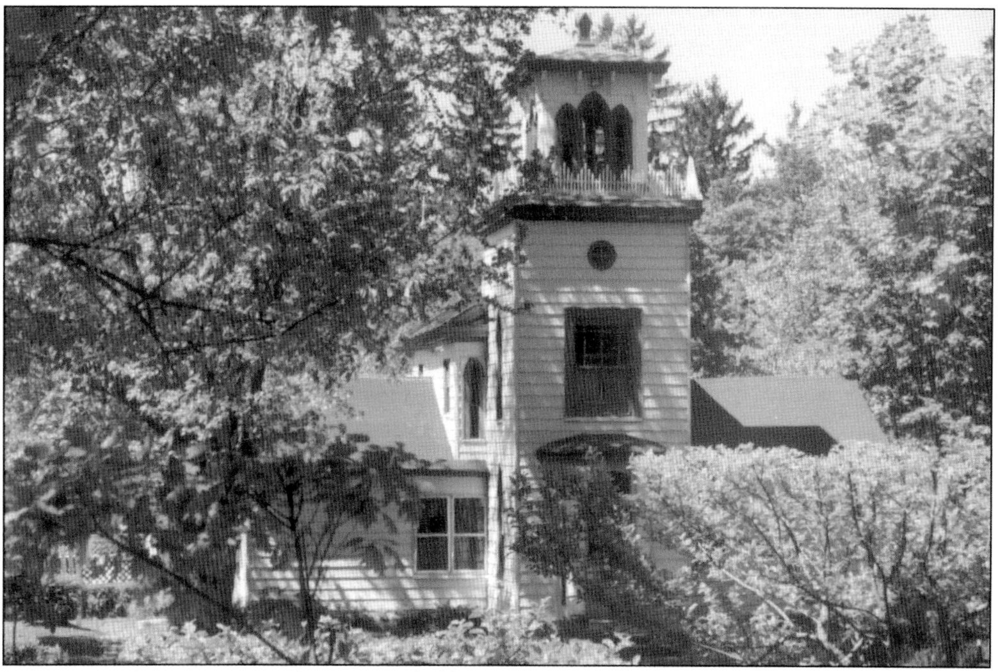

BROOKSIDE INSTITUTE. In the 1860s, children of many local families received their schooling at Brookside Institute, a private school. The institute was conducted by Harvey H. Boone, a son-in-law of Albert H. Fox, on whose land the school was built. An interesting feature of the building is the red glass in the three-and-a-half-story tower. Located next to the Fox Mansion, the school is now the residence of the Parry-Hill family. (Courtesy Sand Lake Historical Society Collection.)

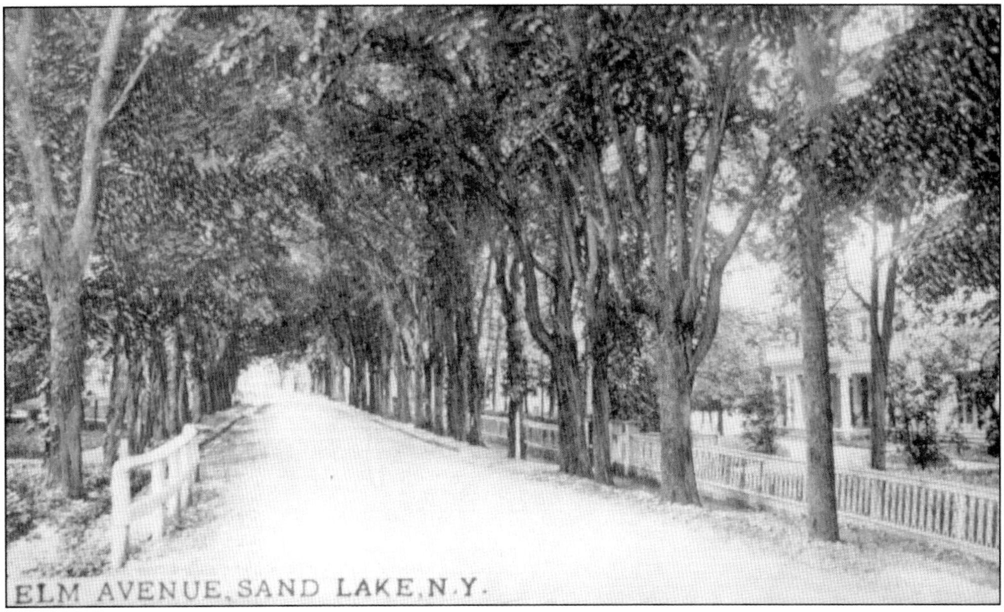

ELM AVENUE. This view looking south shows the numerous elm trees that once lined what is now Routes 43 and 66. The Fox Mansion is on the right. (Courtesy Sand Lake Historical Society Collection.)

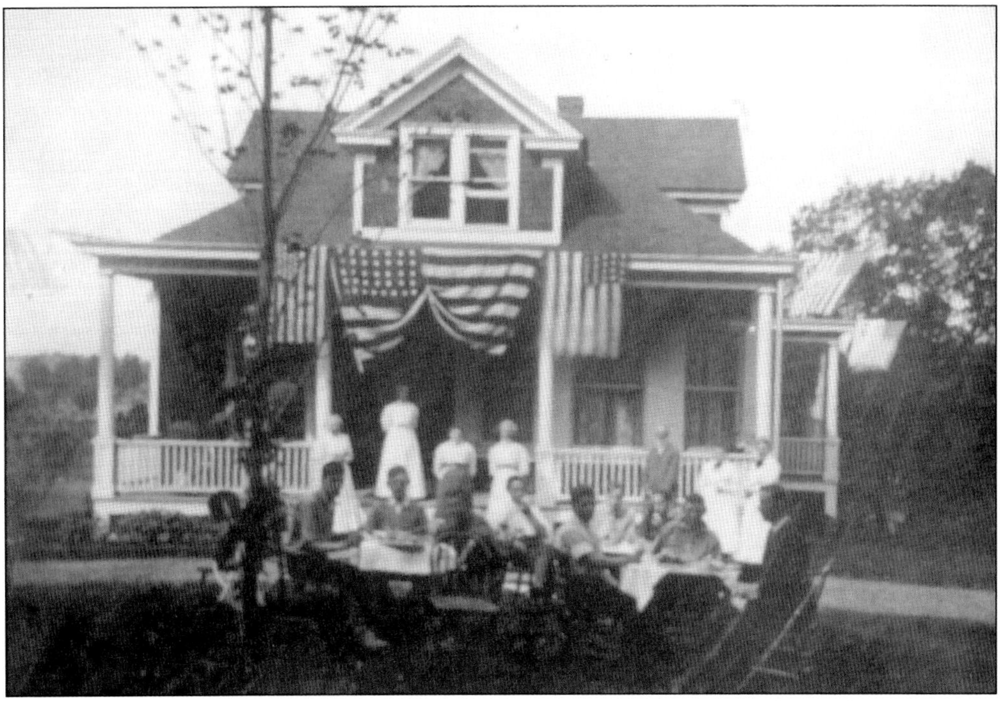

THE AVERILL HOME. Jennie Averill stands on the porch of her Victorian home during a festive occasion. This house was constructed in the 1880s and was purchased by Adam Schumann as a summer home in 1918. Schumann had a sign over the porch, calling the home "Friedwalde," the location in Germany from which many local immigrants came. The Alan Fuess family now resides here. (Courtesy Town of Sand Lake Collection.)

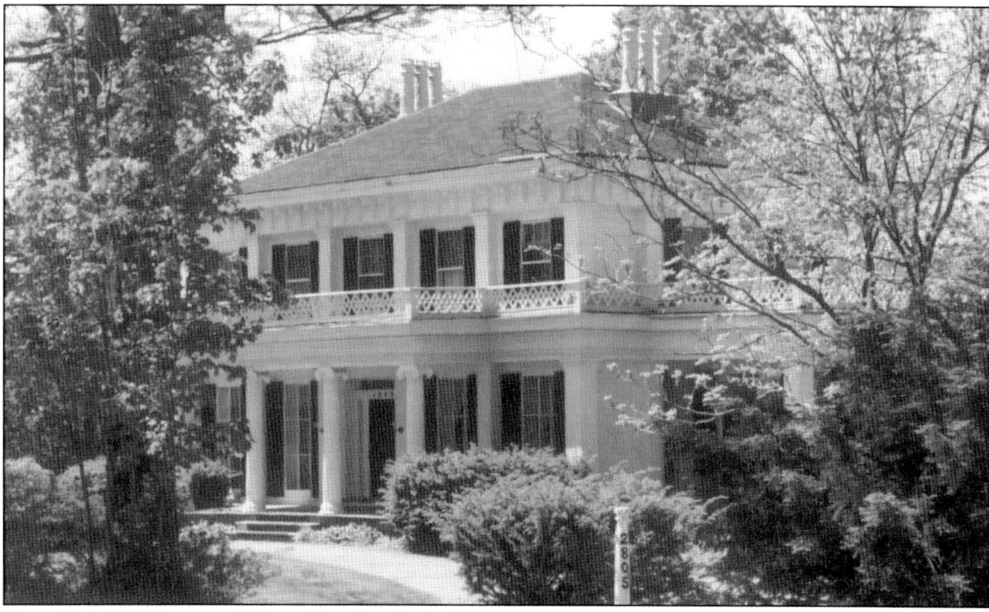

The Fox Mansion. Albert Fox built this Greek Revival mansion in 1840. Fox was a state senator in 1848 and 1849. He and his brother Samuel Fox ran the Rensselaer Glass Works at Glass Lake from 1837 to 1853. The windowpanes in the mansion came from the glass factory. (Courtesy Sand Lake Historical Society Collection.)

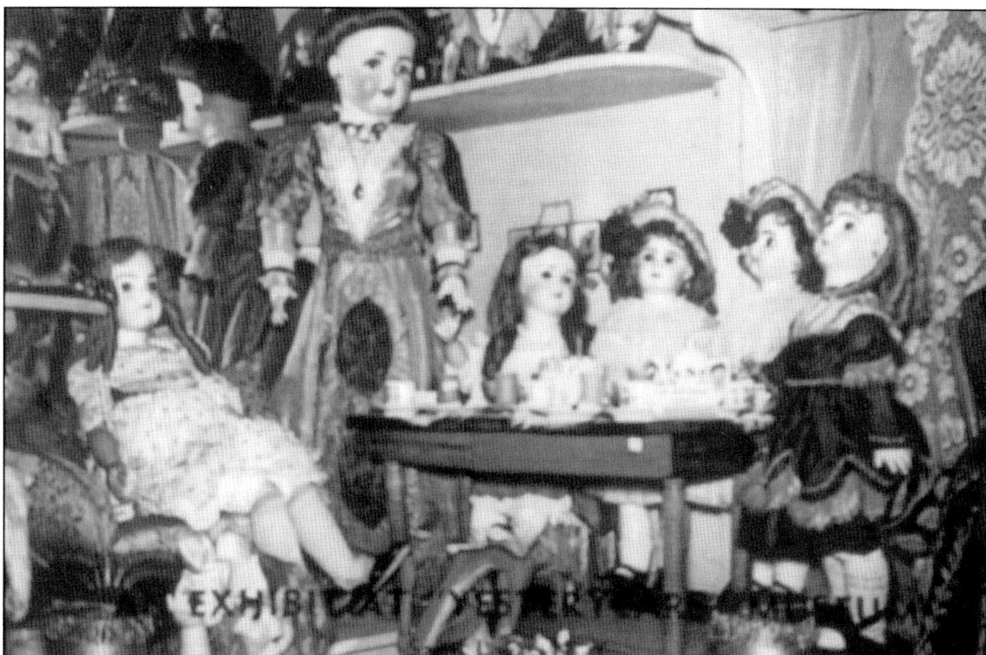

Yesteryears Antique Doll Museum. Lillian Eauclaire Sproule was the curator of the Yesteryears Antique Doll Museum, located in the Fox Mansion. She was renown for her expertise in the repair, design, and reproduction of dolls and toys. Her masterpiece was a reproduction of Queen Elizabeth's coronation gown. The museum gained international fame for its fine collection. (Courtesy Ada and Wesley Miller.)

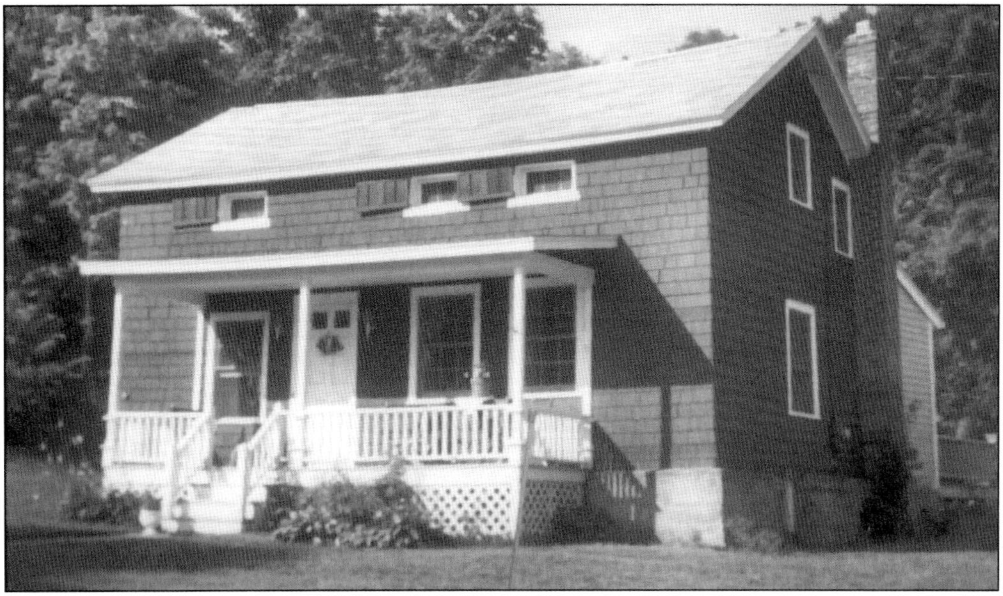

An Original Glass Factory Farmhouse. This house overlooks Glass Lake. Richard Knowlson was the first owner of record, in 1826. Over the years, the house fell into disrepair. In 1988, Dalmar A. Tifft III restored it as accurately as possible to its original appearance. (Courtesy Sand Lake Historical Society Collection.)

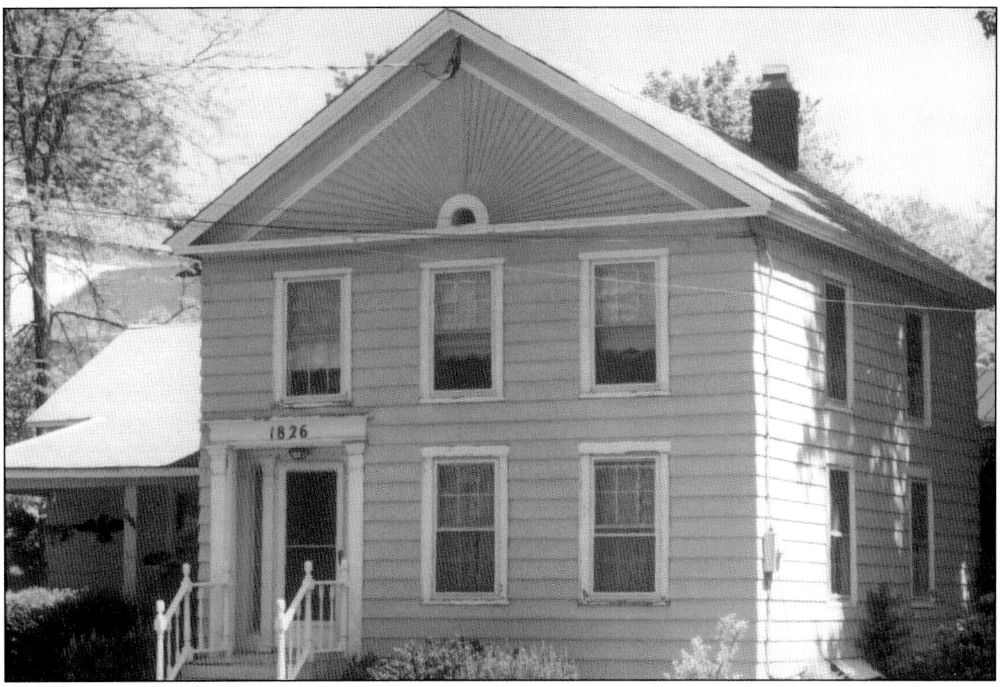

The Lewis Sliter House. This 1826 house was the home of Lewis Sliter, for whom Sliter's Corners was named, before it became the hamlet of Sand Lake. A striking feature of the house is the large sunburst fan on the front. Members and relatives of the Carl Beck family owned the house from 1913 to 1997. The present owner is the Paul Glasser Jr. family. (Courtesy Sand Lake Historical Society Collection.)

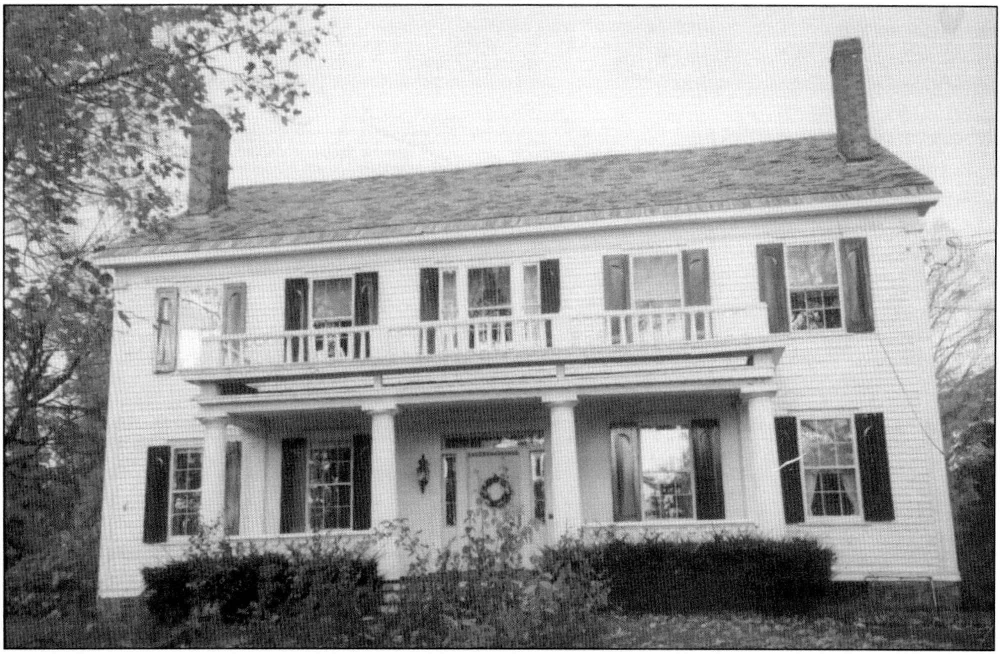

THE KNOWLSON HOUSE. Richard J. Knowlson built this house in the early 1800s. He was a friend of LaFayette and was his escort on his visits to the area. The Knowlsons operated the glassworks, sawmills, and a knitting mill. In the latter half of the 20th century, the house was owned by Dr. Harold Haskell, the Kelley family, and most recently Dalmar A. Tifft III and Mark Hammond. (Courtesy Sand Lake Historical Society Collection.)

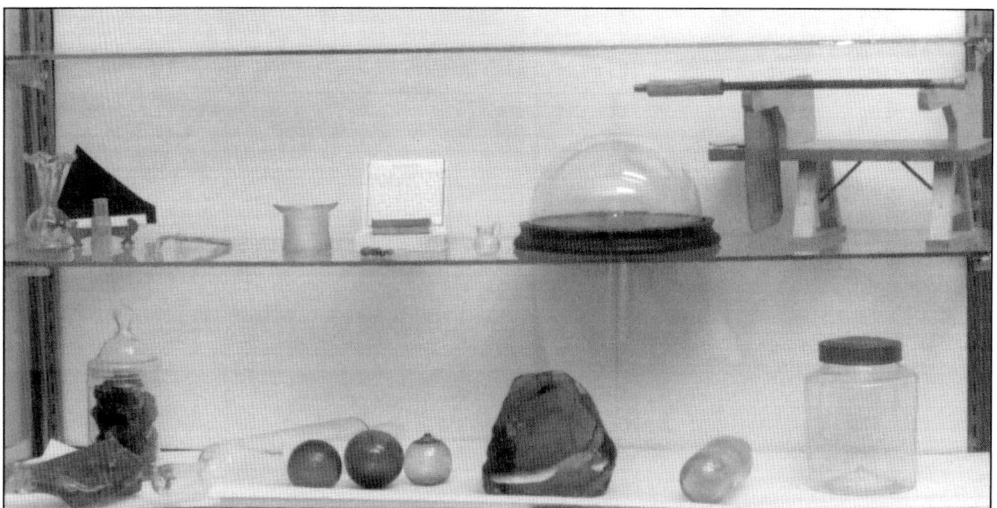

A GLASS LAKE GLASS DISPLAY. The town's collection of Glass Lake glass is on display at the town hall. On the bottom shelf, from left to right, are the following: an assortment of frit (raw ingredients heated and then cooled), a clear glass rolling pin, three darning balls, a large piece of frit, a shot bottle, and a cookie jar. On the top shelf, from left to right, are a vase, a piece of red glass made with gold, a cough syrup bottle, an icicle from trees when the furnace blew up, a hat, some beads, a doll's pitcher, a cylinder glass dome, and a glassblower's bench. (Courtesy Sand Lake Historical Society Collection.)

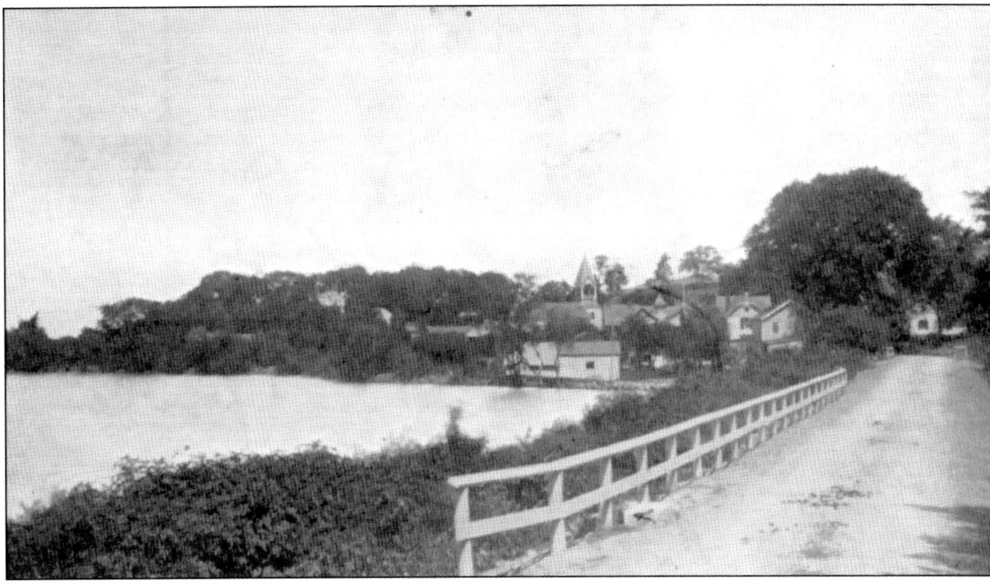

GLASS LAKE, LOOKING NORTH. This view, looking north toward the hamlet of Sand Lake, shows how the area along Routes 43 and 66 appeared in 1906. The spire of the Glass Lake Methodist Episcopal Church is in the center. (Courtesy Sand Lake Historical Society Collection.)

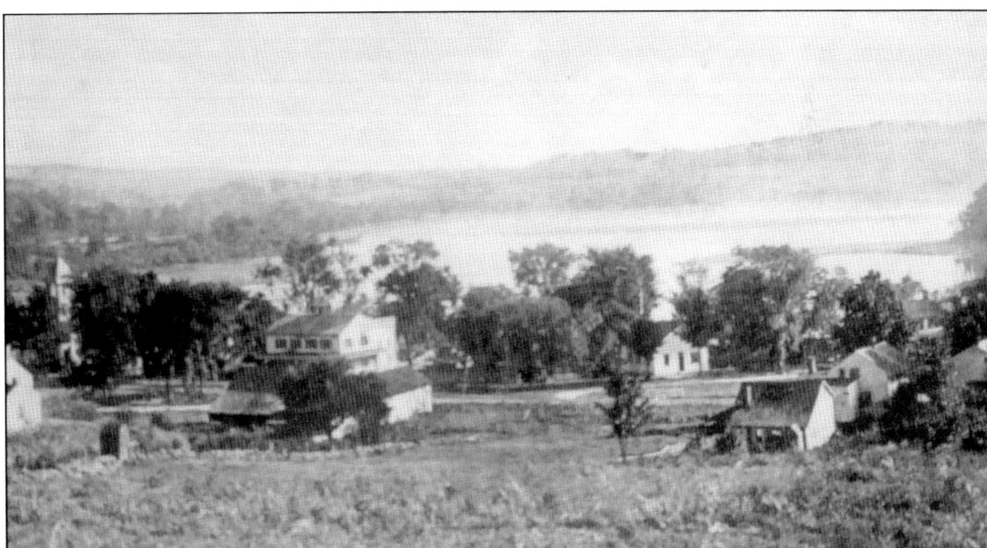

GLASS LAKE, LOOKING SOUTH. This view, looking south, shows the Glass Lake settlement on the far side of current Routes 43 and 66: from left to right, the spire of the Glass Lake Methodist Episcopal Church, the Glass Lake Hotel, and the District No. 8 School. (Courtesy Alice Tifft.)

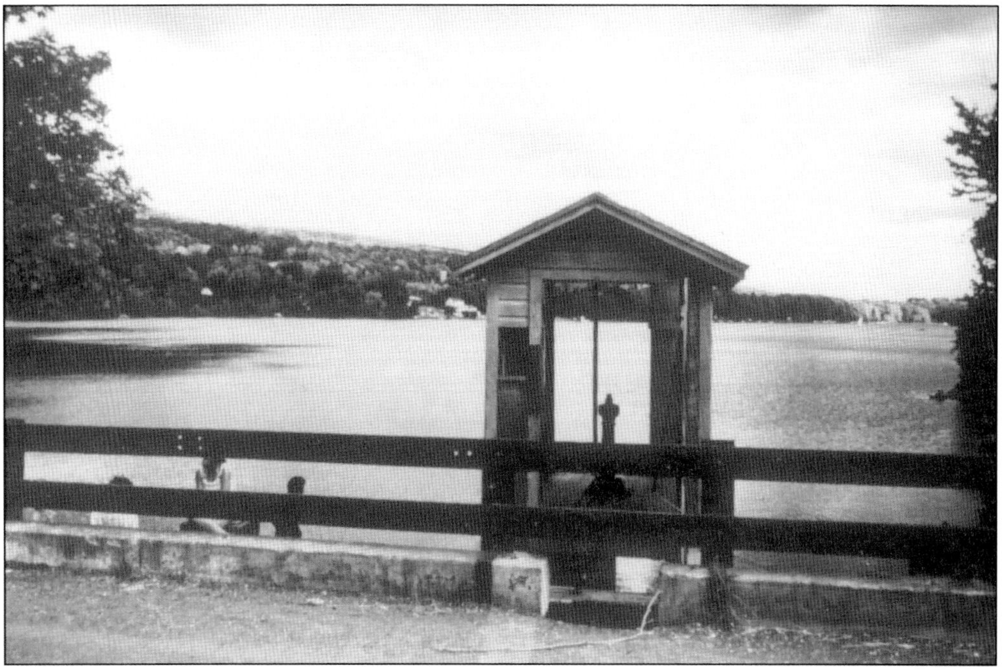

THE GLASS LAKE GATEHOUSE. Glass Lake, called Damm Lack in 1791 and Rouse's Lake in 1839, was a natural lake that was doubled in size in 1865 by the Wynantskill Improvement Association. Water flow from the lakes that fed into the Wynantskill Creek was regulated to operate the waterwheels of the mills at Averill Park, West Sand Lake, and Troy. This is the gatehouse and valve stem at the Glass Lake outlet. (Courtesy Town of Sand Lake Collection.)

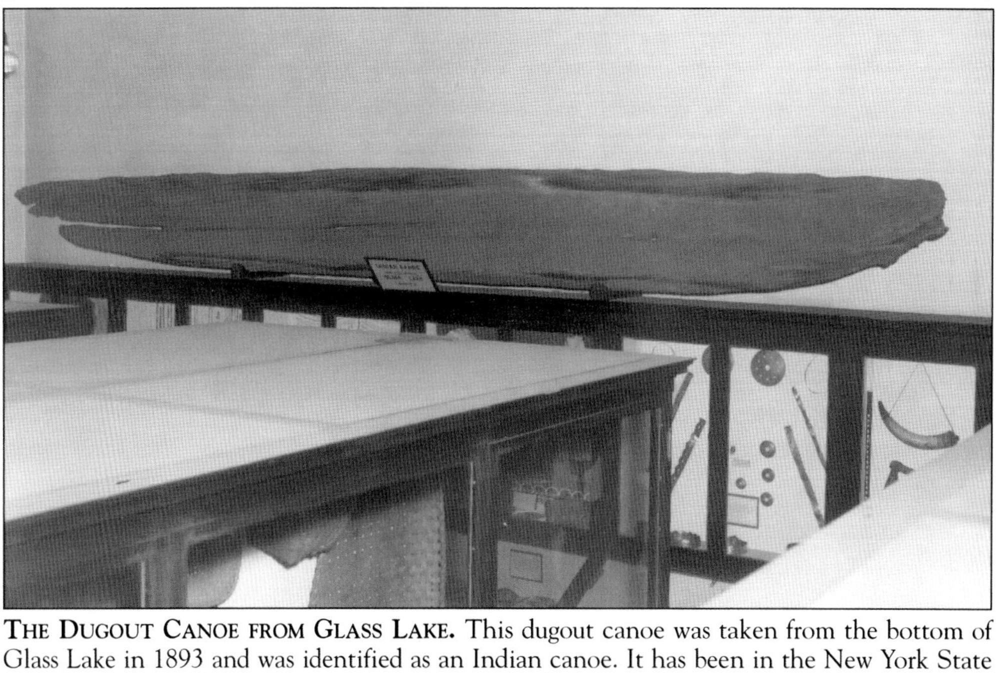

THE DUGOUT CANOE FROM GLASS LAKE. This dugout canoe was taken from the bottom of Glass Lake in 1893 and was identified as an Indian canoe. It has been in the New York State Museum since 1917. The picture shows it atop display cases in the former museum. (Courtesy New York State Museum, Albany.)

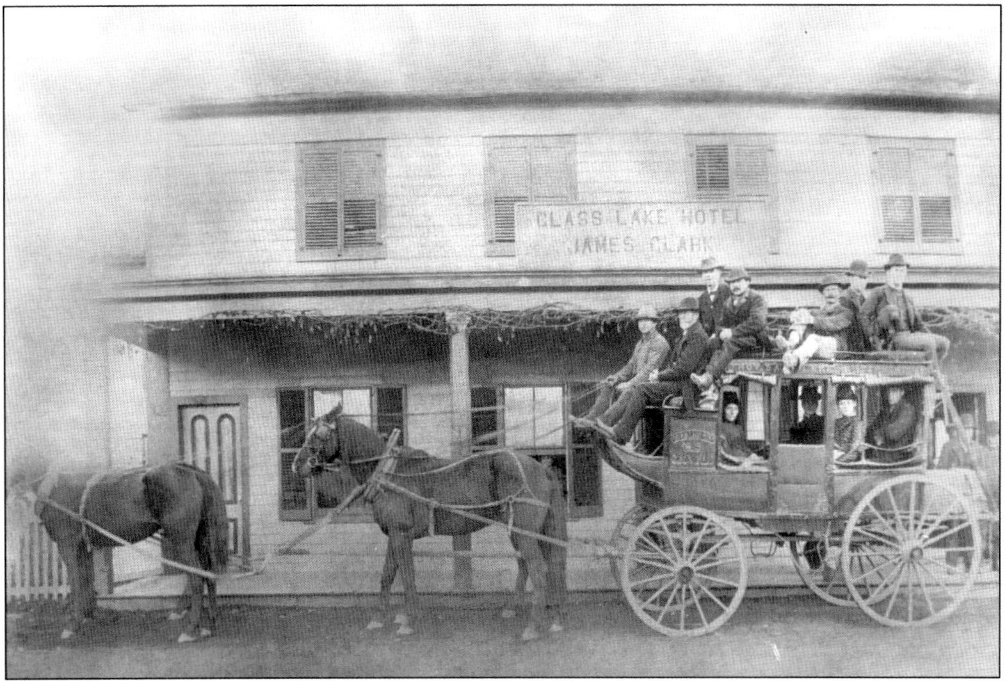

A STAGECOACH STOP. The Troy, Sand Lake, and Stephentown stagecoach stopped at the Glass Lake Hotel and also provided mail delivery by J.L. Myers. In 1876, James Clark owned the hotel and in 1902, proprietor H.E. Martin advertised Sunday dinner—a specialty. (Courtesy Town of Sand Lake Collection.)

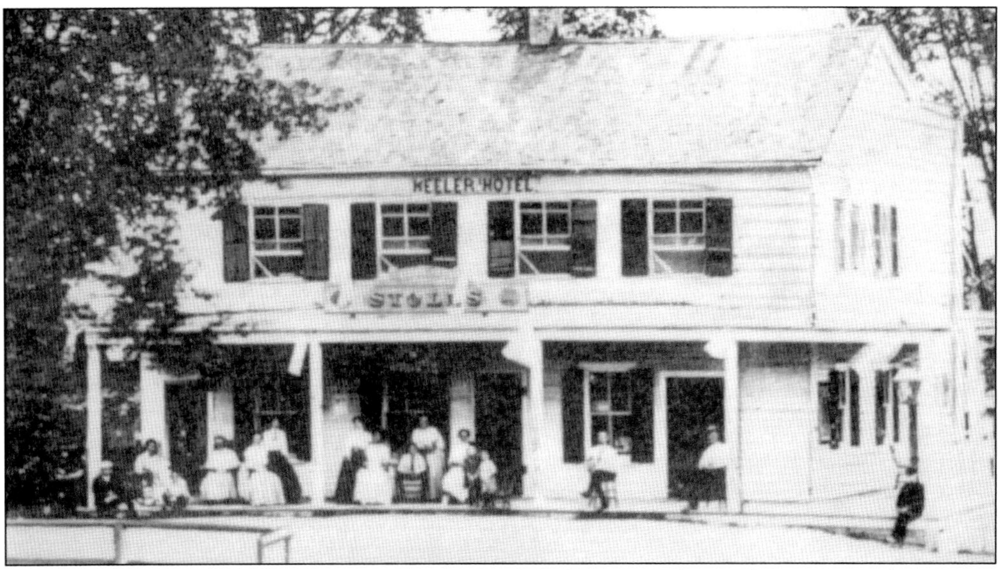

THE GLASS LAKE HOTEL. John Bowers had a public house at Glass Lake *c.* 1820. The present building was built as Mechanics Hall *c.* 1845 to accommodate workmen who had no permanent homes. In 1866, the hall was divided and one part became a residence and the other part was operated as the Glass Lake Hotel. The hotel was run by Joseph Gabler *c.* 1860, John Niehbur from 1933 to 1944, Clayton Teal from 1977 to 1995, and Scott Teal from 1995 to the present. (Courtesy Alice Tifft.)

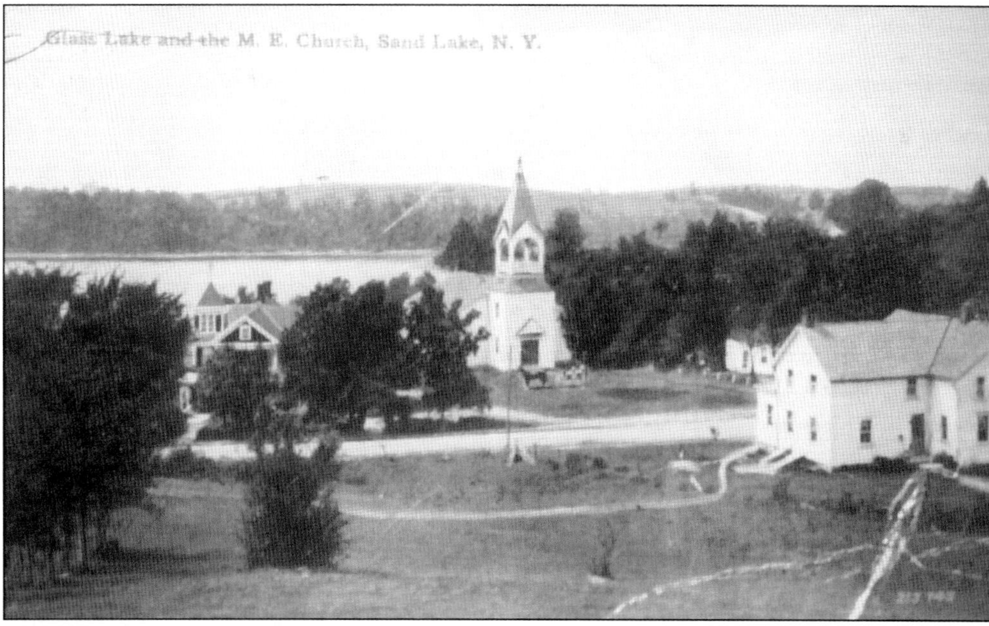

THE GLASS LAKE METHODIST EPISCOPAL CHURCH. This view from the hill shows the church with Glass Lake in the background. Built *c.* 1833, the wooden church was ravaged by fire in 1913 and was then rebuilt. The house on the right is owned by the Ackner family. (Courtesy Sand Lake Historical Society Collection.)

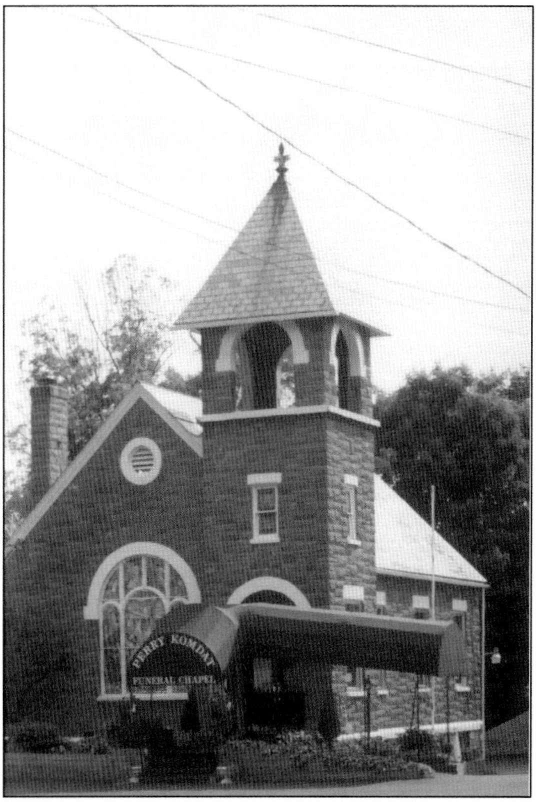

THE GLASS LAKE METHODIST EPISCOPAL CHURCH. After the fire of 1913, a new stone building was erected and dedicated on November 15, 1914. In 1940, the congregation merged with that of Averill Park Methodist Church (see page 51). This building later became the Perry Funeral Chapel and then the Perry-Komdat Funeral Chapel. (Courtesy Sand Lake Historical Society Collection.)

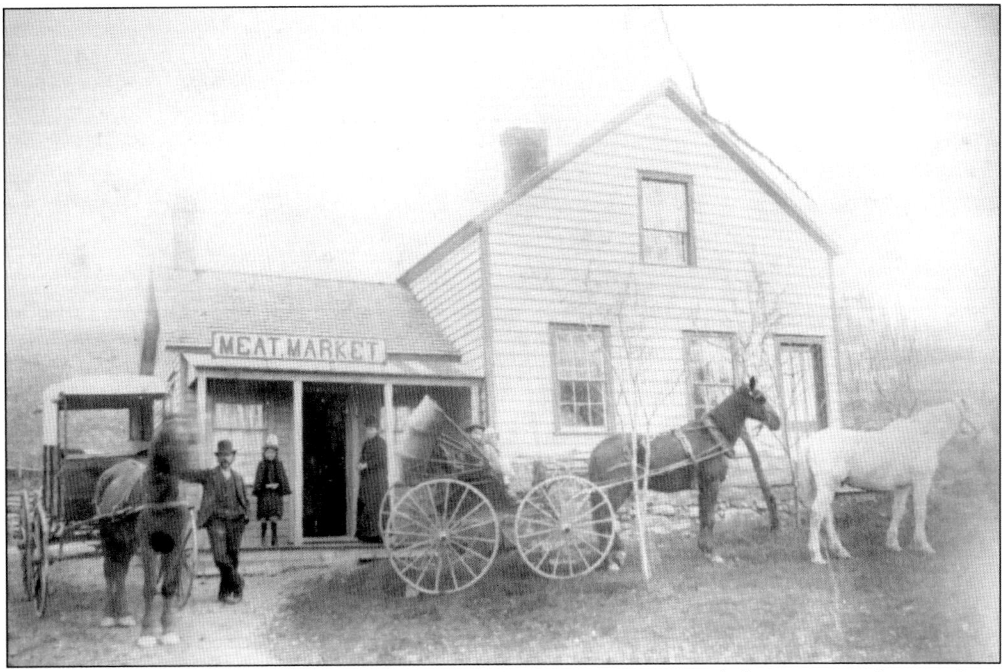

McNARY'S MEAT MARKET AT GLASS LAKE. The McNarys operated this meat market on their farm at Glass Lake. Samuel McNary (see pages 61 and 125) was one of the butchers. (Courtesy Rensselaer County Historical Society.)

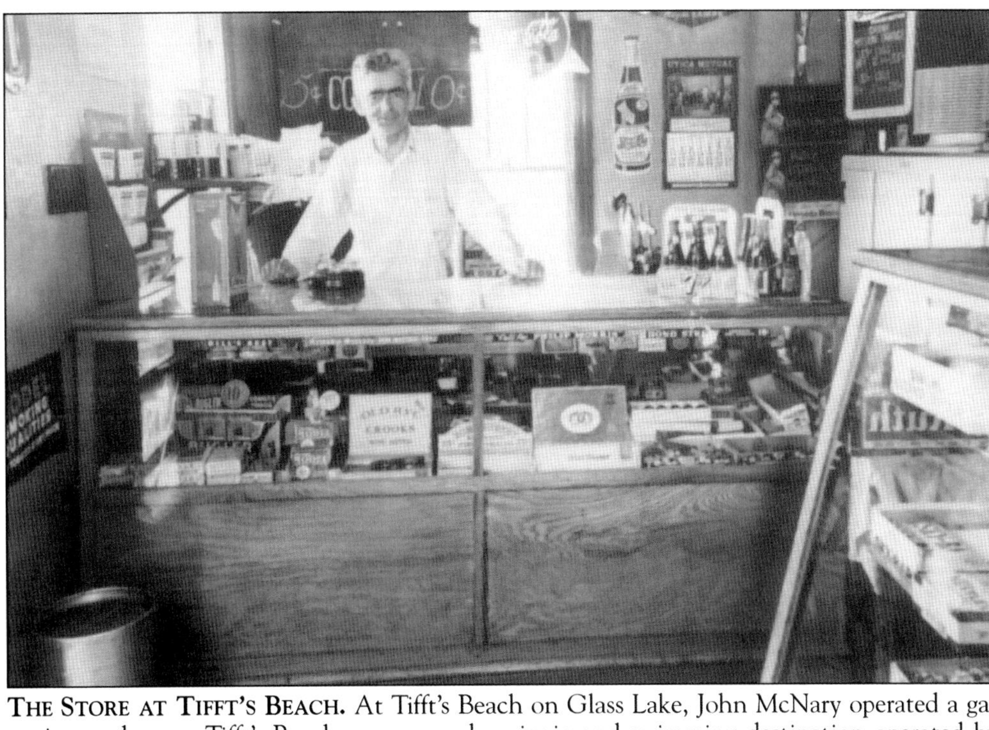

THE STORE AT TIFFT'S BEACH. At Tifft's Beach on Glass Lake, John McNary operated a gas station and store. Tifft's Beach was a popular picnic and swimming destination operated by Harold and Alice Tifft from 1945 to 1992. (Courtesy Margaret McNary Regan.)

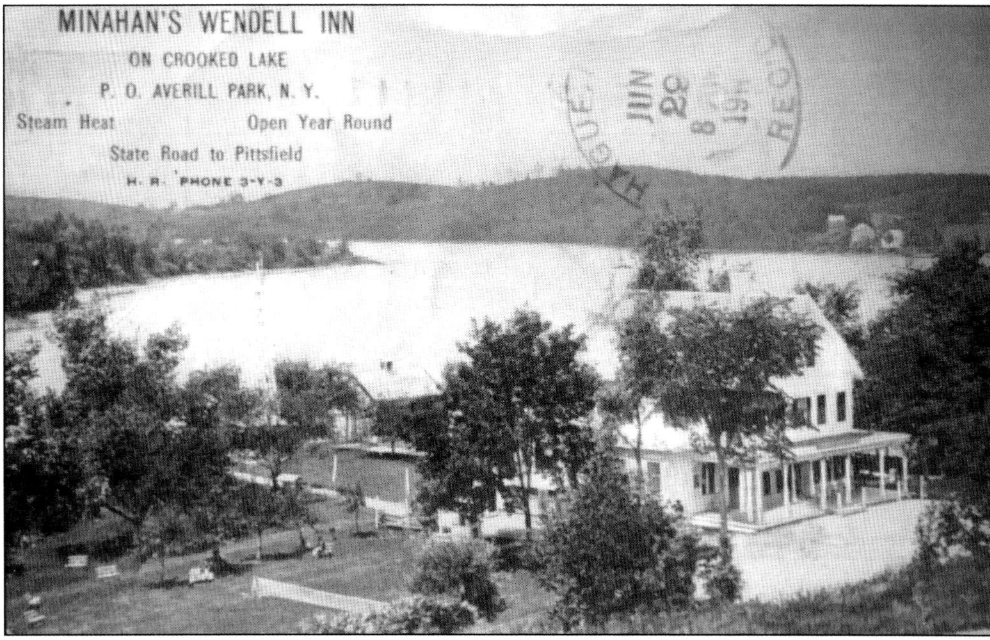

MINAHAN'S WENDELL INN, C. 1910. This hotel began as Upham Tavern. It burned in the late 1850s and was rebuilt by James M. Mosher in 1860. Willet A. Brown purchased it in 1860. Brown's Crooked Lake House had Gov. Theodore Roosevelt and his family as frequent guests. A great outdoorsman Roosevelt enjoyed hiking and hunting on Bear's Head, also called Bare Top. (Sand Lake Historical Society Collection.)

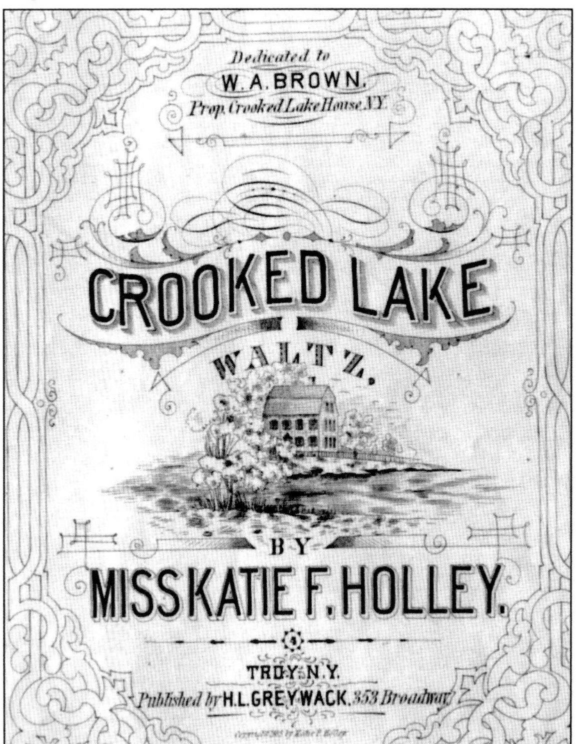

THE "CROOKED LAKE WALTZ." The Crooked Lake House was famous for its Saturday night dances. In 1885, Katie F. Holley dedicated the "Crooked Lake Waltz" to Crooked Lake House proprietor W.A. Brown. (Courtesy Angelo Patti.)

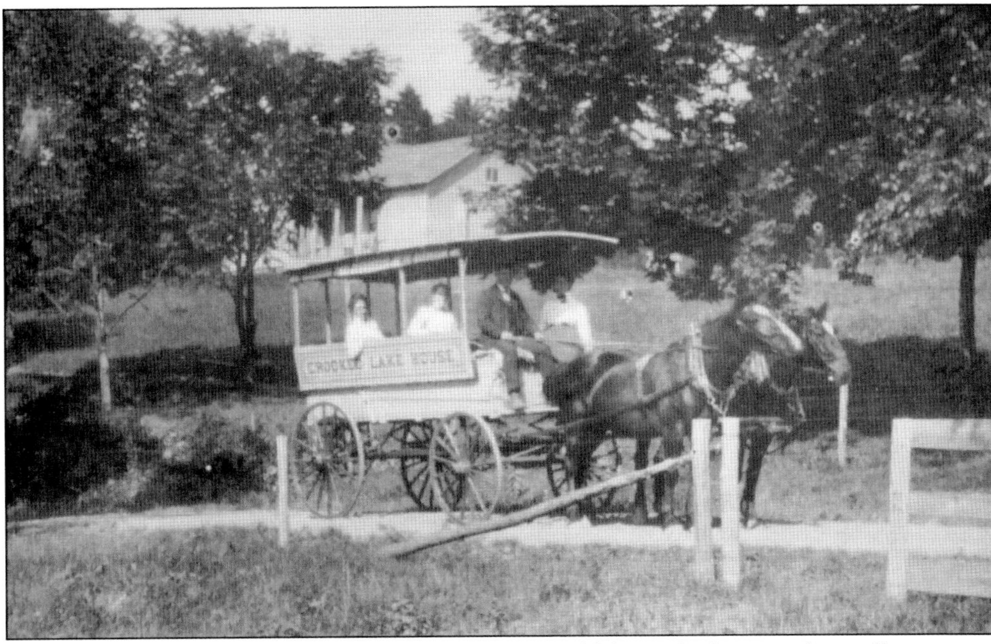

THE CROOKED LAKE HOUSE TAXI. Passengers would be picked up at the trolley station, transported to the Crooked Lake House, and then taken back for their return trip. (Courtesy Town of Sand Lake Collection.)

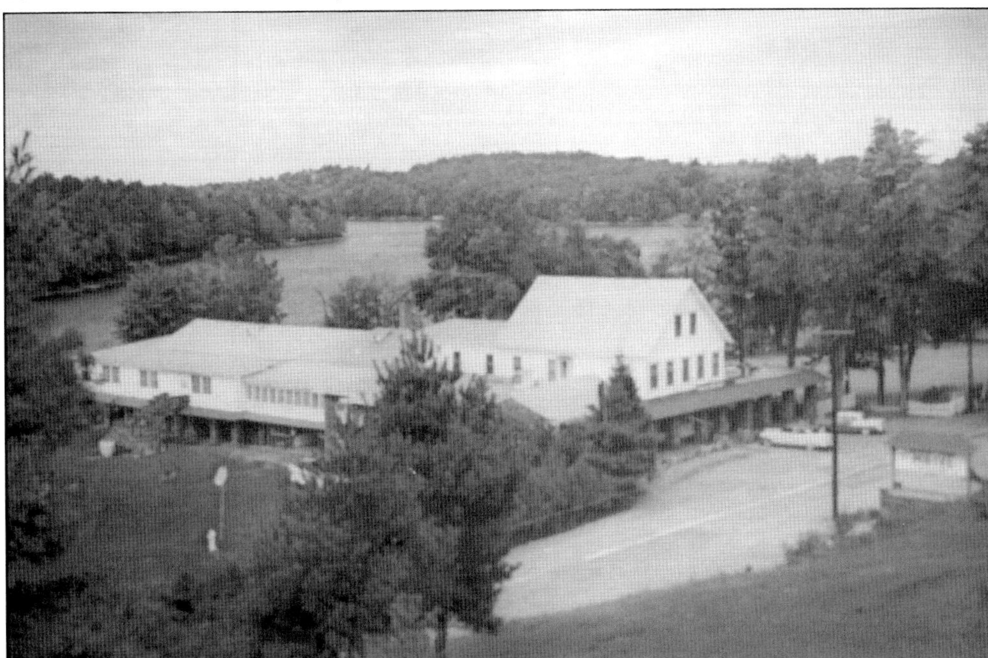

THE CROOKED LAKE HOTEL. Al Coons bought the hotel in 1935 and completely remodeled it in 1947. In the big band era, Glen Miller, Tommy and Jimmy Dorsey, and Stan Kenton played here. The hotel closed in 1981. Dalmar A. Tifft III and Mark Hammond purchased and reopened it as the Crooked Lake House in 1992 . (Courtesy Sand Lake Historical Society Collection.)

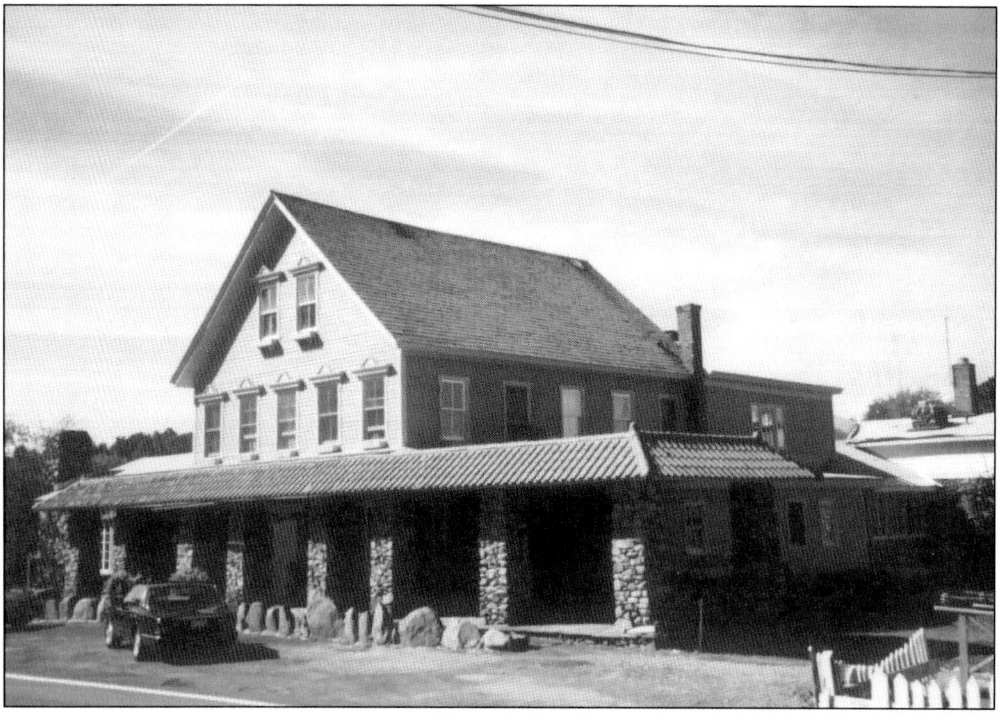

THE CROOKED LAKE HOUSE, 1995. The Crooked Lake House reopened in 1995 and has continued the tradition of having musical groups. Note the stonework, completed by James Clinton Baxter, on the porch columns (see page 74). (Courtesy Sand Lake Historical Society Collection.)

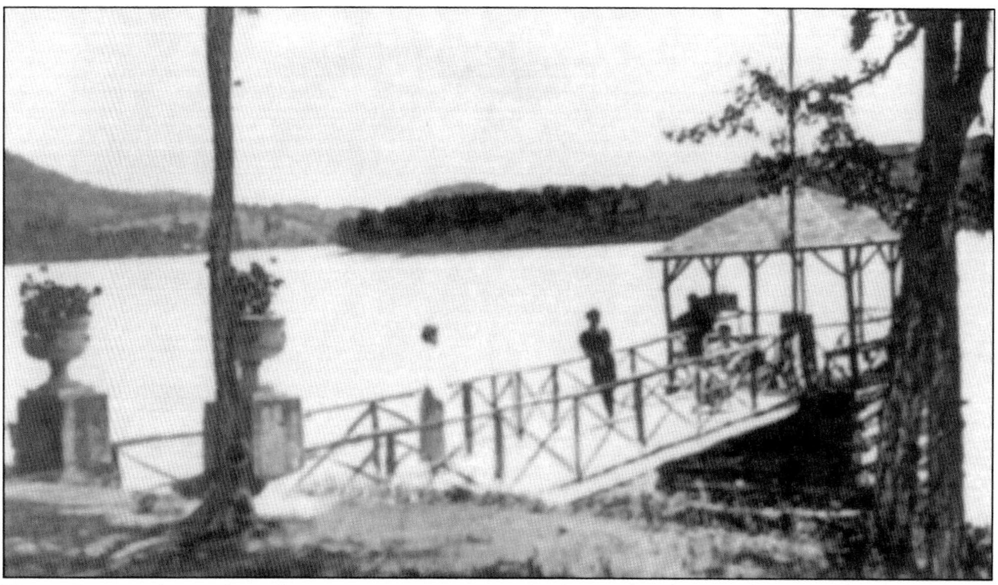

TWIN LIONS. A number of summer cottages were built on the shores of Crooked Lake. Above is the dock with a roof sitting area at Twin Lions. The name Twin Lions came from the twin lion statues at the head of the cottage driveway. (Courtesy Valerie Traver.)

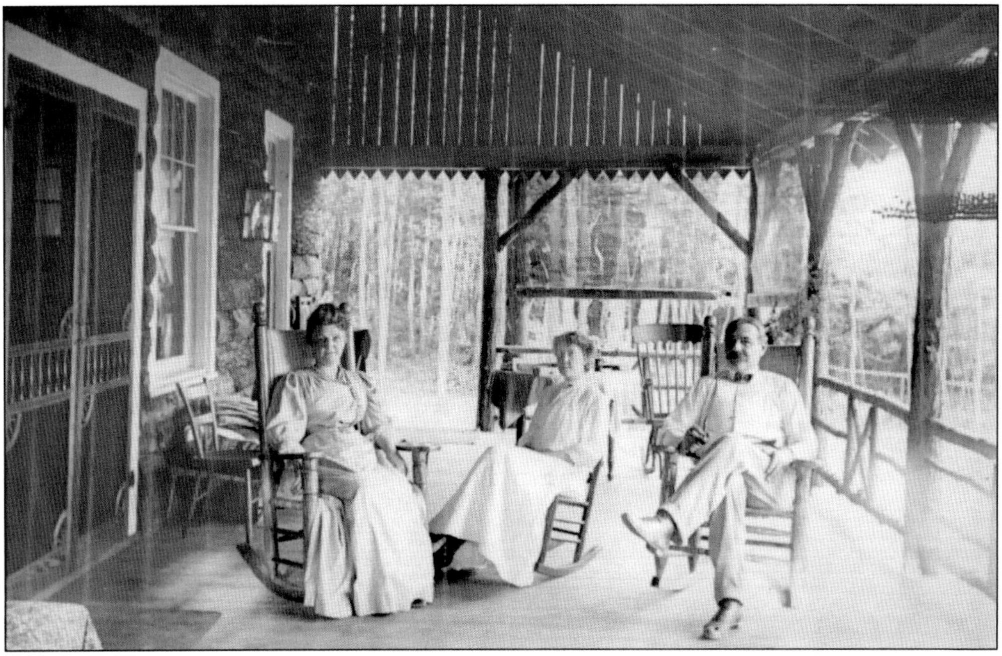

THE WHITEHEADS AT TWIN LIONS. Seated on the porch of Twin Lions cottage with George D. Whitehead are his wife, Elizabeth R. Whitehead, and daughter-in-law Mary Elizabeth Whitehead. The Whiteheads were early owners of Twin Lions. (Courtesy Dan J. Holser, grandson of Mary Elizabeth Whitehead)

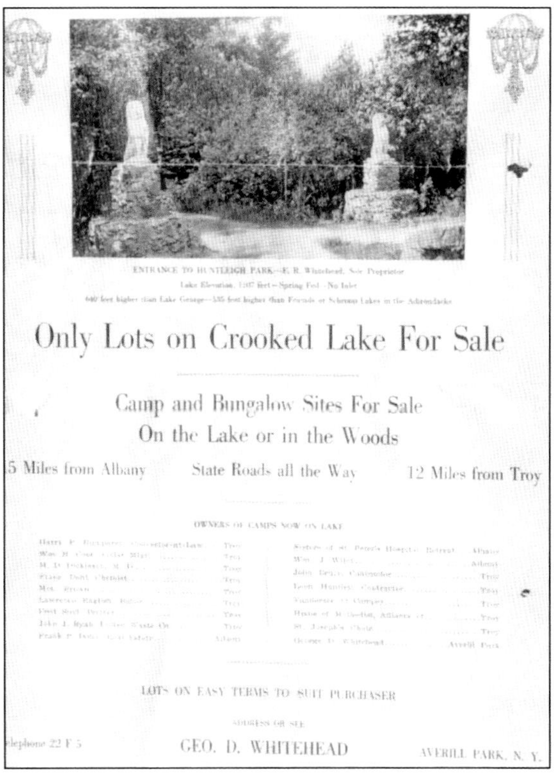

CROOKED LAKE LOTS FOR SALE. On this advertisement offering lots on Crooked Lake, George D. Whitehead shows the twin lions at the entryway to his cottage. Here is a record of property owned in the early 1900s. (Courtesy Dan J. Holser.)

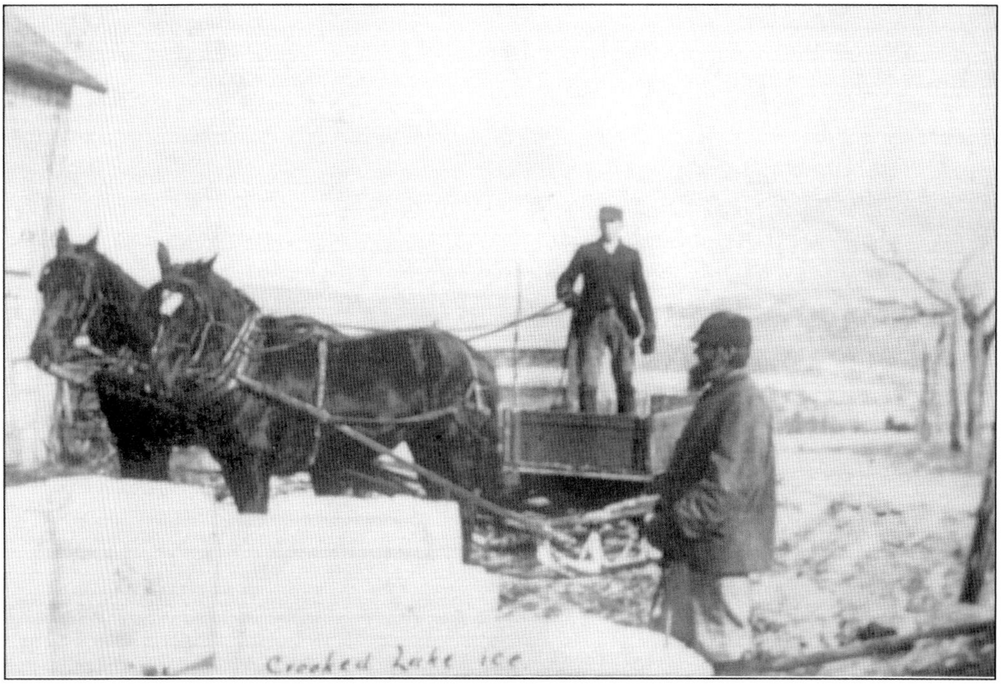

ICE HARVESTING ON CROOKED LAKE. Before refrigeration, ice harvesting was necessary. The Huntley family had a home on Crooked Lake and a store on Schumann Road. They cut the ice, stored it in an icehouse, and used it in the store during the summer months. (Courtesy Town of Sand Lake Collection.)

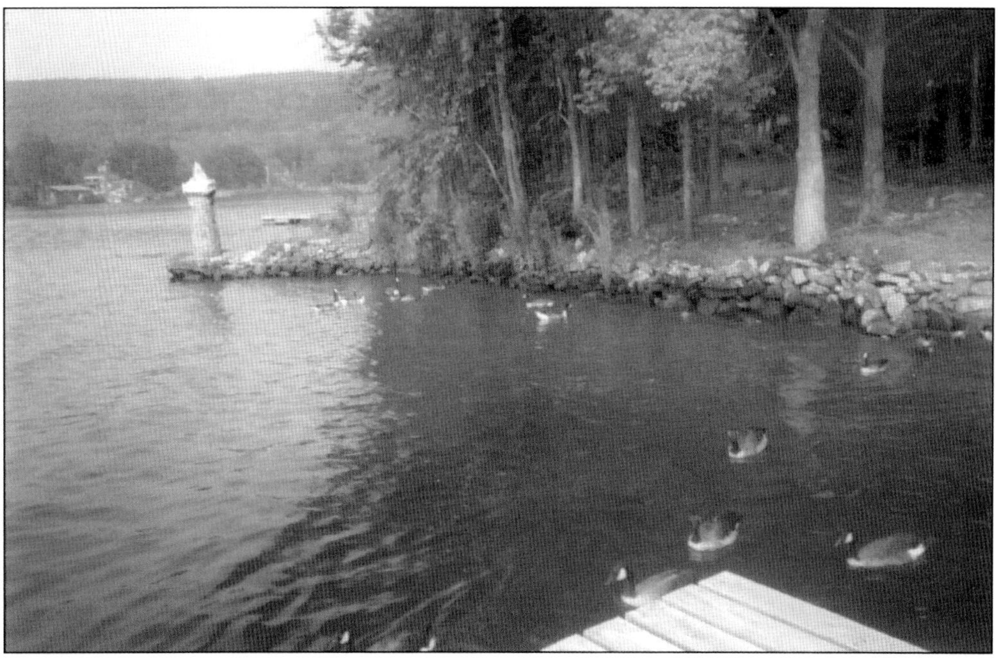

THE CROOKED LAKE LIGHTHOUSE. Earl Hendry built this lighthouse on the point of his property, which is on the south side of the lake. The buildings across the lake are the former Smith farm. (Courtesy Emily Gervais.)

Four

TABORTON

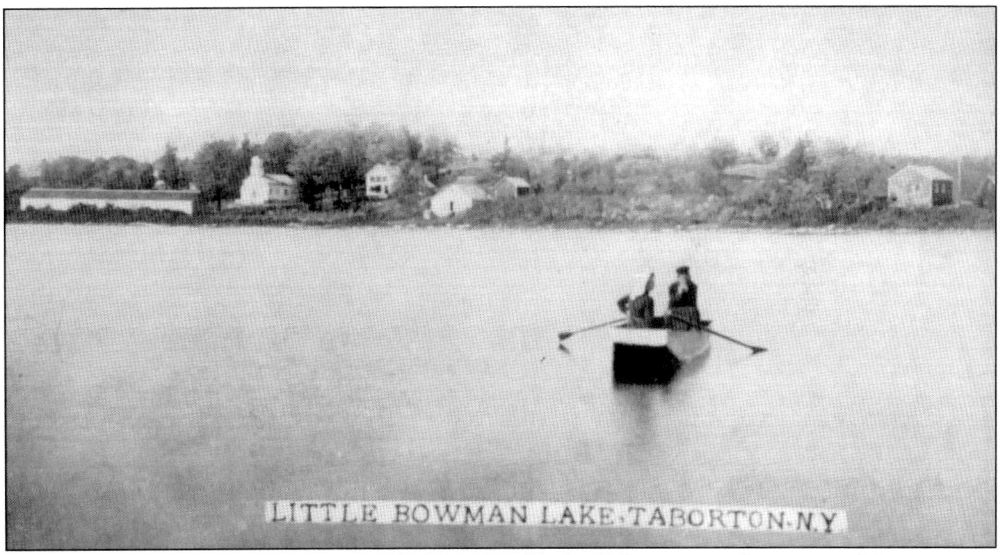

THE HAMLET OF TABORTON. First called East Sand Lake, Taborton was later named Georgetown for lumberman George Horton and finally was named Taborton, meaning "Promised Land" for Mount Tabor, the biblical Mountain of Transfiguration. This view from the middle of Little Bowman Pond shows the center of Taborton. At the left are the horse barns of Zion's Evangelical Lutheran Church, the church, and the parsonage, and to the far right is Taborton School District No. 11. Taborton once was the site of a hunting village for the Stockbridge Indians. Many of its settlers came from Friedewald in Hesse, Germany. They developed their plots of land into self-sufficient farms. They worked in the sawmills and maintained the large charcoal industry. Many mountain homes also provided numerous places for summer visitors to board for a vacation. (Courtesy Gordon "Gunny" Gundrum.)

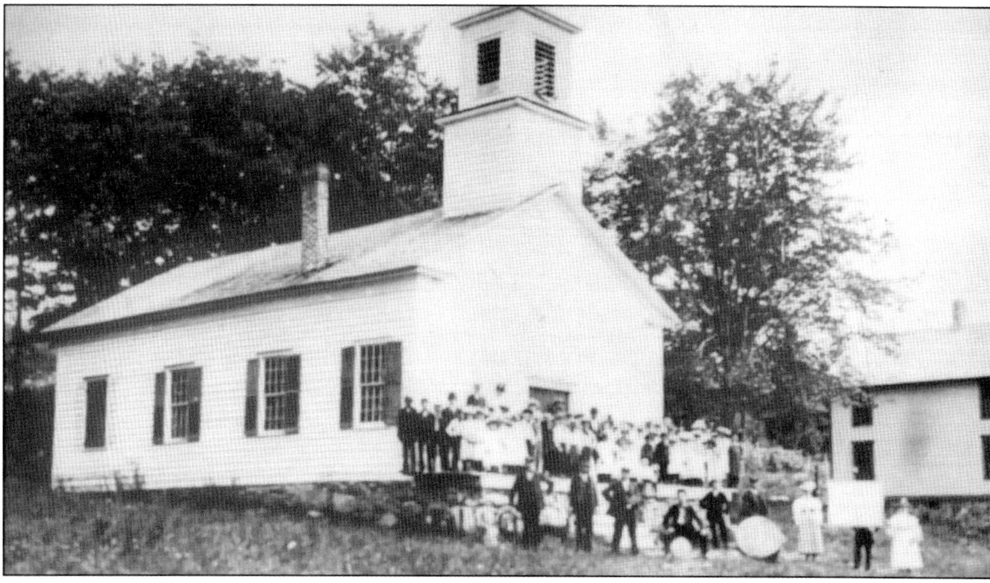

The Evangelical Protestant Meetinghouse. In 1852, services were held in the log meetinghouse every two weeks. In 1865, an acre of land on which the meetinghouse was located was deeded to the trustees, with the stipulation that it be used for the sole purpose of the Evangelical Protestant Meetinghouse. Extensive renovations were made in 1882, and the parsonage was dedicated in 1883. Services were in German until 1917, when services began in English. (Courtesy Gordon "Gunny" Gundrum.)

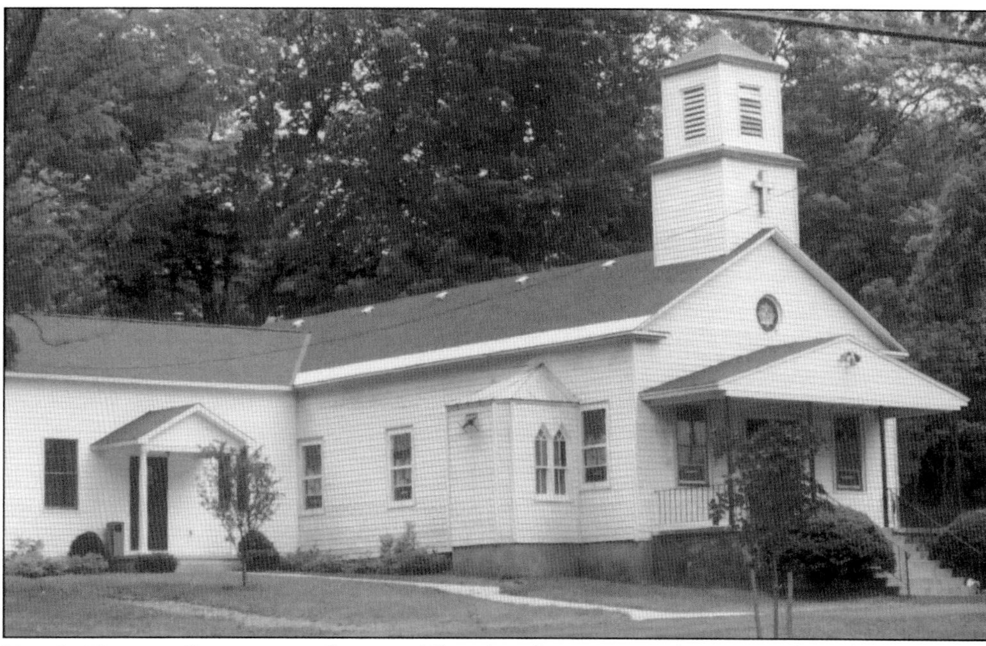

Zion's United Church of Christ. The church, as it is today, was enlarged in the early 1940s and another addition was made in the mid-1980s. The church name changed after a denominational merger. The Taborton Picnic, which began with a parade of the Sunday school children, has continued to be a traditional homecoming event for many to renew Taborton roots. (Courtesy Sand Lake Historical Society Collection.)

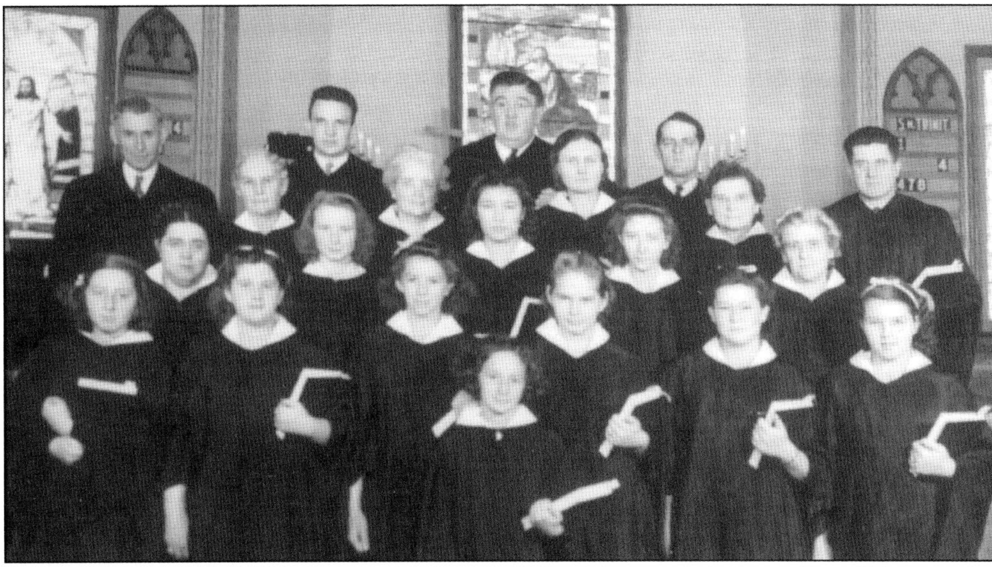

ZION'S EVANGELICAL AND REFORMED CHURCH CHOIR, C. 1945. Rev. Oscar Egli served as the pastor from 1919 to 1947. Choir members, from left to right, are: (first row) May Snyder; (second row) Ruth Snyder, Doris Egli, Shirley Henry, Helen Krause, Ruth Momrow, and Joan Brod; (third row) Emma Brown, Eleanor Bubie, Gladys Brod, Ida Brown, and Anna Egli; (fourth row) Charles Hoffman, Ella Hoffman, Mrs. Augustus Myers, May Senechal, and Freida Walk; (fifth row) Emmot Perry, Rev. Oscar Egli, Charles "Chubby" Smyth, and Nathan Shier. (Courtesy Zion's United Church of Christ Collection.)

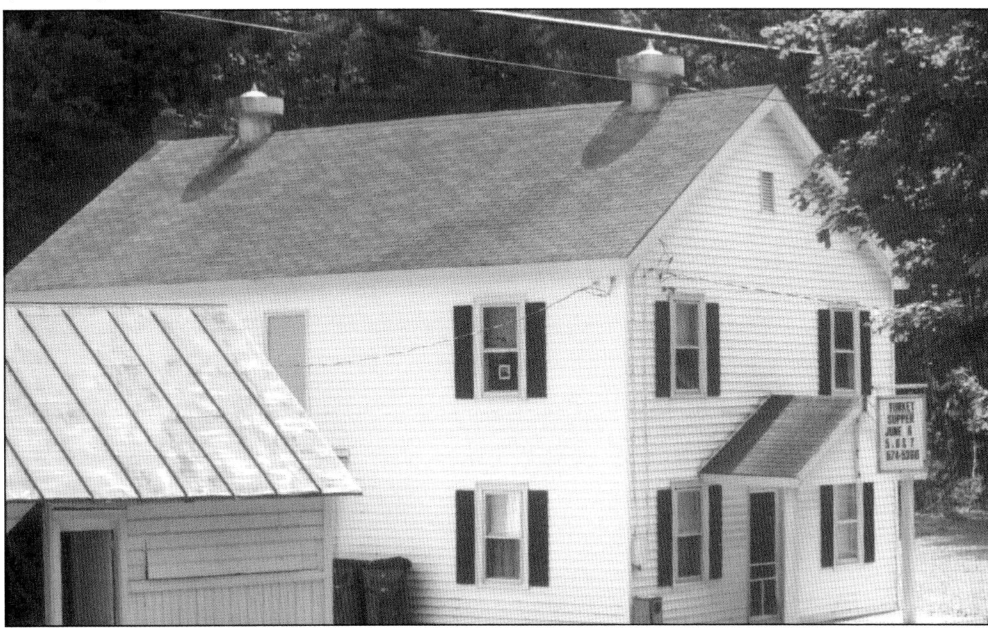

ZION'S CHURCH HALL. The church hall was erected in 1921 for Sunday school and church activities. Square dances were held on the second floor. The sign advertises one of the turkey suppers, which enjoy a reputation for excellence. Oral history gives credence to the strong positive influence the church and its activities have had on the lives of its people. (Courtesy Sand Lake Historical Society Collection.)

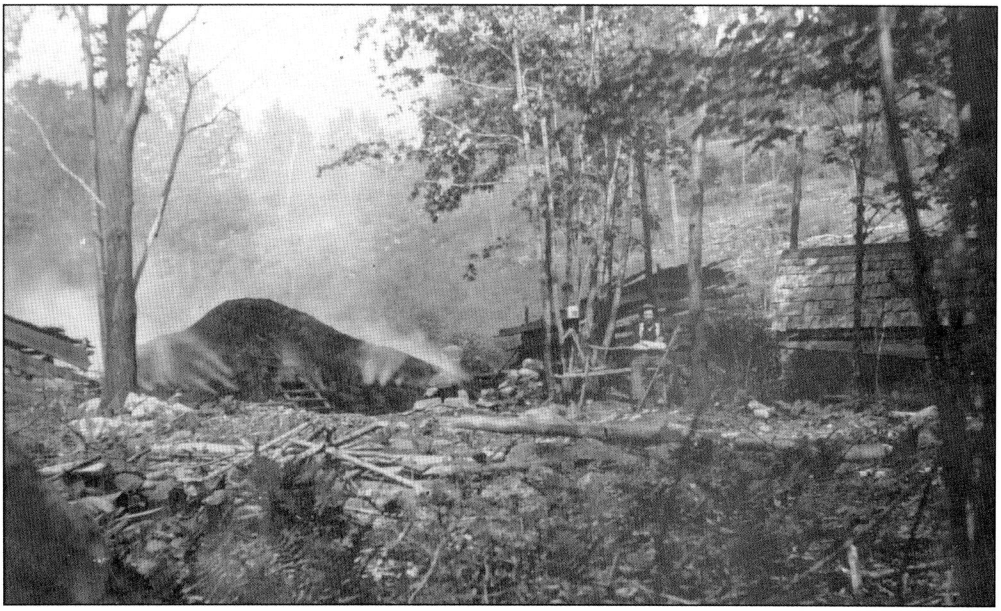

A CHARCOAL PIT SITE. A charcoal pit was a dome-shaped structure about 20 feet in diameter, containing about 20 cords of wood and covered with earth and sod with openings to give some draft when firing began. A continuous two- to three-week camp out at the pit site, pictured above, was needed to maintain the fire at the proper rate. A blaze on the mountain meant that a mishap had occurred and only ashes of the pit would remain. (Courtesy Iona Mosher.)

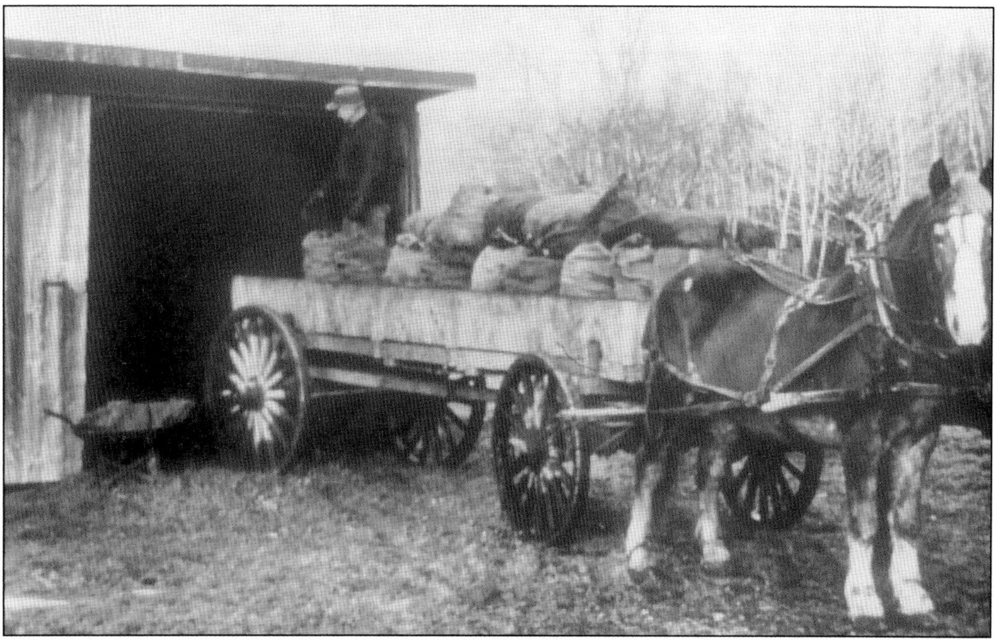

A WAGON LOAD OF CHARCOAL. Sunday night was the usual time to start with a load of charcoal to Troy or Albany. Customers included iron mills, stove foundries, blacksmith shops, hotels, homes, Hudson River boats, and the local Rensselaer Glass Factory. George Dobert, with this load of charcoal, and his son, Eugene Dobert, were the last charcoal burners in Taborton. (Courtesy the George Dobert family.)

PICKING FANCY FERNS. Fern picking was a cash crop for Taborton. In late August or early September, deep in the forest and woods of the mountains, various types of fancy ferns were gathered into bundles of 25 and then boxed, with 40 bundles to a box. In the 1930s, a box brought 35¢. By 1958, the price had risen to $2 per box of 1,000. The ferns were sold to wholesale florists Charles Beck and his son, Carl Beck. (Courtesy Marlene Skaarland.)

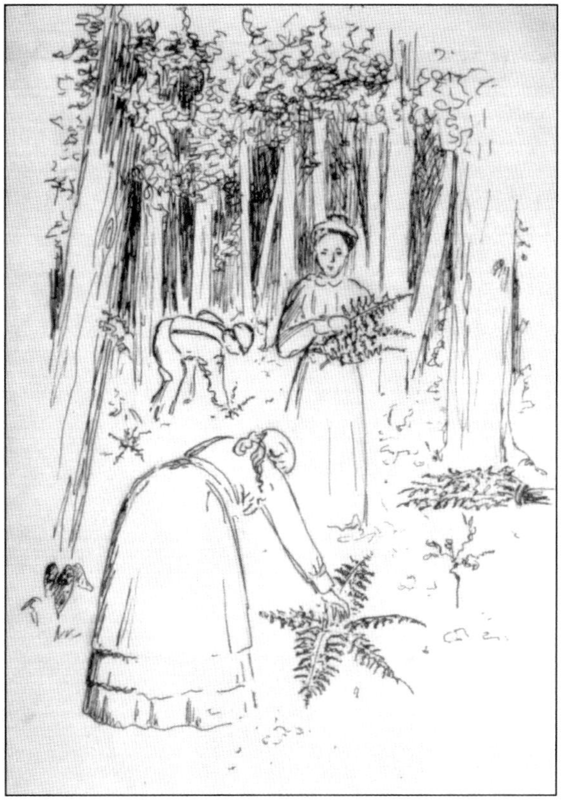

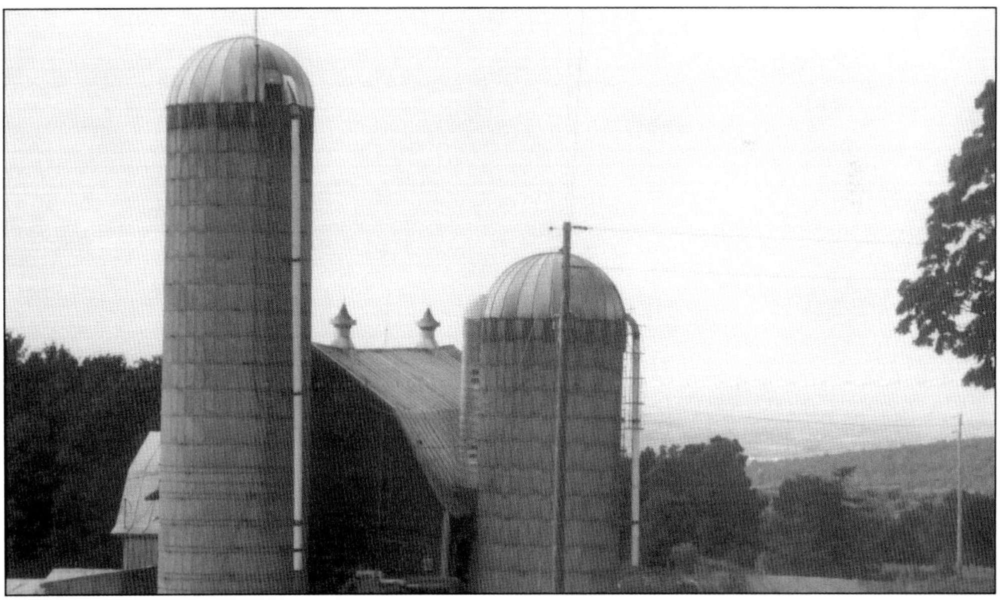

MOMROW'S FARM. Most farms were for family livelihood, with a few dairy farms. Today, Taborton has gradually become a rural suburban area with persons commuting to work. The William Momrow Farm has heifer cattle and sells hay and wood. If the day were brighter the Helderberg Mountains on the horizon would be clearer. (Courtesy Sand Lake Historical Society Collection.)

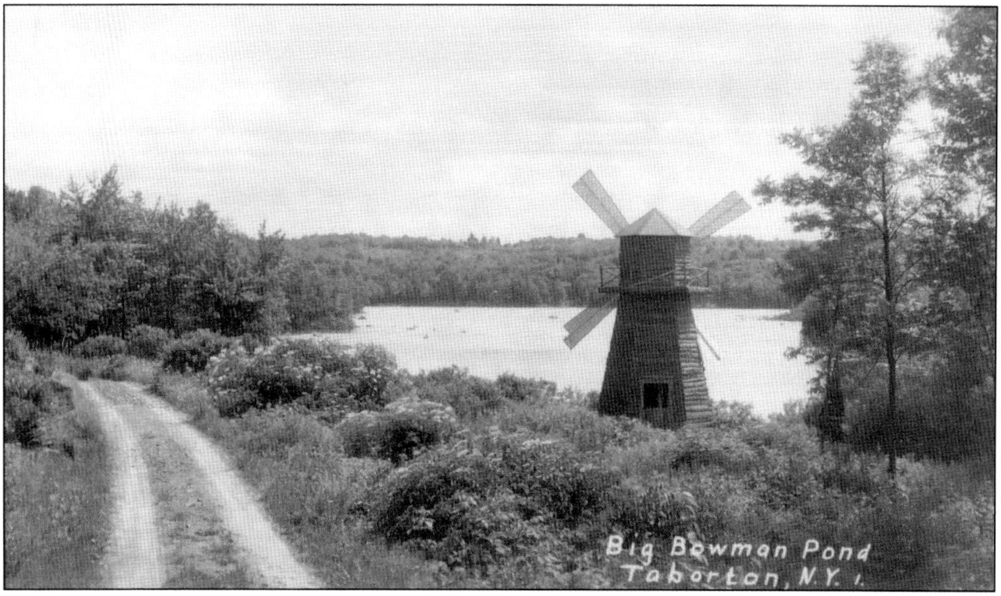

A DUTCH-STYLE WINDMILL. Located on the shore of Big Bowman Pond, this Dutch-style windmill is on the Robert Dawes property. This land was originally leased to Nicholas Feller and Joseph Uline. Then, the Julius Rymiller family operated it as a farm. In 1921, it became the summer home of Prof. Thomas Lawson. He had the windmill built to pump water to a pond next to his house for domestic use. (Courtesy Iona Mosher.)

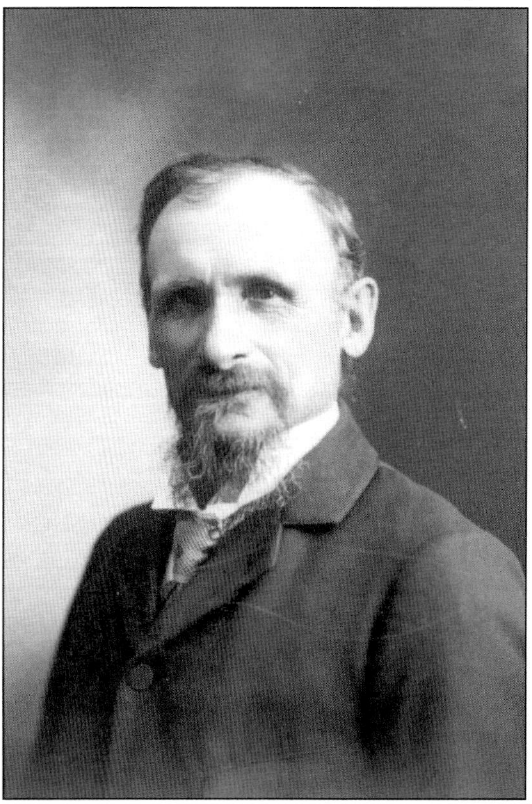

JULIUS RYMILLER. Julius Rymiller was born in 1840 in Taborton, where he lived all his life. He married twice and raised 12 children in a four-room home on Lawson Road. He supported his family by farming and burning charcoal. Later, he became a rural free delivery mail carrier in Taborton. He was buried in Zion's Church cemetery in 1923. (Courtesy Warren Rymiller, grandson of Julius Rymiller.)

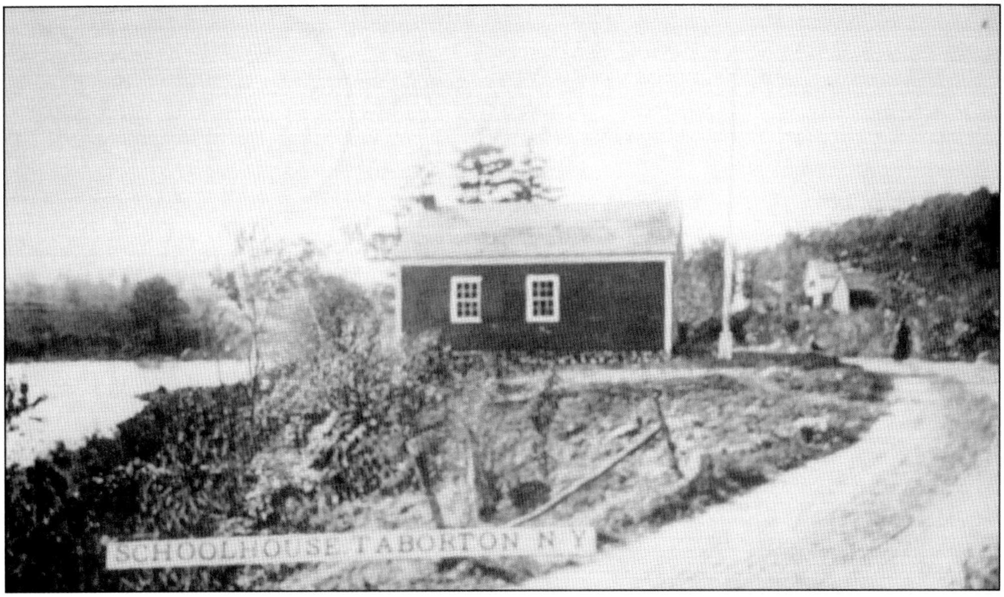

TABORTON SCHOOL. Taborton School District No. 11 was located on the shore of Little Bowman Pond. In 1934, it was annexed to the Averill Park Central School District. (Courtesy Gordon "Gunny" Gundrum.)

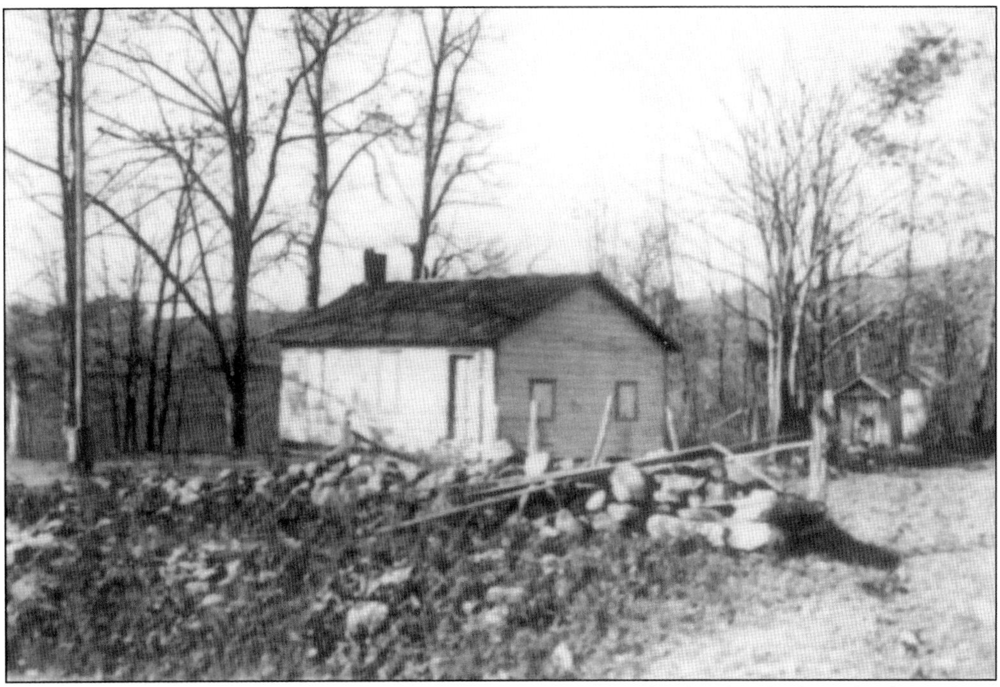

MILLER DISTRICT SCHOOL NO. 9 ON TABORTON ROAD. This land title dates back to 1794, was conveyed to Michael Reichard by Stephen Van Rensselaer, and was in the Reichard family until 1887. One-quarter acre was "excepted" for the use of School District No. 9, called Miller School. It was one of the original schools that consolidated in 1929 to form the Averill Park Central School District. The original building had an addition c. 1972 and is the private residence of the Wayne Schulz family. (Courtesy Town of Sand Lake Collection.)

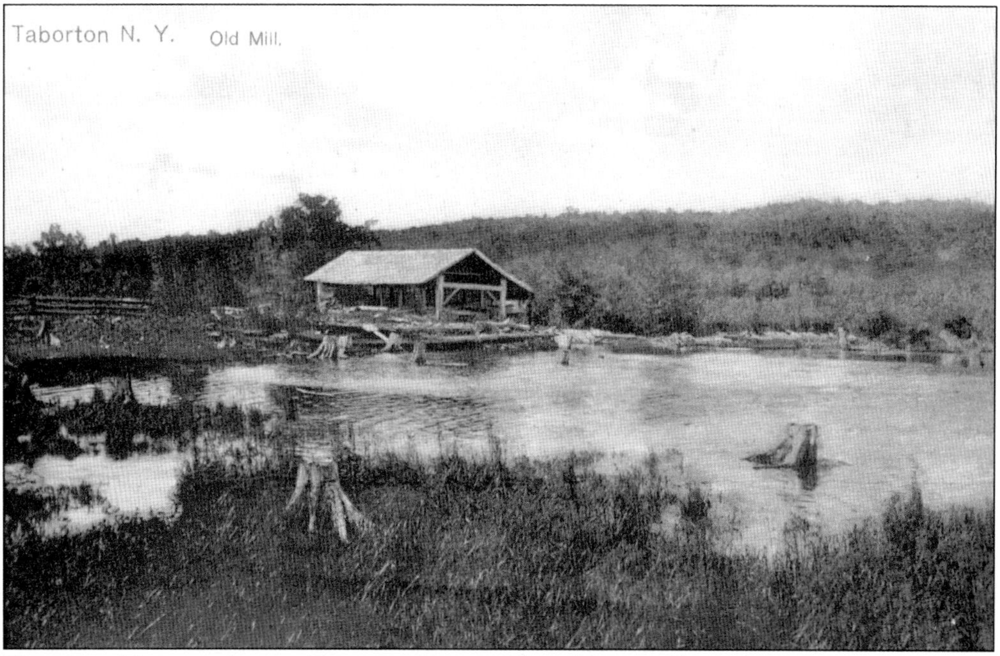

The Old Mill on Little Bowman Pond. This old sawmill was located at the outlet of Little Bowman Pond. Richard Knowlson, Gideon Butts, and George Horton operated sawmills in Taborton in the 1830s and 1840s and had a large lumber business in Troy. (Courtesy Angelo Patti.)

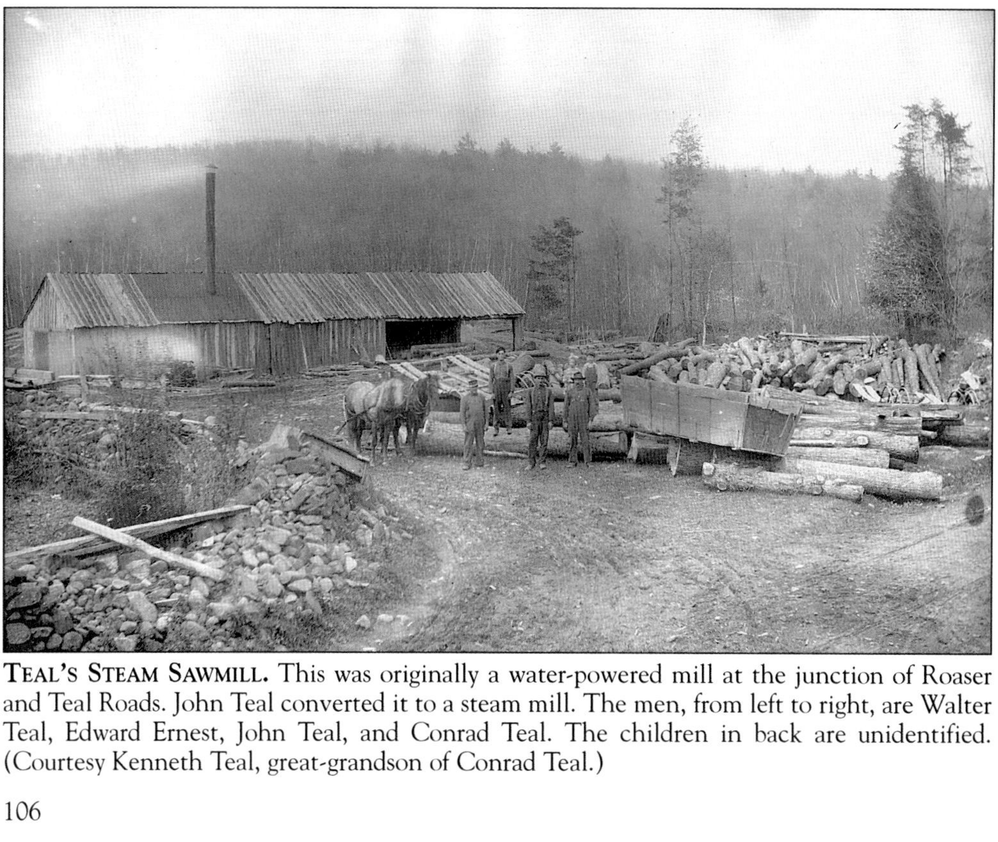

Teal's Steam Sawmill. This was originally a water-powered mill at the junction of Roaser and Teal Roads. John Teal converted it to a steam mill. The men, from left to right, are Walter Teal, Edward Ernest, John Teal, and Conrad Teal. The children in back are unidentified. (Courtesy Kenneth Teal, great-grandson of Conrad Teal.)

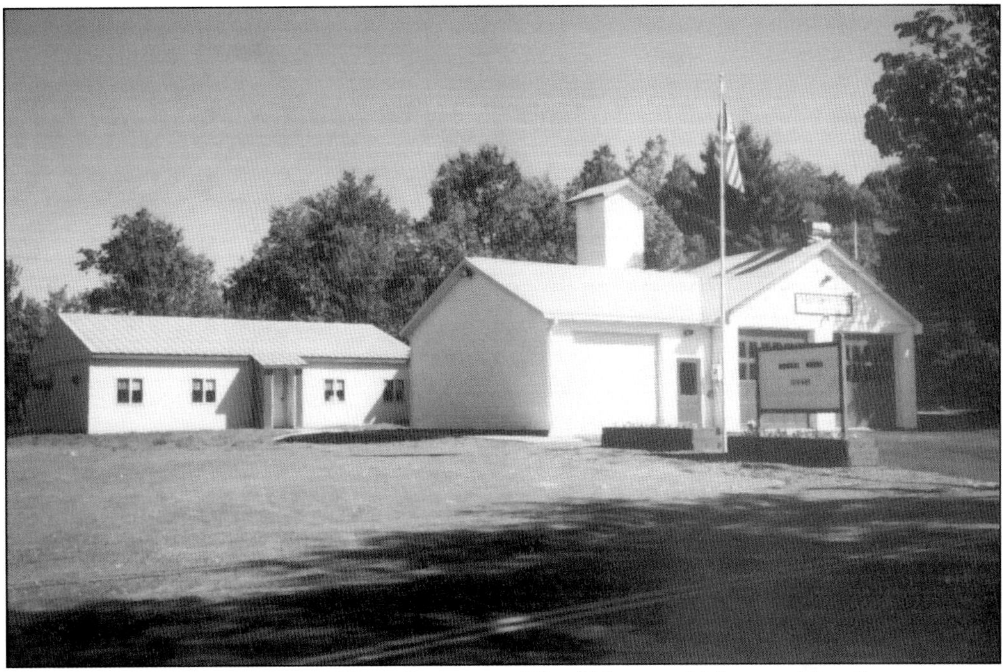

The Taborton Volunteer Fire Company. The Taborton Volunteer Fire Company was established in 1958 and serves the eastern third of the town of Sand Lake and a large portion of the southeast corner of the town of Berlin. The firehouse has a two-bay garage and a meeting hall. (Courtesy Sand Lake Historical Society Collection.)

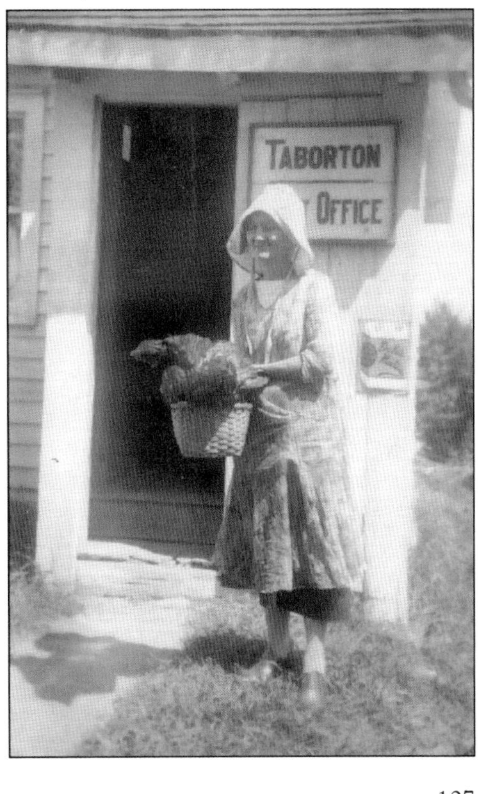

The Taborton Post Office. The Taborton Post Office was established on September 12, 1892. Conrad Malkmes was the first postmaster. His daughter Wilhemenia, or "Minnie," right, was postmaster from 1913 to 1942, when the Taborton office merged with the Averill Park office. A ledger shows merchandise of oats, corn, codfish, flour, flypaper, and candy for sale in the store, which was also run by the Malkmes family. The building is now the home of the Richard McDonald family. (Courtesy Iona Mosher.)

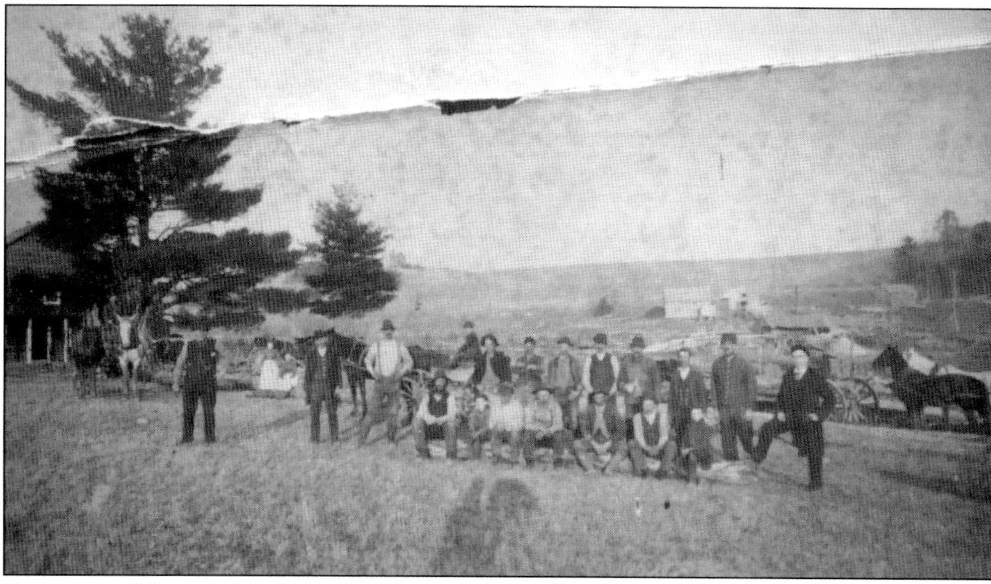

Teamsters Wait for a Load of Wood. Teams of horses and their drivers were hired by the lumber companies as teamsters. It was a full day's work to take one load of wood to customers in the city. (Courtesy Dan J. Holser.)

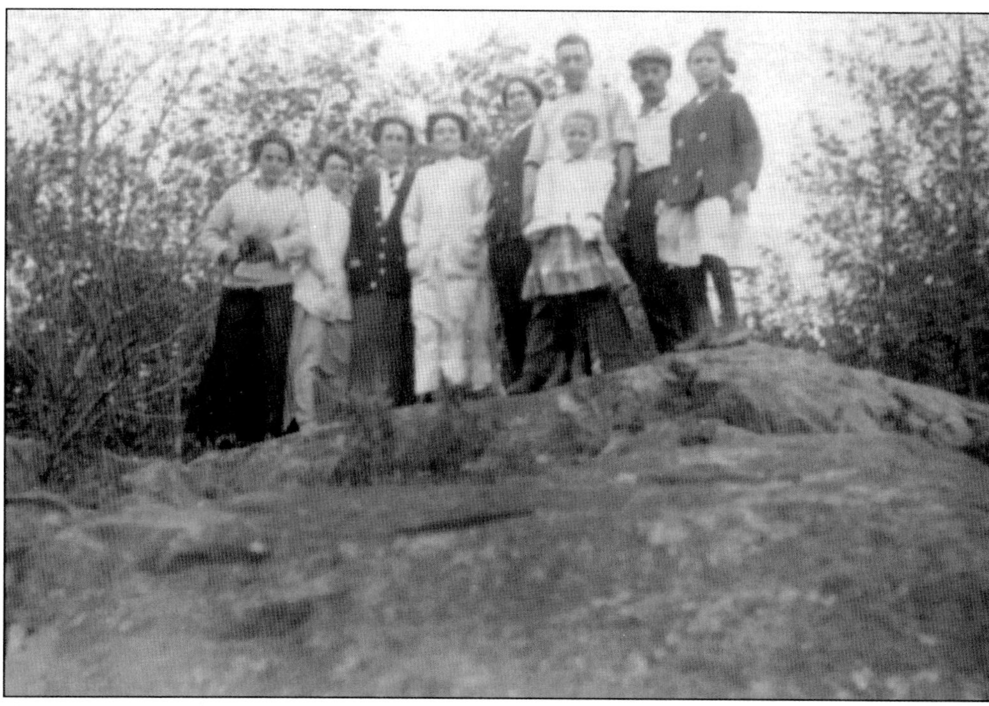

Kipple Rock. To the German-speaking person, it was Gipfel Rock. Gipfel became Kipple after more English began to be spoken. Kipple Rock, the highest point in town, has an elevation of 1,850 feet and is almost as high as Lake Placid, with its elevation of 1,860 feet. The rock has always been a favorite climb for the panoramic western view to the Helderberg Mountains on the horizon. (Courtesy Ernest Hoffman.)

Five

TOWNWIDE EVENTS AND ORGANIZATIONS

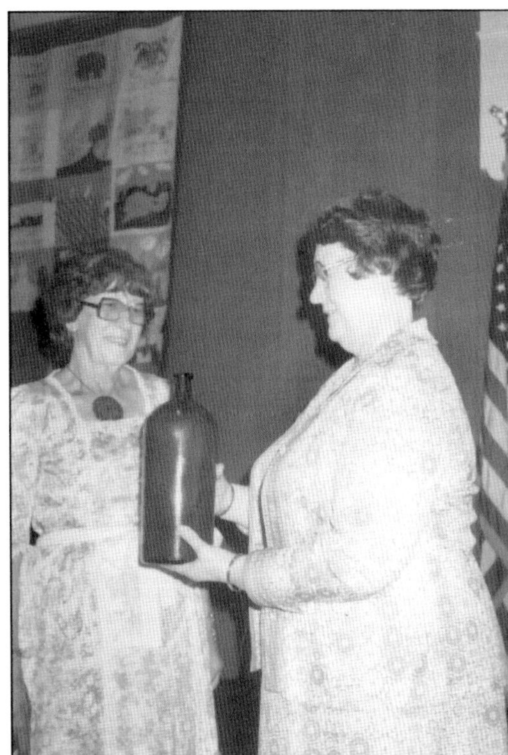

MADOLYN CARPENTER, TOWN HISTORIAN. At the 170th anniversary celebration of the town of Sand Lake in 1982, Madolyn Carpenter (left), town historian, admires a blue glass bottle that Mrs. Robert Wells brought to show. The big question is whether it came from the Rensselaer Glass Factory. The town historian researched many queries such as this during her 20-year tenure from 1975 to 1995. As archivist, genealogist, and researcher, she was involved with all the events and organizations in town, both past and present. She was always striving to preserve the record of the past and present for future generations. (Courtesy Town of Sand Lake Collection.)

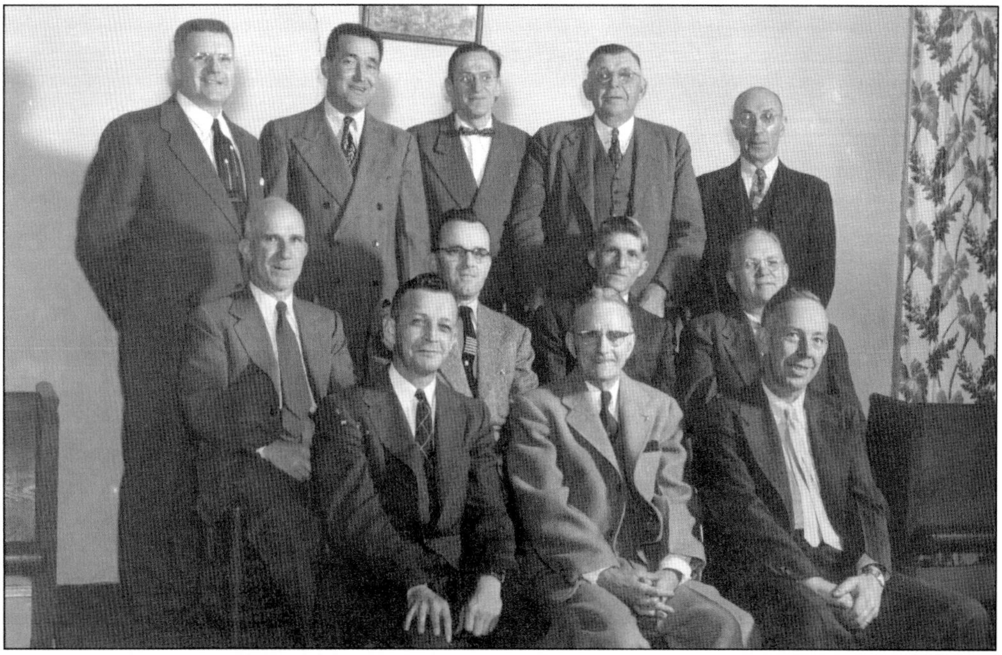

THE TOWN BOARD, 1966. Pictured, from left to right, are the following: (front row) Sidney Gallant, justice; Joseph Fitzgerald, supervisor; and Arthur Bashford, justice; (middle row) unidentified; Joseph Warren, town clerk; Henry Stanley, assessor; and Rockwell White, auditor; (back row) Earl Stiles, tax collector; Charles Hack, assessor; Carl Wicks, justice; Albert Flaxmyer, road commissioner; and Henry Henkel, justice. (Courtesy Town of Sand Lake Collection.)

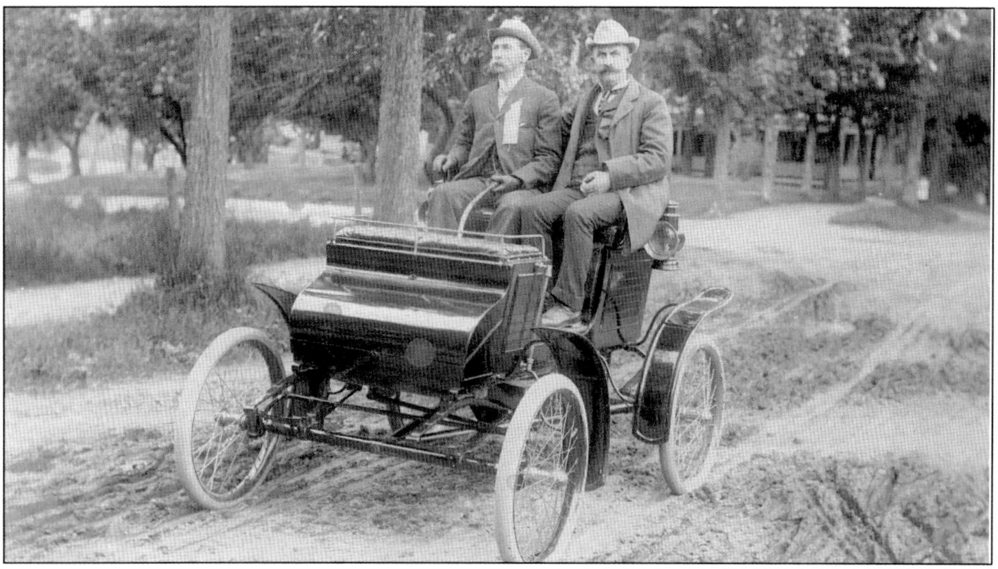

ARTHUR PECK AND GEORGE WILSEY. The Mutual Insurance Association of Sand Lake, Poestenkill, Berlin, and Stephentown was organized in 1878 and was a forerunner to the Capital Mutual Insurance Company. Arthur Peck, left, was secretary-treasurer for 36 years and treasurer for 14 additional years. George Wilsey, right, was an insurance underwriter. (Courtesy Edna DiDomenica Pierce.)

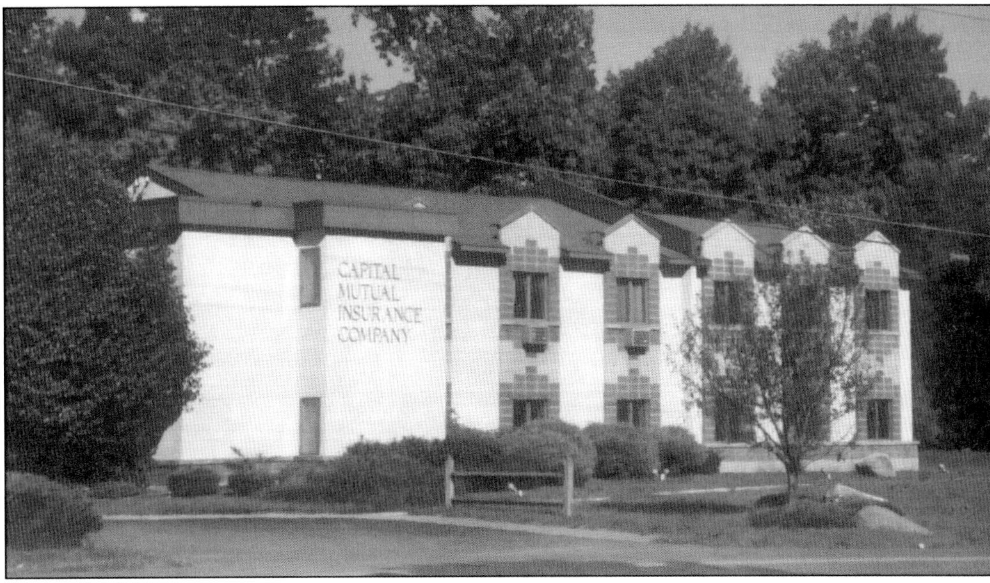

THE CAPITAL MUTUAL INSURANCE COMPANY. Beginning in 1878, the Capital Mutual Insurance Company had its roots in Sand Lake (see page 110). The firm entered into a holding company relationship and, in 1999, moved to Albany. Rather than proceed with plans for a new town hall, the town board decided to use the vacant insurance company building for town offices and a library. Renovations were completed, and the building became the new town hall in August 1999. (Courtesy Sand Lake Historical Society Collection.)

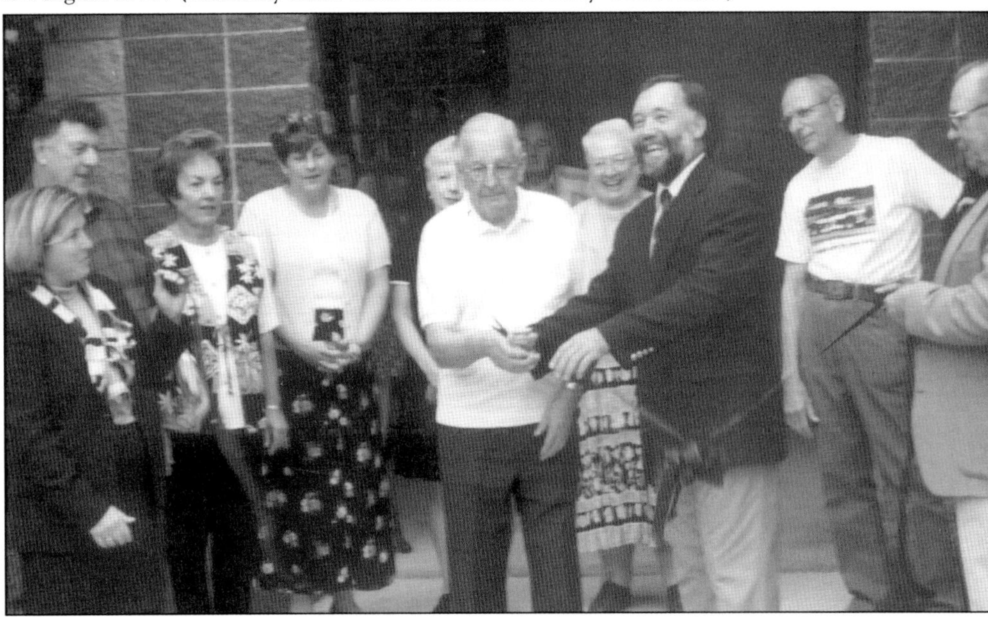

THE DEDICATION OF TOWN HALL, 1999. At the dedication of the new town hall on August 21, 1999, are, from left to right, Flora Fasoldt, councilwoman; Joseph Trupia, councilman; Nancy Dunn, councilwoman; Christine Kronau, town clerk; Dorothy Biittig, receiver of taxes; Sidney Gallant, former town supervisor; Douglas Kelley, supervisor; Henry Rowe; Judy Rowe, town historian; John Udwary, former supervisor; and John "Jack" Welcome, councilman. (Courtesy Town of Sand Lake Collection.)

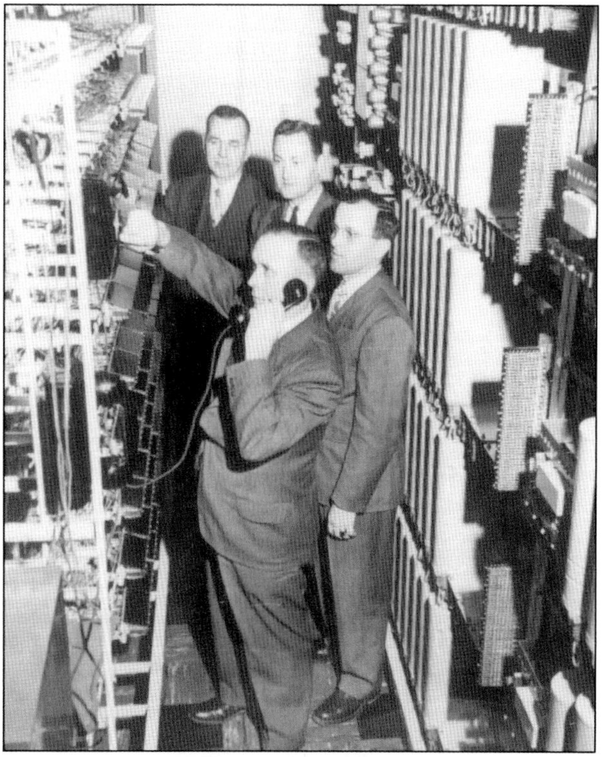

THE DIAL TELEPHONE SYSTEM INSTALLATION, C. 1950. Prior to the dial system being installed in the telephone building on Orient Avenue, the previous phone system was located above the Larkin Funeral Home. In front are Raymond Miller, supervisor, testing the new dial system, and Joseph Warren, town clerk, looking on. Two telephone officials are standing in back. (Courtesy Joseph Warren Sr.)

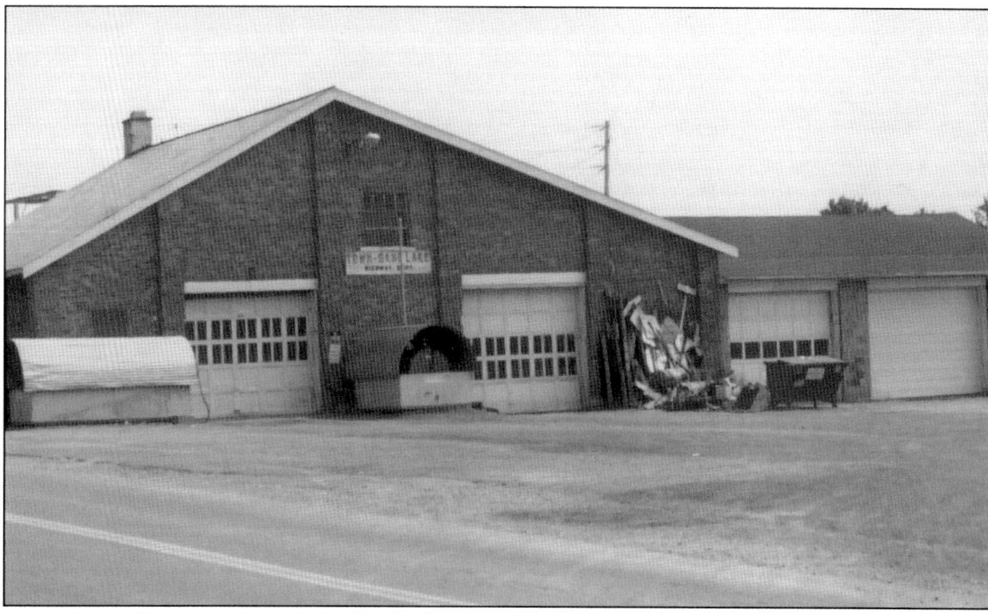

THE TOWN BARN. After 1925, the hydroelectric power plant was torn down (see page 22) and Clifford Hastings, plant owner and town supervisor, donated materials to the town for the Town Barn on Eastern Union Turnpike. It is almost a replica of the old power plant and was completed in 1933 as a Works Progress Administration (WPA) project, providing income for many masons and laborers during the Depression. (Courtesy Sand Lake Historical Society Collection.)

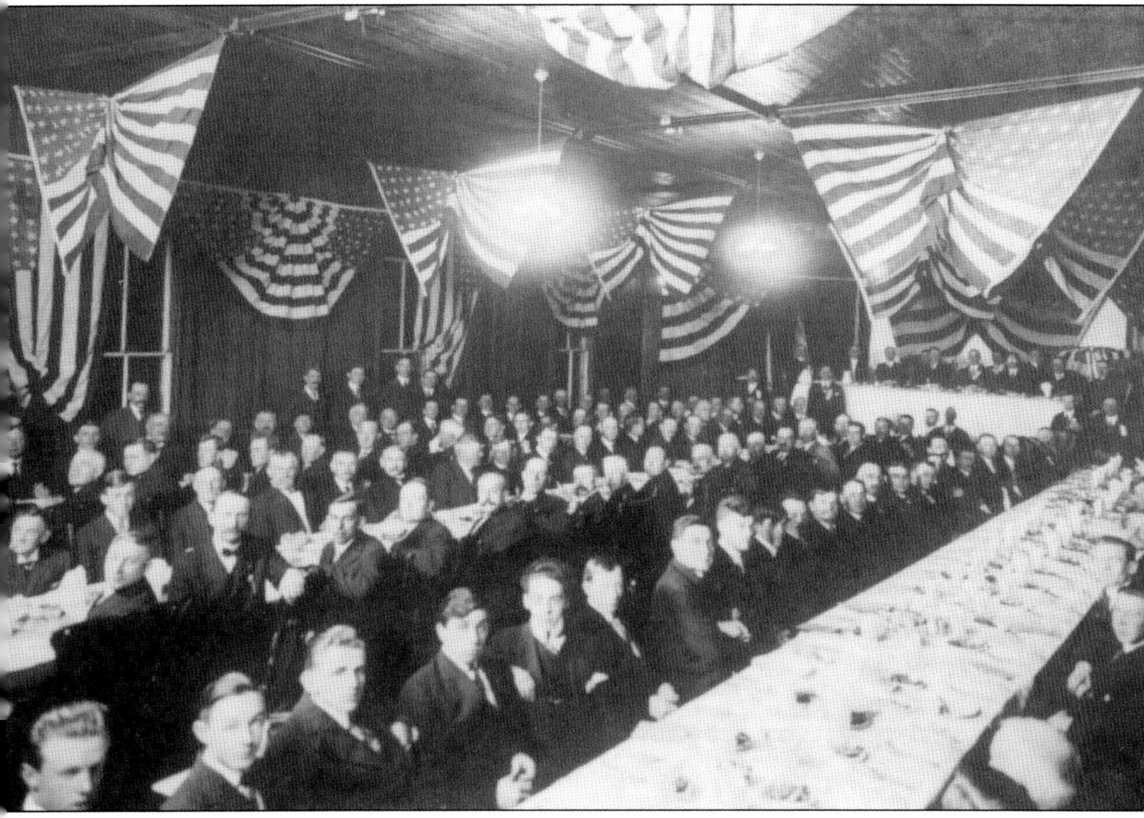

Town Presents Medal. A medal, inscribed on one side "For Service" and on the other "Presented by the people of Sand Lake to their loyal fighting son," was given to soldiers, sailors, and marines of World War I and five Civil War veterans at Faith Community Hall on September 13, 1919. Seated, from left to right, are the following: (first table, facing camera) Walter Baker, unidentified, Leon Smith, unidentified, Ted Brazee, Lawrence Gruber, three unidentified men, George Cann, George Brownhardt, Joseph Kehn, unidentified, Richard Lay, Harrison Lay, Howard Lester, and unidentified; (back to camera) three unidentified, ? Dobert, unidentified, Arthur Butler, Harry Tillson, and Frank Barnum; (second table, facing camera) unidentified, William Adams, Charles Smith, Edward Hack, George Schreiner, William Schreiner, John Lewis, and Rev. John Crippen; (back to camera) unidentified, Frank Fredenburgh, Lloyd French, Floyd Foster, unidentified, Willis Larkin, and James Cotton. (Courtesy Town of Sand Lake Collection.)

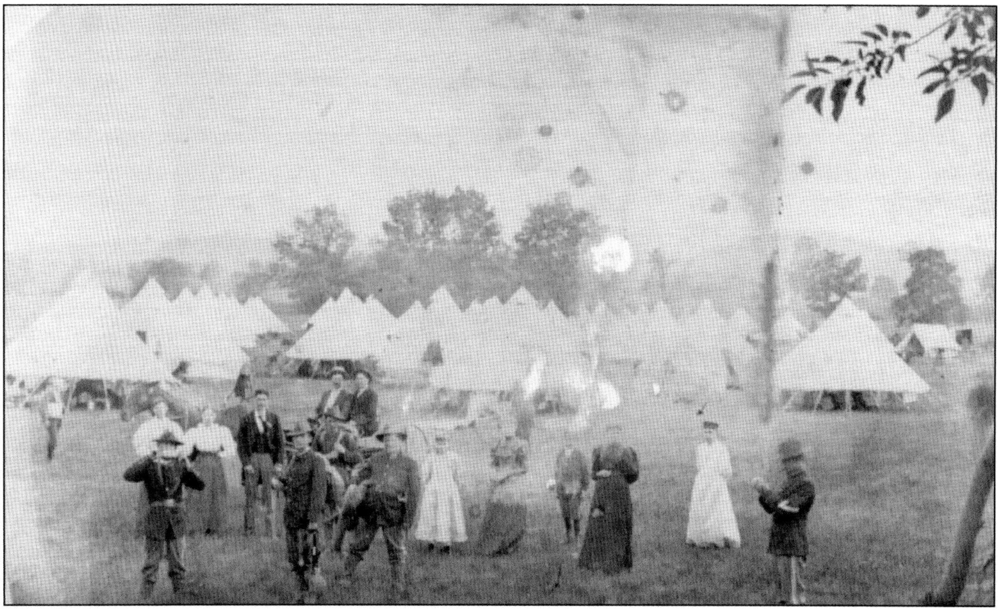

A MILITARY ENCAMPMENT, C. 1873–1884. Soldiers gather for a training encampment during the period after the Civil War, *c.* 1873–1884, on the area which previously was Younghan's Race Track (see page 29) and currently is the location of the West Sand Lake School. (Courtesy Beverly Hastings.)

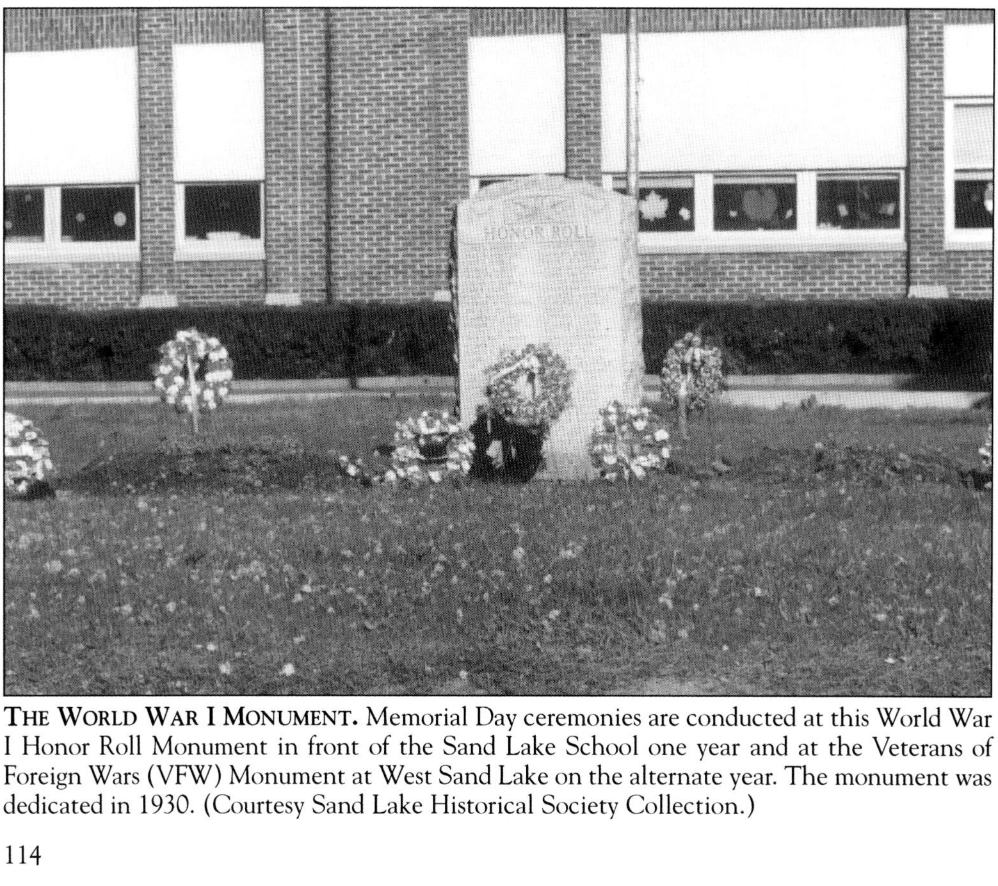

THE WORLD WAR I MONUMENT. Memorial Day ceremonies are conducted at this World War I Honor Roll Monument in front of the Sand Lake School one year and at the Veterans of Foreign Wars (VFW) Monument at West Sand Lake on the alternate year. The monument was dedicated in 1930. (Courtesy Sand Lake Historical Society Collection.)

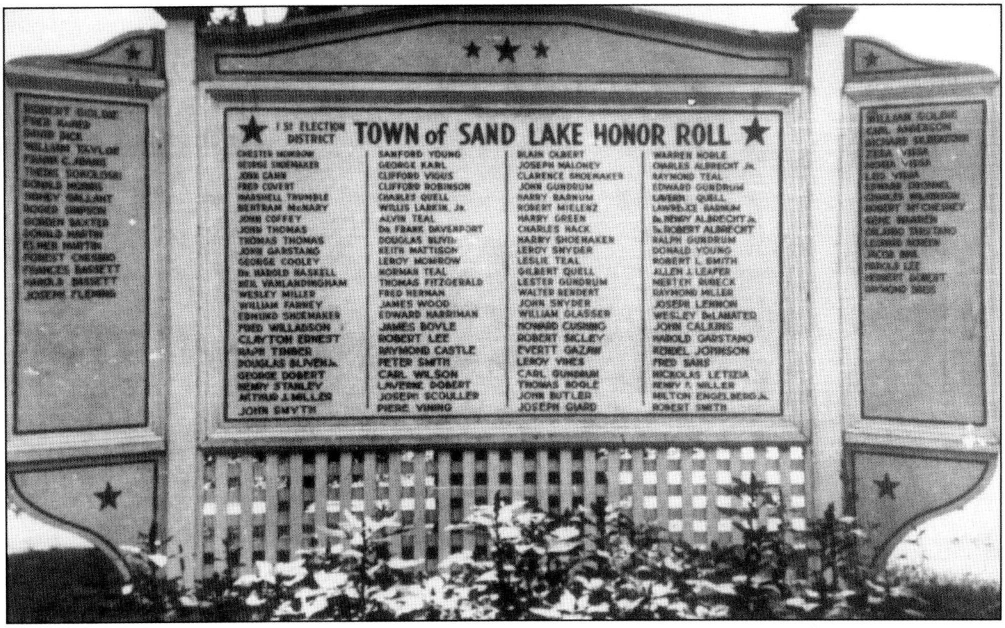

THE WORLD WAR II HONOR ROLL. This First Election District Honor Roll for World War II veterans was located at the junction of Route 43 and Eastern Union Turnpike. (Courtesy Sand Lake Historical Society Collection.)

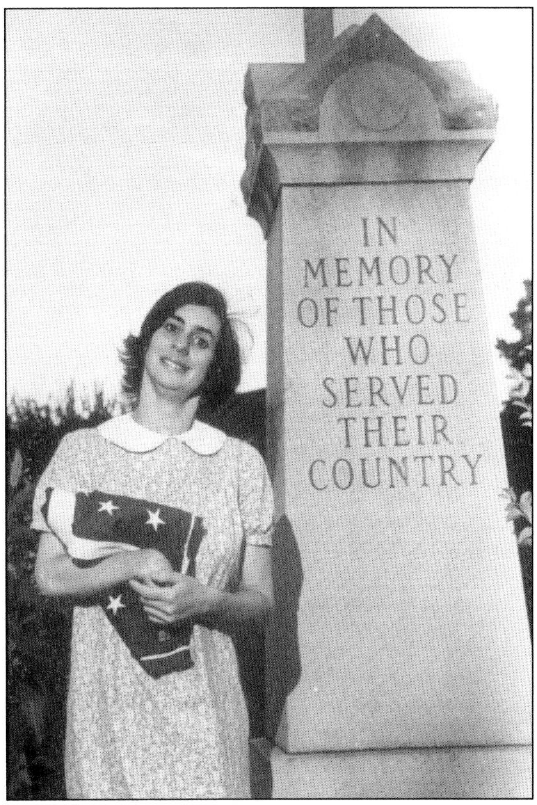

ONE MILE TWICE A DAY. Carolyn De Rosa holds the flag she has raised and lowered at the Veterans of Foreign Wars Monument, erected by the Lt. Perry William Post 3025 at West Sand Lake Corners. She walked the mile from her house to the monument twice a day, weather permitting. In 1980, the town honored her with a Thank You Resolution for 15 years of service. (Courtesy Carolyn DeRosa; Brian Triller, *Times Union* photographer.)

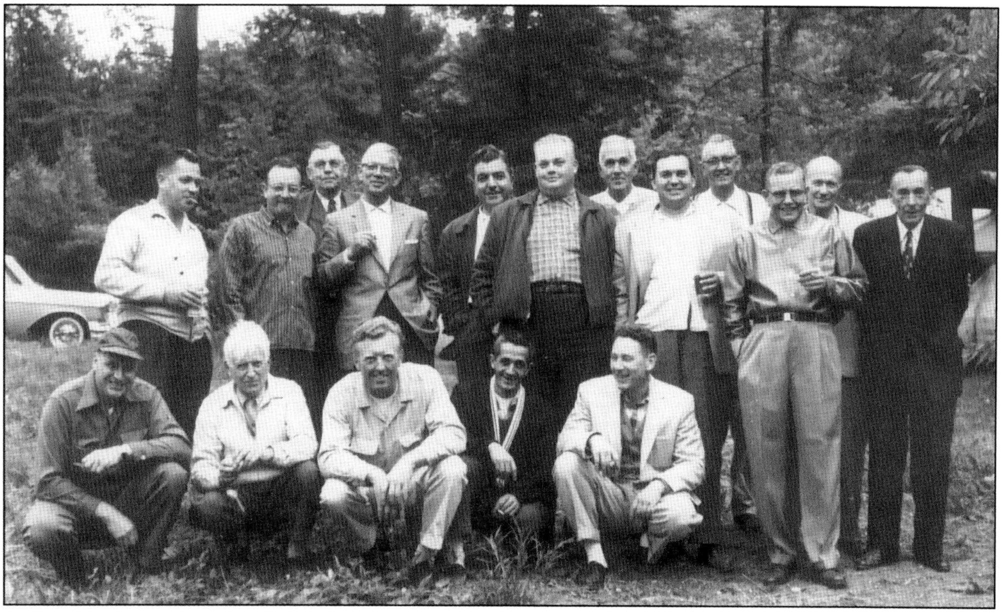

AVERILL PARK MERCHANTS, 1958. Enjoying a clam steam at Brookside Park, from left to right, are the following: (front row) William Glasser, Raymond Eastman Sr., Harry O'Donnell, Willie Stelleto, and Raymond Eastman Jr.; (back row) Bernard Baniak, ? Linden, Albert Flaxmyer, Roy Kern, Zane Bedian, Dr. John Reid, Benjamin Silberg, Aubrey Primeau, two unidentified men, Elmer Rendert, and unidentified. (Courtesy Town of Sand Lake Collection.)

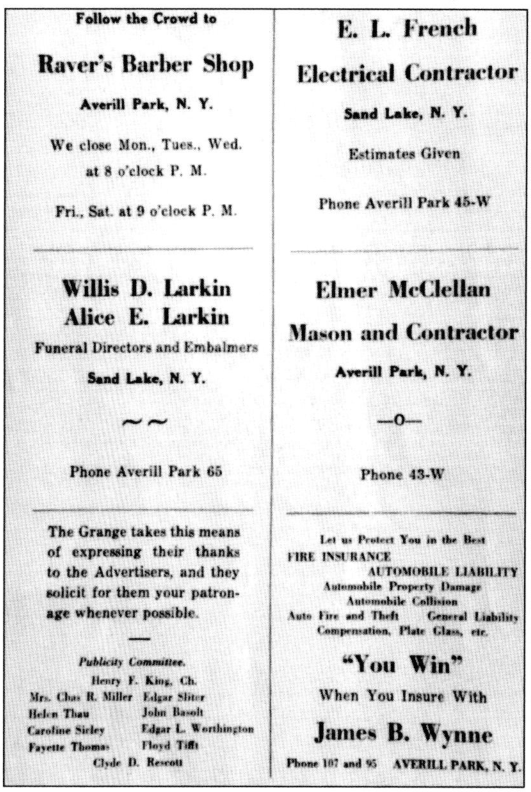

Follow the Crowd to

Raver's Barber Shop

Averill Park, N. Y.

We close Mon., Tues., Wed.
at 8 o'clock P. M.

Fri., Sat. at 9 o'clock P. M.

Willis D. Larkin
Alice E. Larkin

Funeral Directors and Embalmers

Sand Lake, N. Y.

~~

Phone Averill Park 65

The Grange takes this means of expressing their thanks to the Advertisers, and they solicit for them your patronage whenever possible.

—

Publicity Committee.

Henry F. King, Ch.
Mrs. Chas R. Miller — Edgar Sliter
Helen Thau — John Basolt
Caroline Sirley — Edgar L. Worthington
Fayette Thomas — Floyd Tifft
Clyde D. Rescott

E. L. French

Electrical Contractor

Sand Lake, N. Y.

Estimates Given

Phone Averill Park 45-W

Elmer McClellan

Mason and Contractor

Averill Park, N. Y.

—0—

Phone 43-W

Let us Protect You in the Best
FIRE INSURANCE
AUTOMOBILE LIABILITY
Automobile Property Damage
Automobile Collision
Auto Fire and Theft — General Liability
Compensation, Plate Glass, etc.

"You Win"

When You Insure With

James B. Wynne

Phone 107 and 95 — AVERILL PARK, N. Y.

PROGRAM ADVERTISEMENTS, 1933. A page from the West Sand Lake Minstrels program in 1933 has several Averill Park businesses advertised. (Courtesy Town of Sand Lake Collection.)

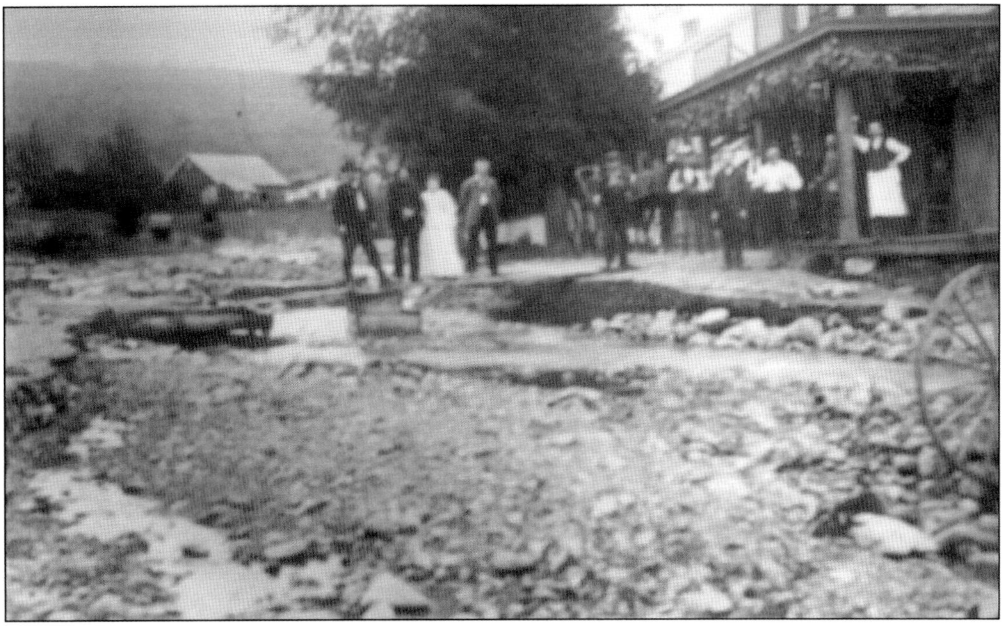

THE FLOOD OF 1891 IN FRONT OF THE GLASS LAKE HOTEL. A cloudburst struck Sand Lake on August 21, 1891. The Wynantskill was swollen to the dimensions of a river. Several banks of Glass Lake disappeared. Water filled the cellar and was up to the first floor of Crape's Hotel. The general store of Huntley and Olmstead collapsed. Seven bridges above West Sand Lake and one below were washed out. (Courtesy Edna DiDomenica Pierce; the *Troy Record*, January 8, 1946.)

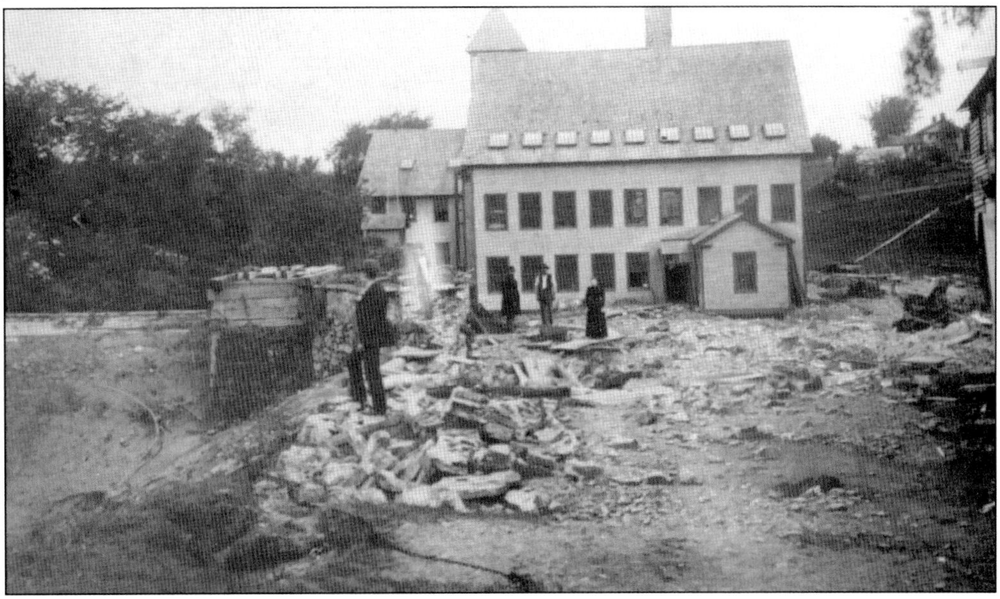

THE FLOOD OF 1891 AT KANE'S MILL, AVERILL PARK. In Averill Park two bridges across Kane's pond were destroyed. Dams at Knowlson's Mill, McLaren's Mill, and McConihe's factory were destroyed. At West Sand Lake, near the gristmill on the main highway, a gully 100 feet wide and 30 to 50 feet deep was gouged out, and the bridge below Milo Hastings' gristmill went down the Wynantskill. (Courtesy Dorothy Leitgeb; the *Troy Record*, January 8, 1946.)

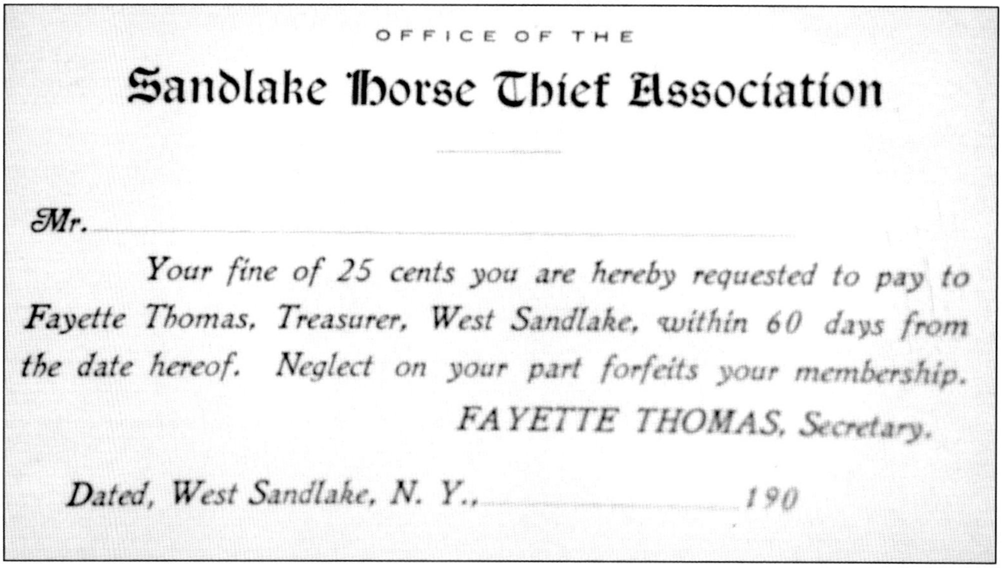

OFFICE OF THE

Sandlake Horse Thief Association

Mr.

Your fine of 25 cents you are hereby requested to pay to Fayette Thomas, Treasurer, West Sandlake, within 60 days from the date hereof. Neglect on your part forfeits your membership.

FAYETTE THOMAS, Secretary.

Dated, West Sandlake, N. Y., 190

THE SAND LAKE ASSOCIATION FOR THE MUTUAL PROTECTION AGAINST HORSE THIEVES. This association was incorporated in 1849. Minutes reflect a $25 reward for apprehension of the thief and $50 for the recovery of a mare stolen on October 29, 1863. The notice above is a fine for nonpayment of dues. The association continues to meet annually on the Sunday afternoon prior to Election Day. (Courtesy Town of Sand Lake Collection.)

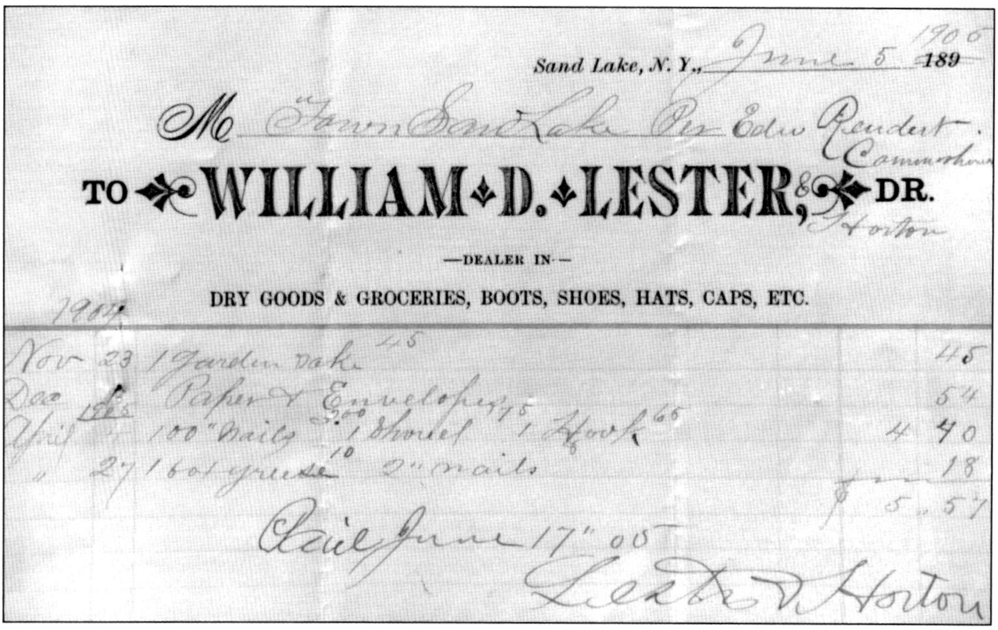

Sand Lake, N. Y., June 5 1905

M Town Sand Lake Per Edw Rendert. Commissioner

TO WILLIAM D. LESTER & Horton DR.

—DEALER IN—

DRY GOODS & GROCERIES, BOOTS, SHOES, HATS, CAPS, ETC.

1904

Nov 23	1 Garden rake	45
Dec	Paper & Envelopes	54
April	100" Nails 3.00 1 Shovel 75 1 Hook 65	4 40
" 27	1 box greese 10 2" nails	18
		$ 5.57

Paid June 17" 05

Lester & Horton

WILLIAM D. LESTER LETTERHEAD. This receipt has "& Horton" written in after William D. Lester on the letterhead and was for the Lester & Horton Store. Edward Rendert, town highway commissioner, paid $5.57 for a garden rake, paper and envelopes, nails, shovel, a hook, and one box "greese" purchased in 1904 and 1905. (Courtesy Town of Sand Lake Collection.)

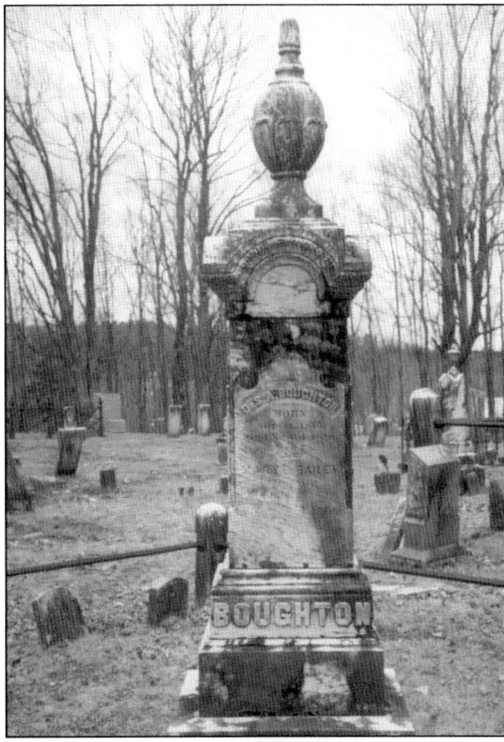

DOWN WITH THE RENT. At the height of the Anti-Rent War, Dr. Smith Boughton, known as "Big Thunder," led a major resistance to the Van Rensselaer landlords on both sides of the Hudson River. Dressed in a calico dress and wearing an Indian mask to hide his identity, he gave a stirring speech on July 4, 1844, at Hoags Corners against paying any more rent to the Van Rensselaer patroons. His grave site is at Sand Lake Union Cemetery. (Courtesy Sand Lake Historical Society Collection.)

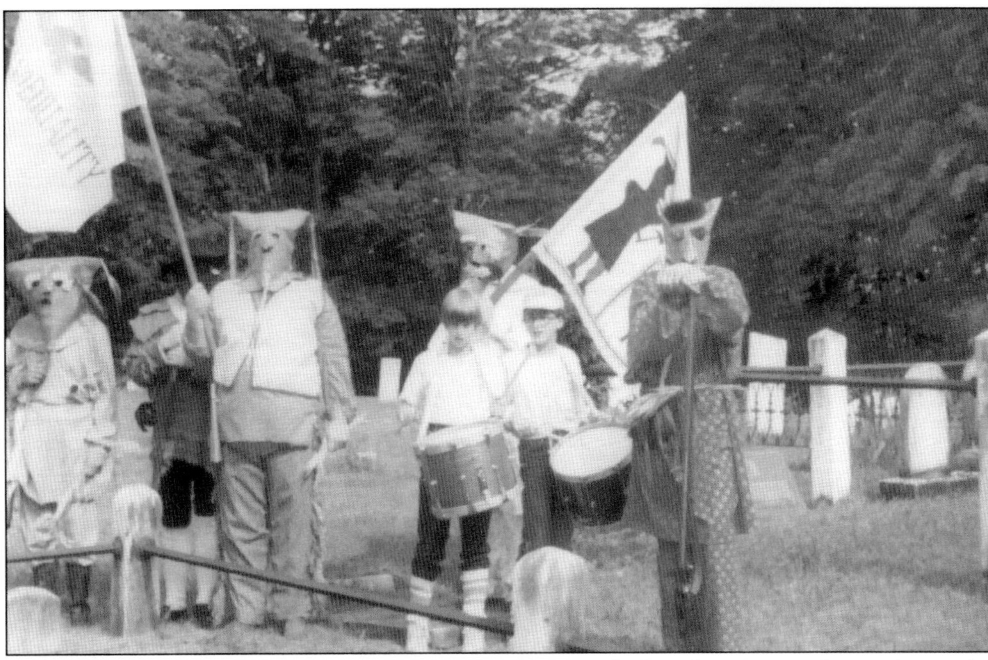

BIG THUNDER DAY. In 1984, 140 years after Dr. Smith Boughton's speech, residents also dressed in calico and Indian face masks and blowing tin horns, began Big Thunder Day at Boughton's grave site in Sand Lake Union Cemetery. The celebration continued at Hoags Corners by reenacting Boughton's call to arms against more rent being levied. Note the logo of the Anti-Rent War on the flag. (Courtesy Town of Sand Lake Collection.)

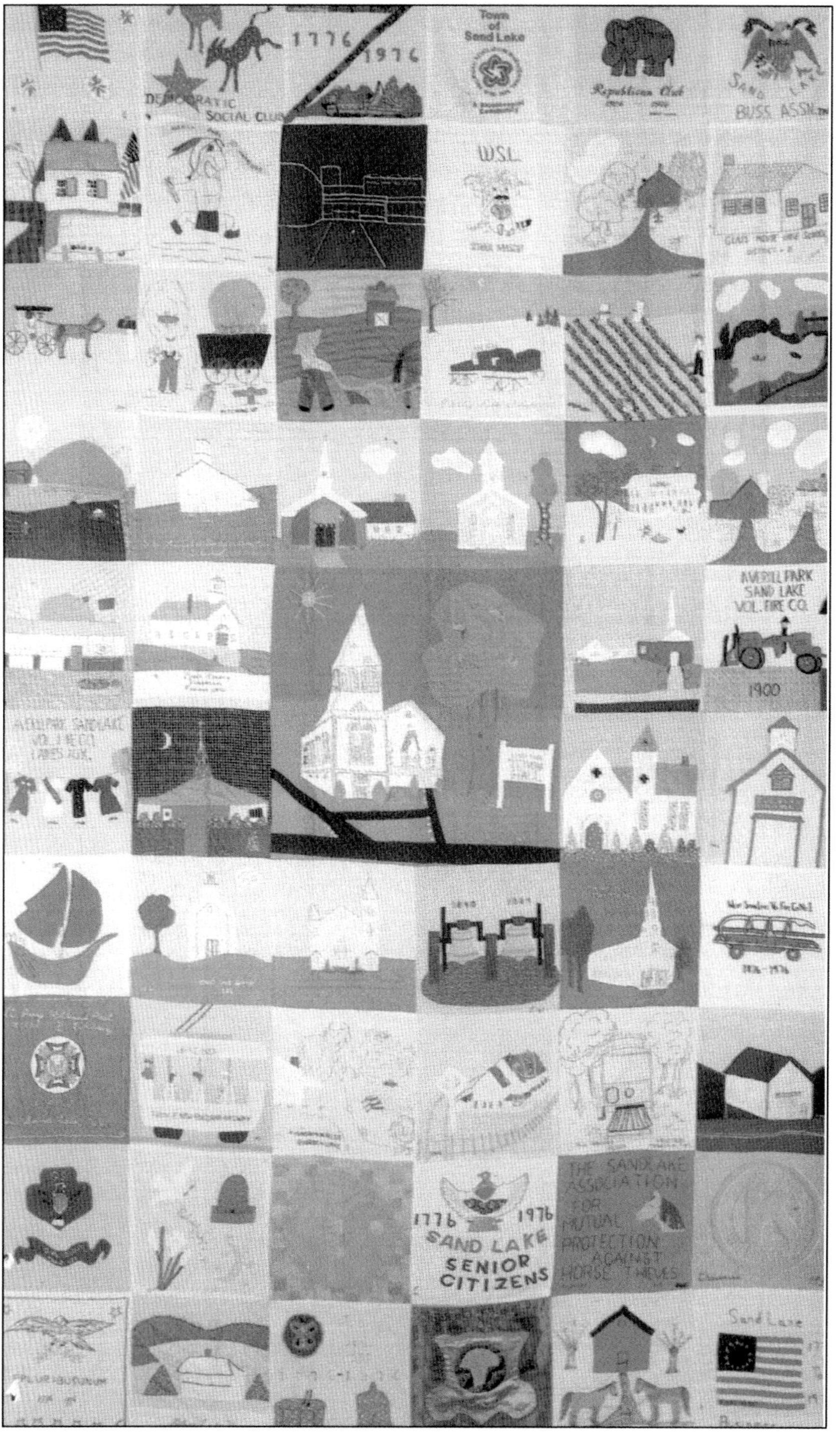

The Bicentennial Quilt. A quilt made to celebrate the bicentennial started out as a raffle but turned out so nice that it was decided to keep it in the town as a wall hanging in the town hall. Many groups and organizations designed squares depicting their part in Sand Lake's history. (Courtesy Sand Lake Historical Society Collection.)

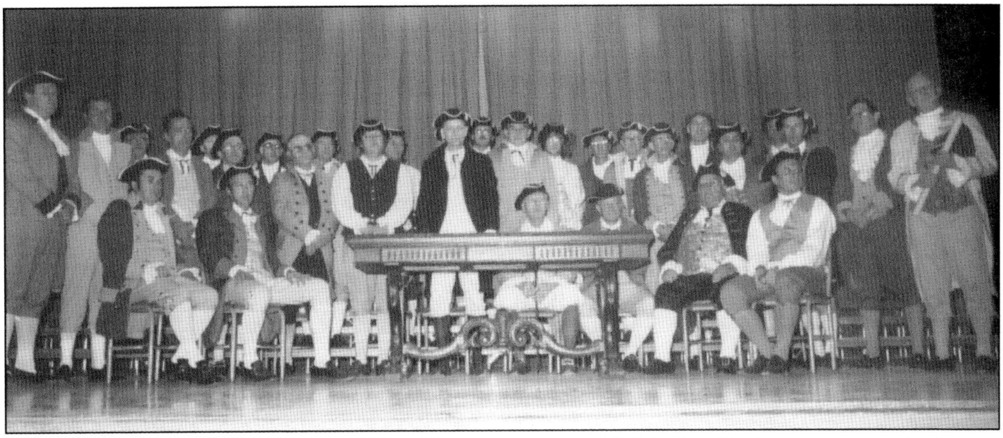

The Declaration of Independence Reenactment, 1976. Sand Lake was recognized as an official Bicentennial Community. A highlight of the celebration was the reenactment of the Declaration of Independence, depicted by 56 men of the town in Colonial costumes on July 4, 1976. (Courtesy Charles Viens.)

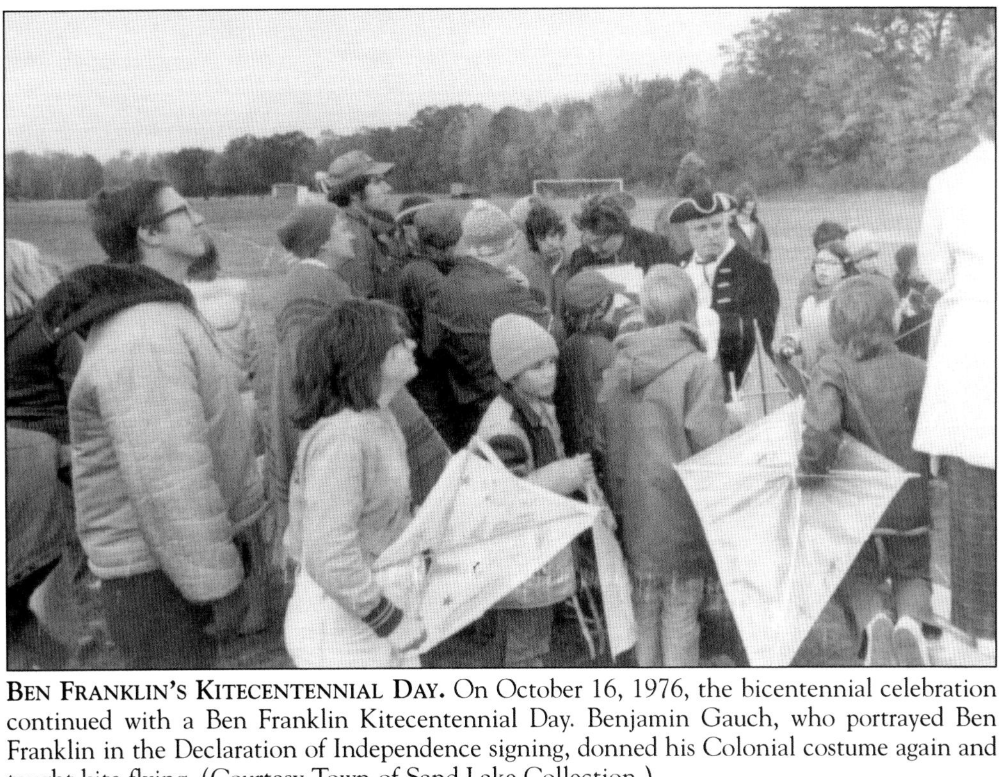

Ben Franklin's Kitecentennial Day. On October 16, 1976, the bicentennial celebration continued with a Ben Franklin Kitecentennial Day. Benjamin Gauch, who portrayed Ben Franklin in the Declaration of Independence signing, donned his Colonial costume again and taught kite flying. (Courtesy Town of Sand Lake Collection.)

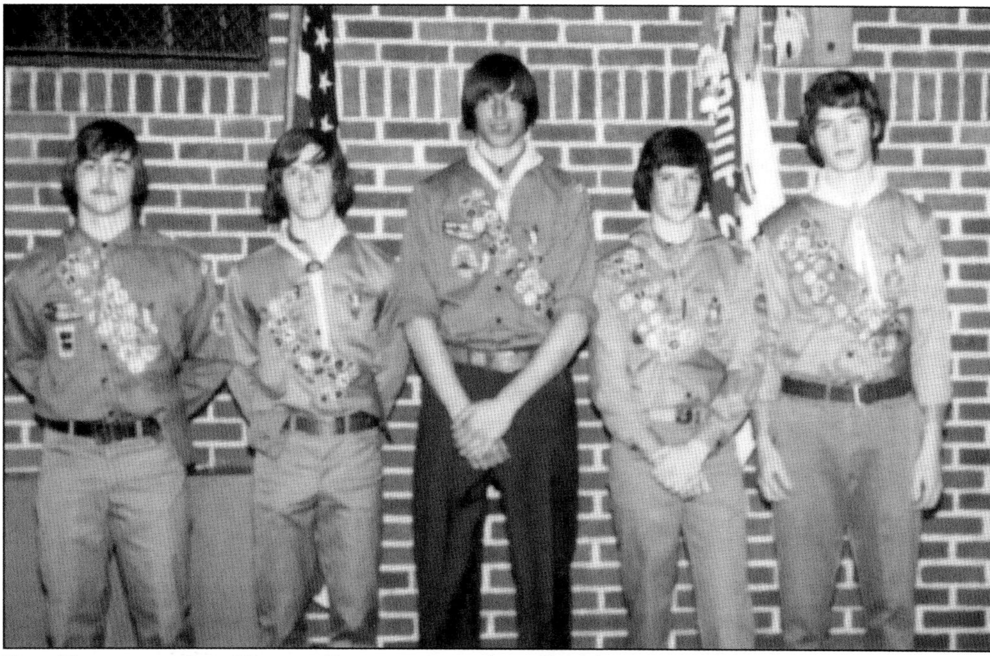

Five Eagles in One Troop. Five scouts in Averill Park Troop 526, sponsored by Sand Lake Kiwanis and led by Gale Mosher, earned Eagle Awards in 1976. The Scouts, from left to right, and their projects are as follows: Jeffrey Mosher, mapped all available water in town for the fire companies; Robert Wagner, instituted a bicycle registration program; Michael Supkis, customized a spanner wrench to link fire hoses; William Marshall, updated the invalid list and delivered identifying stickers; Daniel Case, relayed shortwave radio communication during the Guatemalan disaster. (Courtesy Sand Lake Kiwanis.)

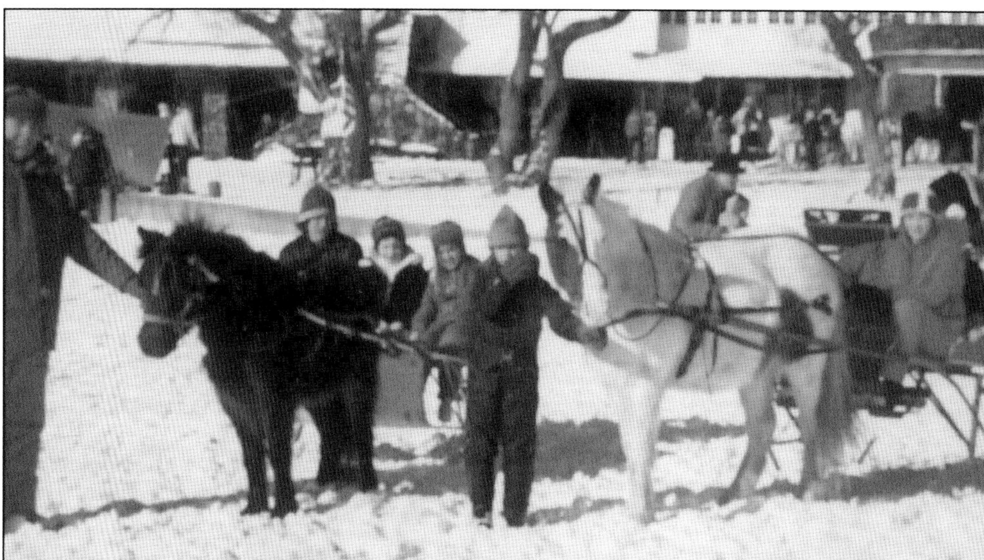

The Kiwanis Winter Festival. A popular community event, sponsored by the Sand Lake Kiwanis, was the annual Winter Festival held for many years at the Crooked Lake Hotel. Being pulled on skis by a horse, or skijouring, was a favorite event. (Courtesy Sand Lake Kiwanis.)

Elroy Face Field. Elroy Face, left, an Averill Park High School graduate, became a major league baseball pitcher, held several baseball records, and played on three All-Star Teams in 1958, 1959, and 1960. With him are, from left to right, Irving Sewell and his grandson Keith Molitor, Harold Schriner, and John Glasser. They are attending the Sand Lake Kiwanis Summerfest on July 25, 1992, when the Butler Park ball field was dedicated as the Elroy Face Field. (Courtesy Irving Sewell.)

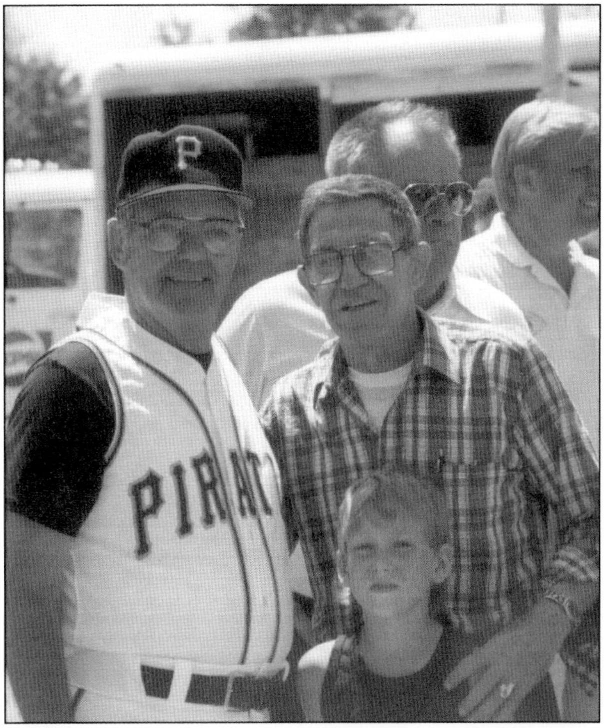

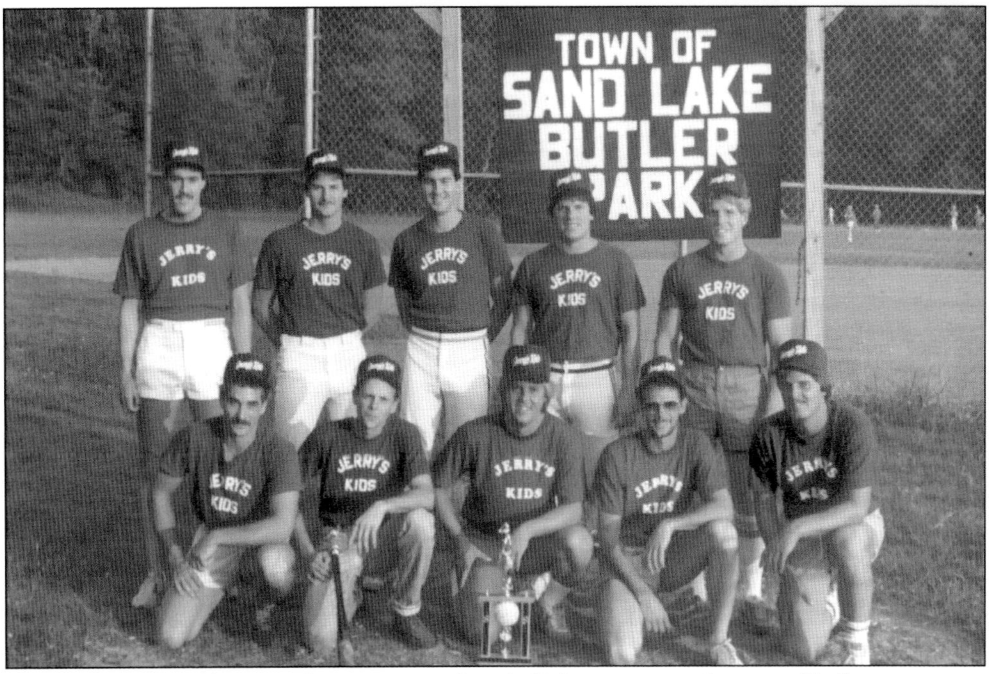

Jerry's Kids at Kiwanis Summerfest. Jerry's Kids participated in a softball tournament during the Summerfest held at Butler Park c. 1984 and won a trophy. From left to right are the following: (front row) Ken Bailey, Blaine "Fudgy" Berner, Jerry Shelgren, Mark Berner, and Ken Gunderman; (back row) Mike Buckley, Tim Mardon, Kevin Ryan, Jeff Bailey, and Glenn Weiss. (Courtesy Sand Lake Kiwanis Club.)

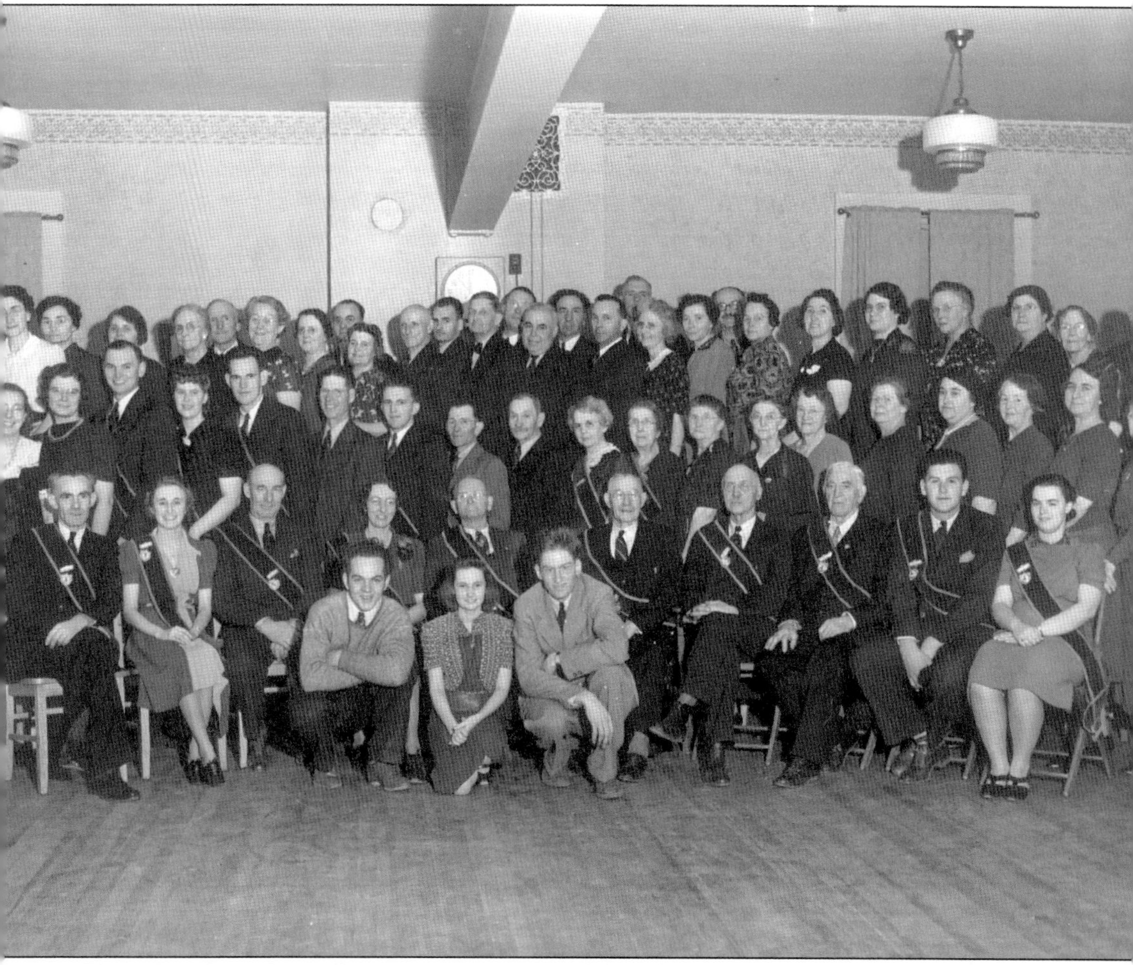

THE WEST SAND LAKE GRANGE, 1939. Pictured, from left to right, are the following: (first row) Ernest Berry, Emily Gardner, and Carl Wicks; (second row) E.W. McLarin, Bernice Houghton, Clyde Rescott, Virginia Tryon, H.D. Vincent, Michael King, G.W.Fredenburgh, J. Henry Lerch, Emmett Sagendorff, and Elizabeth Bubie; (third row) Violet Sewell, Ruth Weinbrecht, Edward Barnes, Dorothy Everett, William Barnes, H.F. King, Russell Jones, Stanley Stevens, L.W. Ferguson, Emily Waterbury, Mrs. Charles Miller, Sara Wagner, Ella Lurch, May Tyron, Edith Wicks, Edna Sagendorff, Mrs. Clyde Rescott, Mrs. I. Raymond Cipperly, and Mrs. Albert Cipperly; (fourth row) Mrs. Charles Smith, Mrs. Elmer Barnes, Mrs. J.E. DeGraff, Mrs. W.J. Bower, Mrs. Alba Fellows, Madeleine Berry, Mrs. H.D. Vincent, Mrs. E.C. Gardner, Charles Smith, Arthur Sharpe, William Bienbrecht, Raymond Miller, Mrs. Raymond Miller, Mrs. Arthur Shaver, Mrs. E.L. Worthington, Mrs. Henry King, Mrs. Clifford Moul, Mrs. William Weinbrecht, Mrs. Harvey Rogers, and Mrs. William Snyder; (fifth row) John Basolt, Clifford Moul, Daniel Karpiak, Wilbur Bower, Raymond Cipperly, Arthur Shaver, and Albert Cipperly. (Courtesy Irving Sewell; *Capital Newspapers* photograph.)

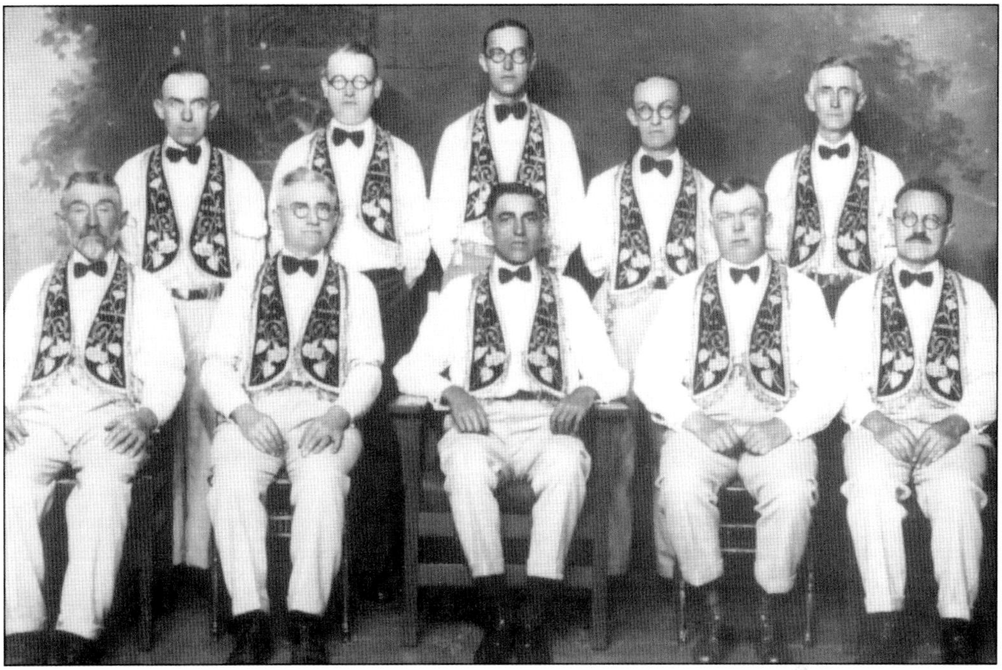

IOOF. In this early 1900s photograph of members of the Independent Order of Odd Fellows, Samuel McNary (see pages 61 and 93), father of Margaret McNary Regan, is seated third from the left and Henry Snyder is fourth from the left in the second row. (Courtesy Margaret McNary Regan.)

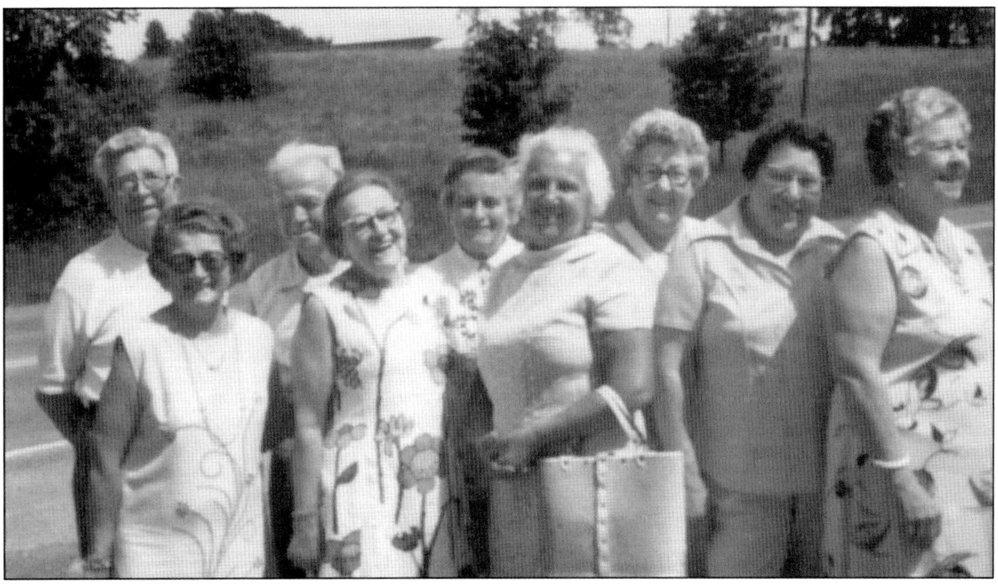

SAND LAKE SENIOR CITIZENS. The election of the first slate of officers for the newly organized Sand Lake Senior Citizens occurred in July 1975. Pictured, from left to right, are the following: (first row) Emily Weiss, trustee; Florence Barnham, historian; Audna Tifft, president; Eleanor Sullivan, first vice president; and Marguerite Lobdell, treasurer; (second row) William Rutherford and Max Schoenberger, trustees; Mary Trumble, second vice president; Ruth Patchin, secretary. (Courtesy Audna Tifft.)

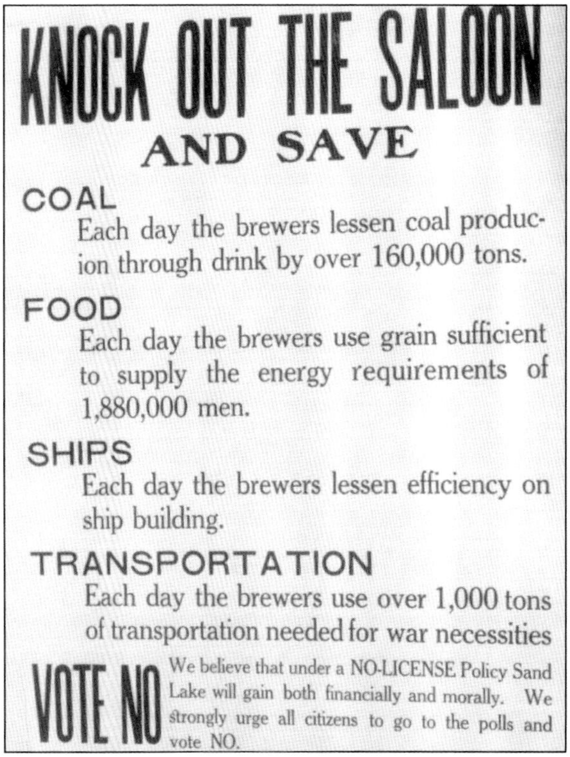

KNOCK OUT THE SALOON, C. 1914–1918. Several of these posters were found between the walls of a local residence. After Prohibition ended, their message had little value. However, for an election during World War I, they were displayed to urge a "no-license" vote based on the projected daily cost to the population for brewing alcoholic beverages. (Courtesy Town of Sand Lake Collection.)

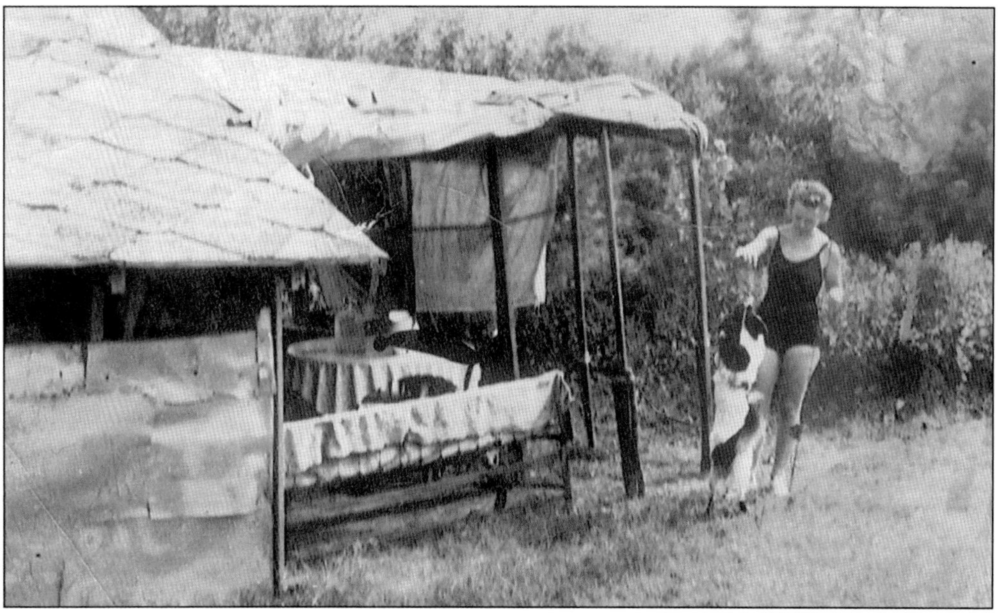

METHODIST FARM, 1937. Adelaide Wilson and her dog Terry are outside their camp at Methodist Farm on Crooked Lake. When the farm first started in 1915, accommodations were tents. In the 1940s and 1950s, campers upgraded to buildings and, still later, some upgraded to trailers. Methodist Farm has two pavilions, which are used by groups and organizations for picnics and outings, and vespers are held on Sunday evening at the chapel. (Courtesy Emily Gervais, niece of Adelaide Wilson.)

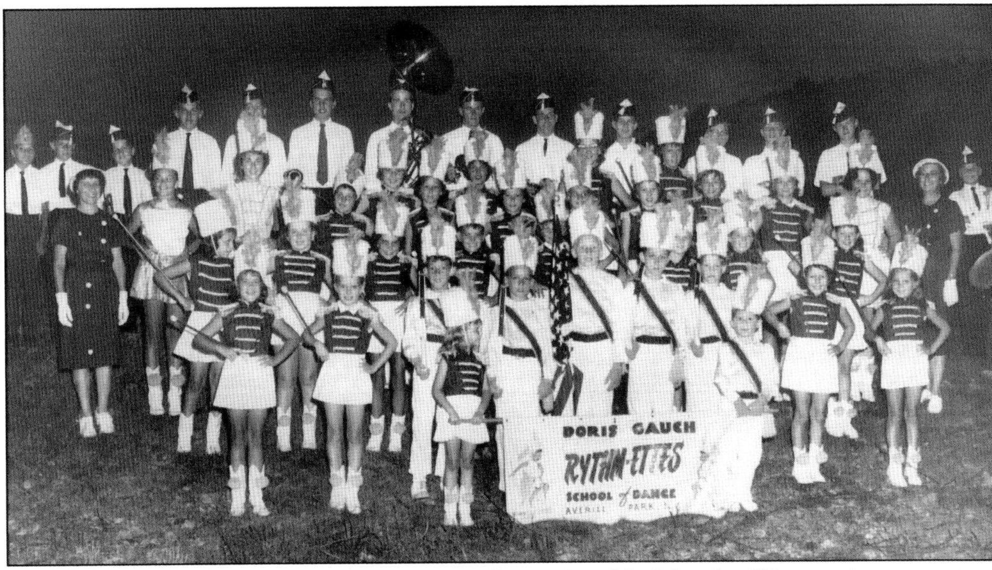

THE RYTHM-ETTES SCHOOL OF DANCE. Doris Gauch's School of Dance always received much applause at the Memorial Day and Firemen's Field Day parades. (Courtesy Averill Park and Sand Lake Fire Company.)

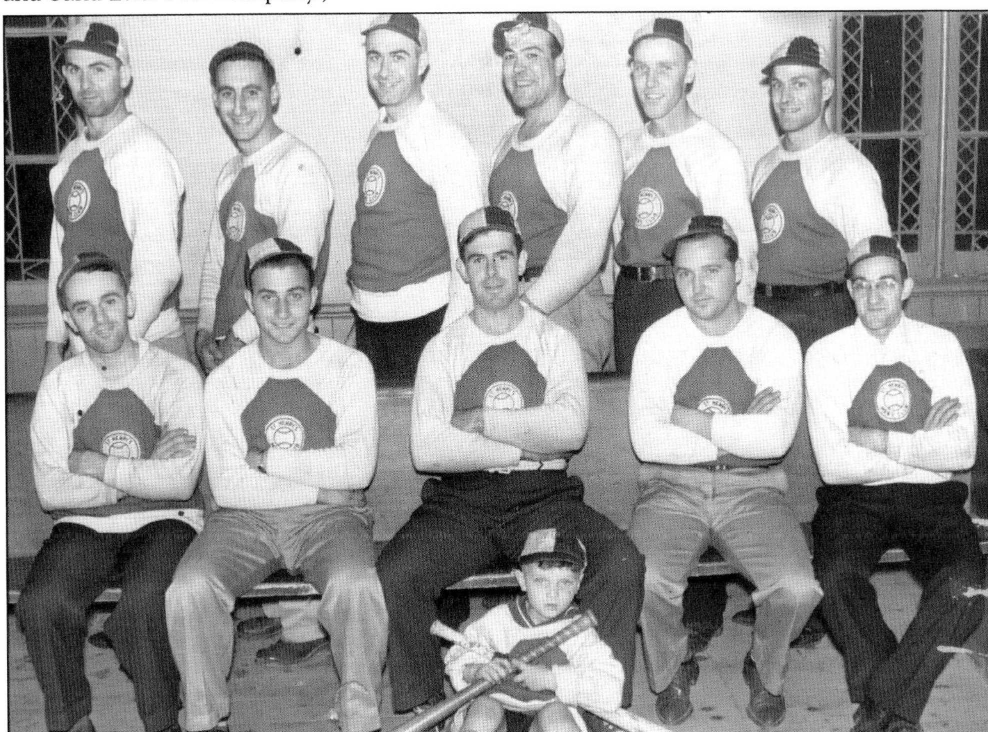

ST. HENRY'S BASEBALL TEAM, C. 1940. Churches in town had baseball teams, which played each other. Pictured, from left to right, are the following: (front row) Joe Warren Jr.; (middle row) Joe Warren Sr., Joe Castalda, Jack Coffey, Tim Frasier, and Buster Warmt; (back row) Laverne Quell, Joe Castalano, Dr. Ed Minehan (dentist), John "Tarz" Albanese, Francis "Snook" Warren, and Franklin Smith. (Courtesy Town of Sand Lake Collection.)

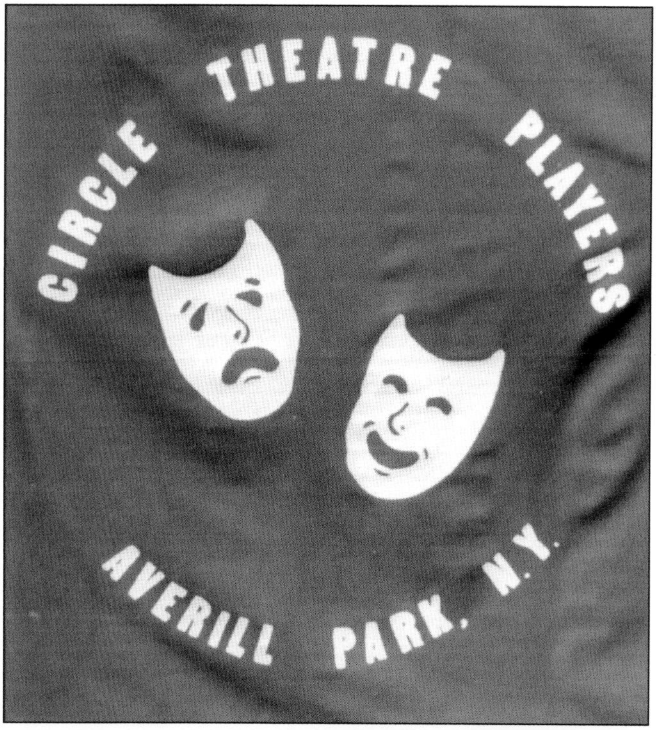

CIRCLE THEATER PLAYERS. Circle Theater Players (CTP), a community theater group, began performing chancel dramas at the Church of the Covenant. In 1981, with Bertram McNary as its director, it went public and the play sold out. Two weeks before its second production, the director died. Joan Fuess stepped in and has led the CTP ever since. Twenty successful years later, the board is seeking its own theater building. (Courtesy Circle Theater Players.)

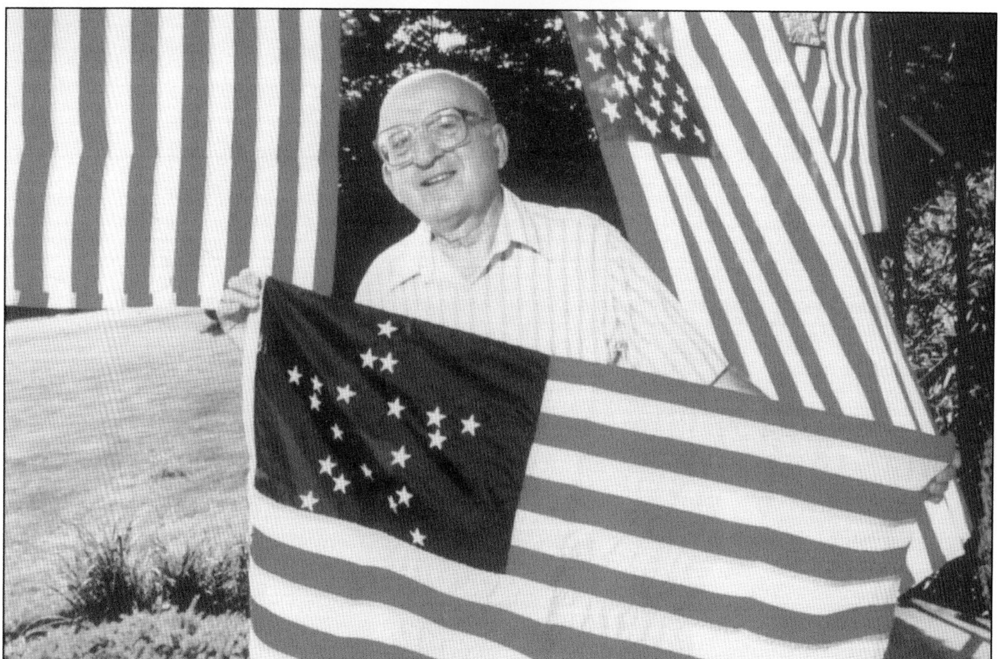

JOHN KACHARIAN, FLAG PROTOCOL EXPERT. John Kacharian is a historian of the flag and also an expert on protocol for displaying the flag. He is holding the Great Star Flag, *c.* 1818. Hanging on his porch, from left to right, are the Star-Spangled Banner Flag, the present American Flag, and the first Stars and Stripes Flag. (Courtesy John Kacharian; Tom Killip, photograph, the *Record*, July 4, 1995.)